The Shark God

The Shark God

*Encounters with
Ghosts and Ancestors
in the South Pacific*

CHARLES
MONTGOMERY

HarperCollins*Publishers*

The epigraph for chapter 4 from James McAuley, "Captain Quiros," *Collected Poems* (copyright © Norma McAuley), is reprinted with permission from HarperCollins Publishers Australia.

The epigraph for chapter 5 is reproduced with permission from Northrop Frye's *Notebooks and Lectures on the Bible and Other Religious Texts*, copyright © 2003 University of Toronto Press.

The epigraph for chapter 10 is reproduced with permission from *Solomon Islands*, 3rd ed., © 1997 Lonely Planet Publications.

First published in Canada in 2004 by Douglas & McIntyre Ltd.

Designed by Christine Weathersbee

ISBN-13: 978-0-7394-7979-7

Printed in the U.S.A.

What indeed do we not owe to the influence of the departed?
They are not dead. Thousands of them live for us,
they still speak to us out of every century, and from far down
the ages, till we have reached the furthest bounds of history.
Somehow they seem all round us.
                    —HENRY MONTGOMERY, *Life's Journey*

Contents

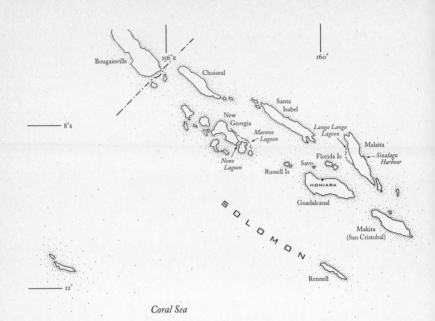

Bougainville 156°E Choiseul Santa Isabel *Langa Langa Lagoon* Malaita *Sinalagu Harbour* New Georgia *Marovo Lagoon* Florida Is *Nono Lagoon* Savo Russell Is HONIARA Makira (San Cristobal) Guadalcanal S O L O M O N Rennell

160°

8°S

12°

Coral Sea

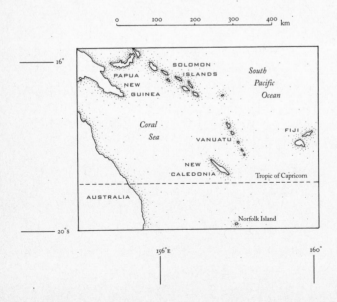

0   100   200   300   400   km

16°

PAPUA NEW GUINEA SOLOMON ISLANDS *South Pacific Ocean* *Coral Sea* VANUATU FIJI NEW CALEDONIA Tropic of Capricorn AUSTRALIA Norfolk Island

20°S

156°E

160°

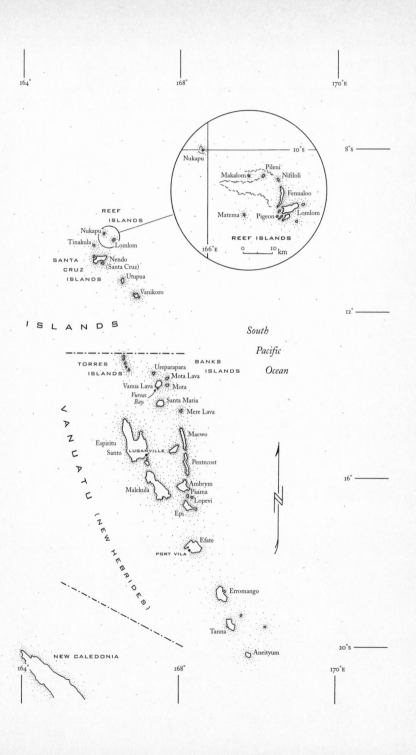

The Shark God

1

A Packet of Sand

Hunters for gold or pursuers of fame, they all had gone out on that stream, bearing the sword, and often the torch, messengers of the might within the land, bearers of a spark from the sacred fire. What greatness had not floated on the ebb of that river into the mystery of an unknown earth!

—Joseph Conrad, *Heart of Darkness*

The story should begin in Oxford.

Oxford, in the muted light of early spring, not far from the pincushion spires of the old Bodleian Library, past the long sandstone wall and the constellation of early spring narcissus, through the marble rotunda and the oak-paneled anteroom, up the creaking staircase to the attic. That's where I found the envelope that set the journey in motion.

I remember the oath—you can't just wander into the attic of Rhodes House or any other part of the Bodleian Library without taking the oath, which includes a promise not to set fire to the books. It's understood that you will not touch the older manuscripts with your fingertips, since oil from human skin is like acid to the wrinkled flesh of old parchment. I raised my hand and swore.

But the envelope. I found it in file c/nz/mel2, a cardboard box full of tattered letters, newspaper clippings, and journal extracts. Inside it was a postcard from Egypt, stamped at Port Said: Jan. 30, 1884. There was no image on the front of the card, just the address of one Reverend Prebendary Plant, the vicar of Weston-on-Trent. The envelope also contained a sheet of cream-colored paper folded many times over and sealed with red wax. The seal was broken.

I made a little fortress of books and albums so the archivists could not see me, then I carefully unfolded the paper. Inside it was another piece of paper, folded to the dimensions of a matchbook. It had also been sealed with wax, and this seal was broken, too. I opened it and peered inside.

It contained perhaps a spoonful of sand and splinters, as though someone had taken a walk on a beach, then scraped the sole of his shoe and swept the remains into that little packet. I reached in and ran my finger through the grit. The splinters were so dry they crumbled on touch. I turned the paper over. Handwritten on the back of it: "Sand and wood from the spot where Bishop Patteson died."

A story: John Coleridge Patteson, the first bishop of Melanesia, had been welcomed ashore on the tiny atoll of Nukapu on a sunny afternoon in 1871. He was led to a palm-thatched hut and offered a grass mat, on which he lay down to rest. The bishop closed his eyes, as if to ready himself for the blow that would shatter his skull, as if he was waiting to die and be resurrected as the martyr-hero of the western South Pacific. The blow came. Everyone agrees on that one detail. Dozens of versions of the story eventually emerged, and they once captivated England as thoroughly as those of the martyrdom of Livingstone in Africa. Preachers, politicians, and pundits turned their attention to the South Pacific.

Queen Victoria was petitioned to deal with the "atrocity." A warship was dispatched to bomb Nukapu and burn its village to the ground. Money, recruits, and a new mission ship sailed across the miles. Patteson's martyrdom was carved into stone and set into stained glass. Yet the circumstances surrounding the bishop's murder were—and still are—shrouded in mystery.

I took a pinch of the sand and rolled the grains between my thumb and forefinger. Nukapu. I imagined the reef, the island, and the murder that was a transforming moment in the history of the South Pacific, a moment that tied together the dreams of an ancient culture, the crimes of a generation of rogues, and the aspirations of hundreds of spiritual adventurers, including my own great-grandfather.

I was ten years old when the first piece of the story came to me. My father, who had spent most of his life as a sailor, had found his final port on the west coast of Canada. He and my mother bought a swath of pasture and forest on Vancouver Island. He felled the last of the great firs, planted his fields with clover, built a barn for his Herefords, and then he died.

A few weeks after the funeral, my mother discovered my father's dispatch box in a corner of the attic. She hauled the black tin trunk down to the dining-room table and began to sift through it. I remember watching her and seeing the worry on her brow. I know now that she was terrified my father was receding, drifting away on the sea of memory. She wanted to imprint my brother and me with something of our father's character—something that would remind us that we were part of a story that did not end with his death, a story that would bind us to him, or at least to his name.

The box didn't offer much. My father ran off to sea when he was fifteen. He had served on troopships in the Atlantic and Indian oceans during World War II, dodged German submarines in the Mediterranean. He had fed dinner leftovers to sharks off the coast of Sicily. One letter, posted in Cape Town, described a showdown with a water buffalo in Mozambique. What else? He once had a girlfriend in Athens. He bought a Super 8 camera in Tokyo. He spent decades at sea, but the scraps in his box didn't begin to fill in the blanks. It was as if he had not wanted his tale to be told.

But there were other stories in the box. Diaries. Bits of paper. Newspaper clippings from the Victorian era. Photos of stone mansions in Ireland and India. Soldiers on tanks. Tea parties on vast lawns. Buggies drawn by camels. There were books about God: volume after volume of theological musings and fatherly advice for Christians, palm-sized booklets with titles like *Visions* or *Life's Journey*, and guides for young missionaries headed for distant colonies. The covers of some were stamped with the same nautical scene: a square-rigged ship sailing toward an island populated with diminutive natives. The sea was rough, but the sun smiled down on the ship, whose sole passenger stood at the bow, waving an open Bible toward shore.

These were my great-grandfather's writings. Unlike my father, the Right Reverend Henry Hutchinson Montgomery had taken pains to ensure that his descendants would remember him. In fact, though the bishop was buried in 1932, he had always presided over our household. There he was, floating in a whorl of crimson brushstrokes above the dining-room table. A royal blue cloak printed with exquisite thistle bouquets hung from his shoulders. A pancake-sized medallion and a gold cross dangled from his neck. His face was weathered, cheeks hollowed with age, but there was a soaring, powerful dignity to him. He kept his white beard tidy and trimmed. The bishop looked down over his long nose, not at you but into—what was it, a prayer book? He wore a gold, cone-shaped miter. We never cursed in front of him.

It was under that portrait that I sifted through the black trunk to discover the story that would make me forget all about my father's mystery years. It didn't look like much on the outside: a pocketbook bound with blue cotton and frayed at the crown. The cover, polished by years of jostling among other unread volumes, reflected the lamplight. The title was stamped across it in gold, as brilliant as the day it was printed:

The Light of Melanesia.

The pages were the color of smoke, and brittle. Some were decorated with floral motifs, thistles, and mermaids. The text was faint. But the photos were mesmerizing. Faded monotones showed muscular black men clutching spears or dozing on sleek outrigger canoes. Those men were naked but for the feathers that poked from their frizzy hair like peacock plumage, curls of—was it shell? bone?—that hung from their earlobes and noses, and shocking phallic sheaths that shot up from their loins. Bare-breasted women emerged like shadows from still lagoons. A gang of magnificent, barrel-chested men carried a long pole adorned with rings of feather money. Then, beyond a village of grass huts, past an explosion of jungle, a ship with three masts waited at anchor.

The writing was difficult. I didn't read it all, just enough to understand that this was an account of a journey made more than a century ago; that back in the days when the world was a wild and treacherous place, when white men in top hats and ties confronted cruel savages on the rocky shores of remote islands, when black magic and powerful spirits still ruled the shadows, the bishop had followed the ghost of the martyred Patteson to the darkest corner of the South Pacific. It was an adventure sanctioned by God Himself. The story I fashioned from the raw material of those pages went like this:

By 1889, the British Empire was nearing the apex of its power. It controlled a fifth of the world, but much of that domain was still lacking the spiritual guidance of the Church of England. The archbishop of Canterbury consecrated the forty-two-year-old Henry Montgomery as bishop of Tasmania and sent him off to the empire's distant fringe. The bishop was happy in the antipodean colony, which was like a bit of Cornwall dropped off the coast of

Australia. He had a comfortable manor house and a great stone cathedral in which to preach. He had a wife and four children. But after three years, he left them all. He caught a steamer to New Zealand, where he set sail for the Tropic of Capricorn aboard the mission schooner *Southern Cross*. The objective: to bring the One True God to the heathens of the Melanesian archipelagos, hundreds of islands shrouded in violence, fear, and—equally shocking to the Victorian missionaries—nakedness, promiscuity, and sloth.

The bishop cataloged the horrors of this most perilous mission field. Dozens of traders and evangelists had already been murdered on the shores of the islands that were scattered across 1,200 miles of ocean between Fiji and New Guinea. Some, like Patteson, were clubbed to death. Some were pierced with arrows tipped with human bone. Others were held underwater until their bodies stopped shaking. The most unlucky were cooked and eaten. The natives had not been behaving well toward each other, either. An epidemic of head-hunting had spread east from New Guinea through the Solomon Islands. Entire villages had been wiped out. Hundreds of miles of coastline were left desolate by the skull-collecting chiefs of New Georgia. Old women were killing their own grandchildren.

It was clear to the bishop that the Evil One had reached the islands long before the missionaries. It wasn't just war and violence that marked his presence: Satan had imbued his servants with the most sinister of powers. Black magic was rampant. A sorcerer could kill a man by shaking a handful of cobwebs at him. People worshipped sharks, stones, invisible spirits, and the dead, all of whom demanded constant blood sacrifice. The jungles of Melanesia echoed with the chanting of their followers.

To my adolescent mind, Melanesia was a fabulously sinister and magical place. Good and evil were indeed clashing in the South Pacific, and in 1892, goodness required a new champion: it had been twenty years since the murder of Bishop Patteson. Now

Patteson's replacement had succumbed to the ravages of tropical disease and retreated to England. The archipelago was desperate for a bishop. The white priests the *Southern Cross* had dropped on so many hostile islands needed reassurance. The natives had to be shown that their bond with the Almighty had not been broken. The mission frontier needed to be pushed even farther into the archipelago of bloody ritual and bubbling volcanoes so that Patteson and the other Christian martyrs would not have died in vain. There was really no choice for my great-grandfather but to sail across the miles and repeat the journey of his heroes.

Henry Montgomery wrote to his children from the deck of the *Southern Cross*. "Remember," he told them, "that your father visited all these islands, and that his heart went out to the dwellers among these lonely scenes, praying ever that they might be brought to know their Father in His son Jesus Christ." He reminded his children that they were special. "You have all been taught that we must be true and pure and upright because we are Christ's disciples; but next after that reason there is no incentive to live nobly which is so powerful as the possession of a great family tradition. You come from a family of 'gentlemen'; you know that word does not signify mere outward refinement: it tells of a refined and noble mind, to which anything dishonourable or mean or impure is abhorrent and unworthy."

This was the kind of story my mother had wanted me to find. I held on tightly to the bishop's counsel for years. Sometimes, after hours spent shoveling Hereford manure, I would kick off my gum boots on the porch and pad quietly into the dining room to stand and look at the old man, and know that here was proof that I was connected to a confrontation with the spirit world, something grand, noble, and so very far away from the stumps, muck, and drudgery of the farm.

I didn't think much about religion, or that there might be anything less than heroic about the bishop's journey. I didn't consider that his story might be an argument, a construction, a myth. I just imagined his schooner at full sail over that vast, beckoning ocean, and a hundred thousand cannibals, sorcerers, and ghosts waiting beneath the palms. And I let the bishop's story ebb and flood through my dreams, as vivid and enduring as *The Jungle Book* or *Treasure Island* or *Star Wars*. It remained so for two decades, long after I had shunned the doctrines of the church, long after I had relegated my family's god to the pantheon of imagined heroes.

But sometimes a story returns to demand your attention, and you must decide whether to let it live or fade. I found *The Light of Melanesia* again when I was thirty-two. I read it all this time, slowly. The bishop and his brotherhood of spiritual adventurers didn't seem so heroic anymore. Their convictions seemed childish, their God a piece of fancy, their crusade to sell him to people on the far side of the world downright racist. The years—and my postcolonial skepticism—were ripping out pages of my great-grandfather's myth and setting fire to them. The Melanesia of my boyhood dreams threatened to disappear. I became obsessed with the islands. I sought out Oceanists, theologians, mission historians, anyone who might offer a piece of the real story, not just of my great-grandfather and his Victorian brotherhood but also of the islands they had set out to change. I flew to England to search for clues. I thought that if I completed the story, I might be able to put it aside for good.

I began inside Lambeth Palace, the archbishop of Canterbury's brick fortress on the south bank of the Thames. I pored over hundreds of pages of ecclesiastical correspondence in the palace library, and learned that the Victorian bishops were uniformly incapable of writing legibly. I took the train to Oxford. I uttered the Bodleian oath. Then, in the creaking attic of Rhodes House, I was rewarded. There were crates and crates of notes, reports from the Melanesian Mission, logbooks from the *Southern Cross,* and a dozen accounts of Patteson's murder. There was a shoe box full of sketches: faded line drawings of spears, canoes, and carved paddles. There were diary accounts of misty mornings and slaughter on creamy sand beaches. There were woeful notes about the sins into which some missionaries had fallen: "The temptations on a desert island," mourned one cleric. Digging through it all was like peering into the corners of my own memory. Every photo, every story, seemed strangely familiar, as if they had grown from the story I had been telling myself for years, only this story wasn't quite the shape I remembered.

It began with the three heroes of *The Light of Melanesia:* George Augustus Selwyn, the stern visionary who hatched the plan to raise the Melanesians from their darkness; John Coleridge Patteson, whose love for the islanders cost him his life; and Robert Henry Codrington, whose curiosity would inadvertently revive the spirits they had all sought to destroy. Like my great-grandfather, these were men of privilege, molded by England's public schools and altogether certain that Empire was a virtue so long as God was among its exports.

Selwyn was their leader. A product of Eton and Cambridge, Selwyn was only thirty-two when he was named bishop of New Zealand. He was a High Church traditionalist and a firm believer in the principle of apostolic succession. He felt that the bishops of the Church of England, like those of the Roman Catholic Church, were God's designated representatives, and therefore successors to Jesus's own apostles. He dreamed that the "Church of England would speedily become a praise upon the whole earth."

This might explain his reaction to the clerical error on the letters patent that described his new diocese. Selwyn's territory should have extended just past the tip of New Zealand's North Island— about 34 degrees south of the equator. But someone scribbled "34 degrees north" latitude where he should have written "south." This extended his territory thousands of miles through Melanesia, past the equator and the Tropic of Cancer to well beyond Hawaii. It was a mistake, but Selwyn was as ambitious as he was willful. He studied navigation and Polynesian grammar on his voyage from England south to New Zealand. Within six years of arriving, he was hitching rides with the Royal Navy into the heart of Melanesia. He befriended chiefs, charming them with gifts of fishhooks, axes, and calico, then convinced them to let him carry away the most promising of their youngsters to his Christian school in New Zealand. (Most of the recruits were after more axes and fishhooks. In fact, the trade was so central to the bishop's persona that islanders confused his title with the word *fishhook*. They called him "bishhooka.") The strong boys, the ones who didn't drop dead from the flu, dysentery, or homesickness, were molded into an army of black apostles and sent back from New Zealand to the islands, where to preach was to invite ostracism and, occasionally, assassination.

Selwyn's progress was slow at first, and his task was urgent. Catholic and Presbyterian missionaries were already trickling across the Pacific from Tahiti and Tonga, and they were keen to steal his recruits. He needed help. In 1855, Selwyn returned to England to drum up support for his mission. His sermons inspired a young man of impeccable credentials. John Coleridge Patteson was the son of a judge, and a former captain of Eton's First Eleven cricket squad. He was also a village curate and a linguist. The latter skill would be useful: Selwyn's potential converts spoke more than a hundred different languages. Patteson was not yet thirty when he accompanied Selwyn back to New Zealand and then into the unknown islands aboard the mission ship *Southern Cross*. In 1861, Selwyn handed the entire mission over to Patteson and consecrated him the first bishop of Melanesia.

Patteson was even more ambitious than his mentor. Every year he ventured farther into the archipelago. At each new island he swam to shore from the ship's whaleboat with a vocabulary notebook tucked inside his hat and presents tied around his neck. He picked up dozens of local languages, and in them tried to explain to the islanders that they had got the nature of the cosmos all wrong. He told them that if they learned to obey his god, they could live on after death; but if they did not obey, they would go on to endless pain and sorrow. And then he took their children away.

In New Zealand, then later at the mission's new base, six hundred miles north on Norfolk Island, the boys were instructed in the dignified rituals of the Anglo-Catholic liturgy, not to mention the social graces that came with an Eton education. While the students learned how to button shirts and tie shoelaces, how to use knives and forks, how to read, pray, sing hymns, and play cricket, they whispered about the world they had left behind. Robert Henry Codrington, the third hero of *The Light of Melanesia* and headmaster of the mission school, listened to their stories. Codrington was a scholar, a fellow of Oxford, erudite yet remarkably unassuming. The students trusted him, and he collected their secrets with the hunger of an exiled academic. He passed some of those secrets on to my great-grandfather. The rest he consigned to paper, and many of those jottings and sketches languished for years in the attic of Rhodes House. I found them, and they drew me into a world positively vibrating with supernatural power, where ghosts and spirits moved among men and miracles happened constantly.

The boys told Codrington about *mana,* an invisible force that flowed through the atmosphere of life, through objects, people, and actions. It appeared without warning. It helped the ancestor spirits to speak. It could be concentrated and directed for good or evil. Everyone had a little *mana* in him. In New Georgia, islanders were sure it was concentrated in people's heads. That's why the New Georgians chopped off the heads of their enemies and carried them home. Head-hunting was quite logical, if you thought about it: a head full of *mana* was the most useful treasure of all.

The Melanesians had no supreme being, but their islands were thick with spirits who attached themselves to stones, places, animals, or even words. Sometimes the spirits screamed and howled through dark nights. Sometimes, amid hidden groves of tangled banyan, they revealed their mysteries to the members of secret societies who asked for their help. The boys told Codrington about Qat, the ancestor-spirit hero of a dozen islands, who was always ready to come to the aid of seafarers. "Qat!" men shouted from their canoes. "May it be. Let the canoe of you and me turn into a whale, a flying fish, an eagle; let it leap on and on over the waves, let it go, let it pass out to my land." And Qat would calm the sea, speeding the travelers home.

The ghosts of other ancestors inhabited the bodies of sharks, alligators, octopuses, snakes, and birds. With secret knowledge, a man could win the favor of a shark ancestor, and that shark would come when called; it would herd schools of fish into his net. It would also devour his enemies. The ancestors rewarded allegiance with the same fierce loyalty as the Lord of the Old Testament. Just as God had smashed the enemies of Moses, so the ancestor spirits helped Melanesians sink their enemies' canoes.

There wasn't just one holy ghost in Melanesia; there were thousands of them. And Melanesian spirituality was egalitarian. With the right technique, anyone could harness the power of curses, magic cures, and helpful spirits. Anyone could collect and direct *mana*. The ethereal realm wasn't in heaven. It was all around you. It was in you.

But those spirits, as powerful and plentiful as they were, began their retreat even as Codrington's anthropological opus, *The Melanesians*, made their names familiar to academics around the world. Codrington's Melanesian converts grew ashamed of their dances, their secret societies, and their ghosts. In the pidgin English picked up from traders, they began to call their ancestors by the name white men had given them: *devil-devils*. When the students returned home with the new teaching, they destroyed shrines and cast the devil-devil stones into the sea.

One by one, the islands of Melanesia were claimed by the competing mission societies. Sometimes the Anglicans squabbled with Presbyterians and Roman Catholics over God's new kingdom, but eventually deals were cut, islands were traded back and forth, and palm-thatched cathedrals rose on the shores of every major island lying in the 1.5 million square miles of ocean between New Zealand and New Guinea. By the time Henry Montgomery crossed the reef at Nukapu to pay his respects to Patteson's ghost, a sturdy iron cross had been erected on the scene of the martyr's last stand. He was assured that the conversion of Patteson's murderers was a fait accompli. Perhaps that is why he left Melanesia after his three-month tour of the islands—that's right, his was not the hair-raising adventure I had constructed as a boy. My great-grandfather, above all, was a storyteller. He went home to write, to glorify the names of his mission heroes. And the shark spirits and ancestors who had watched over Melanesians for thousands of years receded in the shadow of the new god, while the old knowledge went fallow in Codrington's academic jottings.

Yet something of Melanesia did follow the missionaries home to the northern drizzle. I saw it in my great-grandfather's portrait, in the way he seemed to gaze through the shadows to some unseen light. I saw it in his writing, which was not the same after his brief tour through the region of magic. He had always insisted that the Apocalypse, the Revelation of Saint John the Divine, would be played out in every age. He may once have meant this metaphorically. Not anymore. In Melanesia he concluded that supernatural power was real, and it was usually the devil's work. Sorcerers' use of charms to inflict death or disease was a manifestation of the Evil One's will. He wrote: "I see no cause to disbelieve, in fact, it seems to me reasonable, that Satan, in whose bond they are as heathen, should be able to bestow a hurtful power upon some of them."

Henry Montgomery was proud of the rationalist tradition that had influenced his church, yet he sailed back to Tasmania and then home to England a mystic, desperate to see a manifestation of his own god. He was convinced that something about England's cold climate made it difficult for his countrymen to commune with the supernatural world. He despaired: "It seems to be a fact that the nearer the home of your race is to the Equator the easier it is for your race to see the unseen: and the further from the Equator the harder it becomes." (

He would wait years for his own god to appear to him. But after his retirement to the family estate in Donegal, Ireland, after hundreds of communions, thousands of hymns, and a hundred thousand prayers, the vision finally did come. Henry was wandering in his garden above the shivering waters of Lough Foyle, in the half-light before dawn. He was ready.

First came the ghosts of his ancestors, tramping one by one through the roses. He was not afraid. They spoke to Henry approvingly. They had seen his work and knew it to be good. A mistlike veil settled upon the garden. Daffodils and snowdrops began to stir as though whispering in their own secret language. The ancestors raised their faces and their hands to an unseen spirit, and they urged Henry to follow it into the stone church they had built amid the oaks. He crept to the church door, pushed against its worn grain, and slipped inside. That's when he felt his Lord looking down on him. He fell to the stone floor and covered his eyes. God asked Henry, just as he had asked Abraham: "Lovest thou me?" Henry did not reply. He could not bring his lips to form words. All he could do was weep with shame and awe, and know that the Lord would accept that as his answer. He awoke with the light of Easter morning, feeling a new vigor for the pilgrim path he had followed to Melanesia and intended to follow all the way to heaven.

Tales of visions are like mist and rumors. They offer nothing tangible to hold on to. Oxford gave me something more solid. I had my packet of sand. I had the name of my island. Nukapu was the place where old Melanesia had made its last stand, it was the home of the ghost that drew my great-grandfather across the water, and it was undeniably real. If Nukapu was the place where myths intersected, it might also be the place where they could be measured. I folded the packet and placed it back in its envelope.

I left Oxford on a Sunday. A storm was dragging itself across the hills. The wind was battering the year's first crocuses back into the earth. The bells of the cathedral were calling the faithful to consume the body and the blood of Christ, so that their souls would be washed pure and that Jesus might dwell in them. Those bells rang and rang, but the people didn't come. I marched to the train station, thinking about cannibals, sacred dances, ancestors who didn't vanish after death but who lived on, inhabiting rocks, sharks, sacred groves, and violent storms.

What had become of the islands my great-grandfather's brotherhood of gentlemen had set out to transform? Who had won the battle for souls now that the sacred fire had dimmed here at the heart of the empire? Although I knew it was the worst kind of romantic primitivism, and though I was certain that Melanesian myths were just as illusory as the ones to which my ancestors clung, I let myself imagine an island where gospel and empire had never taken hold, a place where drumbeats and painted skin and searing ritual still marked the survival of the world the missionaries sought to destroy. I imagined barefoot mystics revealing the secret light of their magic. I imagined a vision more powerful than my great-grandfather's. My heart raced, and I was gripped by the urgent thought of secrets disappearing beneath the waves, and the idea that *The Light of Melanesia* might only be the beginning of a story. I boarded the express to Paddington. The train lurched forward. Rainwater streamed across my window, obscuring the spires of Oxford, the ragged sky, and the lethargic Thames, leaving nothing but the rumble and click of the tracks and the whisper of an idea. Nukapu. I was moving south.

2

The Business of Port Vila Is God

Good-bye. I vanish from civilization, hoping to return a
wiser man.

—HENRY MONTGOMERY, letter, 1892

My plan was simple, which is how adventures begin, but not how
they end. I would follow the route my great-grandfather described in *The Light of Melanesia*, the route he and his predecessors
had sailed aboard the *Southern Cross*. I would travel by ship, yes,
and perhaps also by launch and canoe and on foot. I would find
the descendants of the missionary-killers. I would find my heathens. I would cross the reefs and wade to shore on Nukapu, and I
would stand beneath Patteson's cross, where history and myth
would be made utterly clear to me by someone very old and wise.

But where exactly was I going? Melanesia refers not to a country or a single archipelago but a racial theory projected onto maps.
French explorer Dumont D'Urville invented the name Melanésie
to represent the swath of islands of the western South Pacific in-

habited by dark-skinned people. *Melas* and *nesos* are Greek for "black" and "islands." Unlike Polynesians (who populated the many—*poly*—islands to the east), the people whom D'Urville encountered from New Guinea to Fiji were so dark that he imagined they were transplanted from Africa. They weren't, but the name stuck.

There was a map in *The Light of Melanesia* on which were scattered dozens of islands, but no continents. The map had no scale, but a faint arrow pointed toward its lower left-hand corner, and along that arrow was printed TO SYDNEY: 1500 MILES. That put the islands right in the heart of D'Urville's Melanésie. The rest of the script was so minute and so faded that it required a magnifying glass. My glass revealed that the blotches on the lower right-hand corner were the New Hebrides, and the spilled coins above them were the Banks Islands, home of the ancestor spirit Qat. The slugs inching toward the frayed upper left corner of the page were the Solomon Islands. And out in the middle of nothingness, like dust on the page: the Santa Cruz Group. And if you strained, and imagined, then perhaps a smudge next to the loneliest of those flecks read: Nukapu.

We dream places before we search for them. It has always been that way with Melanesia. The first explorers, who are said to have migrated to the islands from Asia as much as twenty thousand years ago, must have been led by faith. They could only paddle so far east past Papua New Guinea before the horizon ran out of islands. They learned to read the waves and the stars, but it was imagination that told ocean argonauts there was more land beyond the edge of their world.

There is less room for imagination nowadays. We have the Internet and global positioning systems to guide us. The Internet told me that the New Hebrides had been renamed Vanuatu, a republic that billed itself as "the South Pacific's Premier Tax Haven." There were eighty islands, four golf courses, and banks promising the utmost in secrecy. The Santa Cruz Group had amalgamated with the Solomon Islands, which were declared emphatically to be "the Happy Isles." A crude government Web site boasted of 992 happy islands and one very large satellite telecommunications dish of which Solomon Islanders were very proud. News reports tended to focus on how Solomon Islanders were apt to burn villages and shoot each other with machine guns. "Death on the Altar" was one headline. I decided to start in Vanuatu and ease my way toward the chaos.

This is how travel writers work: they contact a country's national tourism bureau, they promise to write sunny stories about golf and cold beer and people who never stop smiling, and then they ask for free flights, hotels, meals, and booze. Especially booze. Yes, and then they spend weeks lounging in crisp linen sheets, watching *BBC World News*, and drinking guava punch. It's called a reciprocal relationship.

I do not care about linen sheets, but I do like the idea of flying for free, so I wrote to Vanuatu's National Tourism Office, making promises and asking for help. I caught a 747 from Los Angeles to Fiji—free—then the weekly shuttle to Port Vila, capital of Vanuatu, on Efate Island. That was a two-hour flight, and free as well. But you are not really free when you make these deals. It can take days to extricate yourself from the mechanisms of industrial tourism.

It was dark and humid when I stepped off the plane in Port Vila. An official from the tourism bureau intercepted me at customs, bundled me into her car, and drove me away from the lights of the airport, through a forest, over a hill, and into the arms of Le Meridien Resort and Casino. I was greeted by a pair of giggling teens in Hawaiian shirts, bearing hors d'oeuvres and champagne. My bungalow overlooked a lagoon. The bathtub was bigger than a car, and it had six jet engines. I fell onto a king-sized prairie of linen, opened Robert Henry Codrington's anthropological study

The Melanesians, and gazed at his drawings of pagan dancers. Clad in masks and leaves, they looked like dream monsters from Maurice Sendak's *Where the Wild Things Are*. I fell asleep without supper.

At dawn, I jogged around the golf course, following the high fence that kept the riffraff away from the realm of linen sheets. I hit the breakfast buffet and sat among the Australian bankers and their families. The bankers were fat and exhausted, the wives hideously thin. The bankers stuffed their children with sausages, the wives sipped mineral water. Flies wandered across their shoulder blades. We ate steamed plums and chocolate croissants. *La Traviata* wafted through the palms.

Later, the woman from the tourism office called me with a plan. There was golfing to be done. And a harbor cruise. And shopping. Anything she could do to help, she said. Anything at all. I broke out in a sweat.

"Heathens," I said. "I'm looking for heathens."

"Ah, yes, we have the photos at the cultural center," she said.

"Living heathens," I said.

"Don't be ridiculous," she said. "This is a Christian island."

I hung up the phone and, neglecting to turn off the air conditioner, slipped away, past the laundry girl and the groundskeepers and the resort guards. I ran out the gate and all the way into town.

Port Vila proper was a discordant place, an eager collection of postcolonial cement blocks, duty-free shops, and French supermarkets. It wanted to be Tahiti, or perhaps Waikiki. It had the turquoise harbor full of yachts and pink paragliders, and a smattering of tiny patisseries, where tiny pink princesses with tiny white purses kissed each other on both cheeks. But down in the market, husky Melanesian matrons still followed the dress code introduced by missionaries a century before: Mother Hubbard–style dresses that billowed in the breeze above bare feet or hung from ample breasts like drapery. Their skin was the color of copper or dark roasted coffee. Their frizzy hair was styled into pumpkin-sized Afros.

The streets were full of rough-cut young men who lounged curbside or hooted at each other from the open boxes of pickup trucks. The men braided their hair into loose dreadlocks and twisted their beards into artful knots. They furrowed their brows fiercely in the sunlight. They were sinewy and strong. I wrote in my notebook: "wild-looking." But then I saw their faces melt into generous smiles. The men held hands in the shade. They giggled like schoolboys or Hobbits. Small carved crosses dangled from their necks.

The shops and the giggling were merely a backdrop to the real business of Port Vila, which was religion. The town was crawling with American and Australian missionaries. There were Mormons in pressed white shirts and ties, severe Seventh-day Adventists, burger-gulping members of the Assemblies of God, tongue-speaking Pentecostals, and charismatic holy rollers in business suits. Men shouted the gospel from street corners.

I was standing on Kumul Highway, the town's main street, trying to get my bearings, when the flow of minibuses parted to make way for an acne-scarred white man in his twenties. The foreigner wore jackboots and a white robe, and he carried a flag with a Christian cross stitched on it. With his Aryan aesthetic and severe countenance, he might have been leading a Ku Klux Klan procession, but this white hood was followed by a hundred brown children. They handed out greeting cards depicting a hedgehog in vestments. "I forgive you," said the cartoon hedgehog. The children sang: *"Jesus hem i numbawan. Hem i luvim yumi"*—Jesus is number one. He loves you and me.

The scene would have warmed the hearts of the first missionaries, who were not well received when they arrived in the nineteenth century. John Williams, Melanesia's first evangelist, sighted the New Hebrides in 1839. His interdenominational London Missionary Society had already converted most of Polynesia; Williams thought Melanesia would be just as easily won. His optimism was misplaced. He rowed to shore on Erromango, a day's sail south of Efate, with an assistant. The two men were promptly chased back into the shallows and clubbed to death. Accordingly, the LMS recruited Polynesian teachers to serve as cannon fodder in this spiritual war of attrition. Dozens of Samoans died from disease or treachery on Erromango before the society gave up and a pair of Nova Scotian Presbyterians took over. George and Ellen Gordon landed in 1851. They managed to convert a handful of people in the course of a decade, but then they made a fatal error. When an epidemic of measles broke out and killed hundreds of Erromangans, the Gordons announced that Jehovah was punishing islanders for remaining heathen. The couple were blamed for the epidemic, hacked down with axes, and eaten.

The Erromangans had much cause for hostility. The scum of European civilization had beaten the missionaries to the islands. First came traders, hungry for the sandalwood that grew throughout the archipelago. The aromatic wood was in such high demand in China that traders would do anything to get it. They stole what they could or paid with axes and muskets. As sandalwood supplies were depleted, the Europeans became more creative in their attempts to collect it. In 1848 the crew of the *Terror* kidnapped men from Erromango and sold them to their traditional enemies on nearby Tanna. Other traders figured the wood would be much easier to harvest if they eliminated the middlemen. In one case, a man from Tanna was shut in a ship's hold with sailors suffering from measles, then sent home to his island, where thousands eventually perished from the disease.

Then the white traders started harvesting the Melanesians themselves—they knew the islanders would make hardy laborers for sugar cane plantations in Queensland and Fiji. When young men didn't want to leave their islands, they were lassoed from their canoes like wild horses, dragged aboard the labor-recruiting vessels, and locked belowdecks. Sometimes the blackbirders—as the labor recruiters came to be called—simply shot villagers who wouldn't cooperate. Occasionally they dressed up as missionaries to win the natives' trust. Indigenous populations in the New Hebrides plummeted from the effects of introduced disease and the labor trade.

Depopulation made it easier for European traders and planters to gain a foothold, sometimes acquiring paper title to thousands of acres of land in exchange for a few bolts of calico or bottles of gin. Soon Europeans were fighting each other over the land. When French plantation owners asked their government to annex the islands, Presbyterian missionaries, incensed by the prospect of French (meaning Roman Catholic) rule, demanded that England take over instead. Neither government had the resources or desire to do so, but neither was inclined to concede territory to the other, so they agreed to share the islands in a bizarre exercise in cooperative colonialism.

The New Hebrides Condominium was declared in 1907. The deal gave the islands two heads of state, two bureaucracies, two police forces, two separate legal systems, and two separate national courts, as well as a joint court presided over by a Spaniard, who was fluent in neither English nor French. The system was soon dubbed the Pandemonium for the anarchy it spawned. But it did create a town at Port Vila, where the British commissioner and French consul flew their respective flags across the harbor from each other, hosted cocktail parties, and desperately tried to uphold an atmosphere of sophistication. They banned horse races in the town center and forbade Melanesians to stay out after dark—except when planters happened to be using their black laborers as collateral in poker games. The Condominium lurched along until 1980, when islanders gained independence and began to call themselves Ni-Vanuatu—the people from our own land.

*   *   *

The schizophrenia of the Condominium era was still evident. On the one hand, Port Vila was Melanesian: the prime minister and the bureaucrats were Ni-Vanuatu. And look at all those dark faces, all those dreadlocks, all those shacks serving nightly rounds of kava, the narcotic juice squeezed from the root of a local shrub. Then again, perhaps Vila was French. Quiche was as easy to come by as coconuts and yams. Or maybe it was English. Pubs showed Aussie-rules football matches with English-language play-by-play, even if the commercials were voiced-over in Papua New Guinea pidgin, the lingua franca of the northwest end of Melanesia. The Ciné Hickson played American films dubbed in French. White plantation owners rumbled into town to scour Au Bon Marché for foie gras, then left in their pickups, boxes crowded with dusty black hitchhikers.

Then there were the tribalists: eyebrows pierced violently, noses caked white with zinc, hair bleached freakish shades of blond, arms tattooed with thorn garlands. Australians. They invaded precisely at noon, disgorged from a cruise ship. They descended on Vila with the ferocity of Anzacs at Gallipoli and the steely sense of purpose common to suburbanites on safari. I watched them from the shade of the Cannibal House, where they paid $10 each for the opportunity to take photos of their children standing in a waist-high stew pot, surrounded by spear-clutching "warriors" in loincloths. The warriors hammed it up, pinching their Australian customers under their arms, exclaiming playfully: "Mmm, nice and fat!"

One is supposed to be mortified by this kind of thing. And I would have been but for the Ni-Vanuatu, who were absolutely keen to keep the cannibal mystique alive. It was good for business. Albert, a boat pilot from nearby Lelepa Island, boasted shortly after we met that his people had been among the last to be converted. "My great-grandfather was born in the darkness time, before the Christians came," he told me proudly. "The first missionaries on Lelepa were from England, a husband and wife. They brought their twelve-year-old son with them. My ancestors killed those missionaries and ate them. Ha! Ha! Not the boy, though. They wanted to adopt him, but that boy just would not stop crying. It was awful! They couldn't bear it. So they tied a rock around his neck, took him out, and dropped him in the middle of the bay." Now Albert gave tours of the harbor where the boy was drowned. The tourists enjoyed hearing about cannibalism, he said, especially if the victims were missionaries.

Apparently, Vila's heathen past had been reduced to caricatures and souvenirs. The missionaries had won. A cross hung from every neck. But if all the locals were Christian, why were missionaries still flocking to Vanuatu? Why the weekly revival crusades at the sports stadium? Why was the airport full of black-tied Utahans with name tags supplied by the Church of Jesus Christ of Latter-Day Saints? Why the sense of evangelical urgency in the scrubbed faces lined up for burgers at Jill's American Way Café, why the hallelujah processions down Kumul Highway?

"Because people here still live with so much wrong thinking! We are just trying to offer them what they need: a purer, more powerful gospel message," said my first friend in Port Vila. Kay Rudd lived with her husband, Jack, in the manicured hillside compound of the Joy Bible College. Kay wore farm dresses printed with tiny flowers. Her cheeks were thick and rosy. Jack favored khaki leisure suits. The Rudds were as warm and proscriptive as grandparents. They were missionaries. When I told them I was hunting for heathens, they invited me to their bungalow for ice cream.

"Vanuatu might call itself a proper Christian country. People might claim to be Christian," Kay told me. "But voodoo, black magic, spirits . . . folks still live in utter fear of all these things. And you know, dear, a true Christian doesn't have to be afraid."

"Because ghosts and magic don't exist," I said. "You are helping people overcome their superstitions."

Kay sighed and gave me a look of strained patience. "I didn't say that. Evil is real. But Christians have the power to break its spell. If we can get Bibles into people's hands, in their own languages, they will see they have the power to beat the black magic. They don't have to fear it."

"But everyone I've met in Vila is a Christian already," I said.

"Honey, we are still fighting the battle out on the islands."

The sun had disappeared beneath the banyans. Cicadas screamed from the trees. Fluorescent lights flickered on through distant windows. Kay put away the ice cream and told me an Inspirational Story. It was about Tanna, an island at the south end of Vanuatu.

A Very Bad Thing had happened on Tanna in the 1940s. Just when the Tannese seemed to have given up their ghosts and other devils, just when the missionaries thought they had won the island for Christ, along came a false prophet. The fellow called himself John Frum and made himself out to be some kind of messiah. He promised the islanders that if they abandoned the church and went back to their heathen ways, he would return one day on a great white ship loaded with goodies from America. The islanders bought the story hook, line, and sinker, said Kay. They nailed church doors shut and ran the priests out of their villages. Except for a few tenacious congregations, Tanna was gripped by John Frum fever—and lost to Christianity—for more than half a century.

But in 1996 that white ship from America finally appeared. On board was a friend of Jack and Kay's. His name was John Rush. Tanna's beleaguered Christian pastors decided Rush was the savior they had been waiting for. After all, he was American, he had arrived on a great white ship, and—best of all—he was named John. The circumstances were too close to the Frum myth not to be put to use.

"You get it, right?" said Jack, rubbing his hands together. "John from America: John—Frum—America! When that ship pulled in, it was like a prophecy fulfilled, and the pastors knew it. They figured our John could go to the John Frum chiefs and tell them to stop waiting. Tell them that America was not going to come solve all their problems."

"He didn't want to do it. He really didn't want to be mistaken for John Frum," interrupted Kay. "But the pastors begged him. So he went down to Sulphur Bay, the main Frum village, and would you believe the John Frum people were waiting for him? They rolled out the red carpet. They lined the path with flowers and gave him a big feast."

"John's visit was the beginning of the end for John Frum," said Jack. "That cult is finished now. The Presbyterians have rebuilt the church in Sulphur Bay. God is in. Frum is out. But our John won't take any credit for the good work. He says it was all because of the wise chief who let the Christians in."

"Chief One was his name. Isaac One," said Kay. "They call him that because he never repeats himself. Chief One. Isn't that cute?"

Isaac One. I scribbled that name in my notebook, and I mourned secretly. One more cult down the drain. But the Rudds were so full of down-home cheeriness they were hard not to like. Kay shone with perspiration and motherly concern. I let her hug me good-bye, and then I headed for the harbor.

I wandered along the darkened waterfront, where shadows moved among shadows, murmuring indecipherably and erupting into laughter. Somewhere a loudspeaker creaked and hissed, and occasionally let forth the sad squeal of a Chinese violin. Lights from yachts, canoes, and distant villages shone on the slickened surface of the water, as though this was the edge of the universe, beyond which swirled some terrible struggle between good and evil, white and black magic, unseen and formless but still clashing endlessly just beyond the horizon, singeing every life it touched. That, or it was the edge of nothing at all, an emptiness that could be filled only by the force of imagination.

3

Tanna: A Conflagration of Belief

The Natives, destitute of the knowledge of the true God, are ceaselessly groping after Him, if perchance they may find Him. Not finding Him, and not being able to live without some sort of god, they have made idols of almost everything; trees and groves, rocks and stones, springs and streams, insects and other beasts, men and departed spirits, relics such as hair and finger nails, the heavenly bodies and the volcanoes . . .

—JOHN G. PATON, *Missionary to the New Hebrides: An Autobiography*

When you read the accounts of Victorian adventurers, it is easy to be convinced that life at sea is exhilarating and romantic. The open horizon, the salt spray, the implied danger and possibility of all that heaving ocean. What could be more inspiring?

My great-grandfather wrote affectionately about his three-month tour of the Diocese of Melanesia aboard the mission's flagship, the *Southern Cross*. The three-hundred-ton schooner, the second to bear the name since Patteson's death, was built in 1891. She was fitted with an auxiliary engine, but generally relied on the sails of her three masts, the foremost of which was square-rigged. The ship cut languidly through the waves as it zigzagged from island to island. There were cabins on deck for the white clergy; the Melanesians ate and slept in the hold, so were apt to spend their free time dangling from the rigging or stretched asleep on the ship's dolphin striker. The passages across rough open ocean were trying for the bishop, but he preferred to remember the moments of prayer, the singing of canticles and hymns, the daily Evensong, and the delightful transformation he saw in the natives: "The boys come on board decorated with all sorts of earrings and nose rings, but by degrees these disappear. Before they reach Norfolk Island they have to put on shirts and trousers, and appropriate garments of English pattern are served out to the girls."

There was no sweeter moment for the bishop than dusk, when the *Southern Cross* had anchored in a quiet bay and a sense of peace settled on his mind. "At such times," he wrote, "it was permissible even to sit on deck in those suits, light and not elegant, which men find useful as 'garments of the night' in the tropics." Now and then, from some village hidden among the coconut palms, he would hear the tinkling of a bell, the whistle of a conch-shell horn or the bang of a drum, and he would know that the converts were being called to prayer, and he would be touched.

There was a certain deception in his focus on the bucolic.

This I know: The ocean is not romantic. Not when you have left the calm of the harbor and the swell is up and the vomiting has begun. The ocean is not a gentle mother, not a bucking stallion, not an adversary you can grapple with. The ocean is a great rotting blanket that won't be still. It is a pool of rancid milk. A gurgling toilet. Something to be endured. This is what I learned on my first sea passage.

The MV *Havanna* had been making the three-hundred-mile run from Port Vila southwest to the island nation of New Caledonia—with a stop at Tanna—for three months, and was said to be the finest ship in the archipelago. She created a stir wherever she went. She had seats, the agent who sold me my passage told me excitedly. But the *Havanna* was more a floating warehouse than the ferry I expected. She had an enclosed main deck with room for a dozen shipping containers, and a passenger compartment welded on top, like an afterthought. Her bow fell open like a broken jaw onto the government wharf.

Scots Presbyterians had laid claim to Tanna Island long before my great-grandfather's journey. He had sailed right past. So technically, Tanna was off-route for me. But I was hooked by the Rudds' story about the mysterious John Frum. I wanted to know why the Tannese had given up on their prophet. And so, the moment the *Havanna*'s crew let their guard down, I charged with two hundred others across the loading deck into the maw.

We sailed at dusk. Once we left the harbor, there was nothing to see. There was no squall. There was no lightning. But the spray rose like ghosts each time the *Havanna*'s blunt nose plunged into the undulating shadow of the southeast swell. The ship twisted and rolled unnaturally, and the night was filled with the hollow boom of waves striking the bow, the groan and flex of the hull, and a screeching that sounded like twenty-foot containers sliding across the steel floor of the hold. We did not use our cushioned chairs. We clung to the floor like lovers and vomited into plastic bags, purses, and open palms.

At the first hint of dawn I stumbled out onto the ship's deck. Men stood doubled over the railing. Drool trailed from their chins until it was caught by the wind and flung into the sea. A half-caste woman waved me over and offered me a spongy white ball, which at first I took for a muffin. In fact, it was the fibrous center of an overripe coconut.

"*Mais* this will take that 'orrible taste *long* mouth *blong yu*," the woman said. There was a bit of French and a swath of English. But the finale of her overture was Bislama, Vanuatu's de facto national language. What she had said was: "But this will take that horrible taste from that mouth of yours."

Bislama has been called a pidgin, which is to say it is an amalgamation, a simplification, and a bastardization of other languages by island people. My great-grandfather despised it. He wished Melanesians would learn proper English or at least stick to their own languages rather than using what he called the "vilest of compounds that ever polluted the purity of speech."

But the more I learned about Bislama, the more I realized it was one of the great triumphs of Vanuatu. The moniker originated from *bêche-de-mer,* the name the French gave to the sea slugs they bought from islanders and sold in the markets of Hong Kong. Bislama got its beginnings in the first half of the nineteenth century, when South Sea islanders worked as crew on whaling ships and developed a simple jargon to communicate with Europeans. It is full of nautical references and sailorly slang. When the sun goes down, they say, "*Sun hem i draon,*" as though the sun is drowning in the sea. When something is broken, "*Hem i bagarup.*" Say it out loud: "Him, he's buggered up."

The jargon developed further between 1863 and 1911, when more than fifty thousand Ni-Vanuatu were sent to work on plantations in Australia, Fiji, and Samoa. Those workers who spoke the same language were separated so they couldn't organize against their employers. Separating the *wantoks* ("one-talks," or common-language speakers) was easy: there were more than a hundred distinct languages in the New Hebrides alone. Workers had no choice but to speak to each other using the only words they had in common—English and French—though they used Melanesian grammar and syntax. Then they took the new language home with them.

Bislama may have been the bane of arbiters of grammar, but it gave the Ni-Vanuatu the common tongue they needed to achieve independence. Government documents may be written in English or French, but parliamentary debates are conducted in Bislama.

Everything is a *fala* (fellow), even a tree, a shark, or a girl. A boy who admired a girl told me, "*Hem i wan gudfala gel. Mi likem hem tumas.*" Then I understood that *tumas* did not mean "too much" but "a hell of a lot."

Things are defined by their relationship with other things. The word *blong* (belong) is everywhere—but the word *long* is a preposition, not an adjective. So if you ask a Ni-Vanuatu when colonial rule ended, he will tell you, "*Kantri blong mifala, hem i winim independens long 1980.*" That was the same year the New Testament was translated into Bislama and people began reading the *gud nius blong Jisas Krais.* If you ask a woman where she is going, she might say, "*Mi go nao blong swim long sanbij,*" and you would know she was now off to the beach to wash (*swim* means "wash").

Sometimes Bislama is easier to understand if you imagine it originating with a drunken sailor slurring orders to a Melanesian laborer. Take the initially baffling phrase "*Sarem olgeta doa.*" Now jump back a century, imagine that sailor barking at an islander, "Shut them doors." Perhaps in his hurry or inebriation the words would emerge something like "*Sarem doa.*" Melanesian languages require an extra word to denote the plural, so the reasonable islander would respond to the order by shutting just one door. The sailor, if he hadn't gone and shut the extra doors himself, might happen upon this plural construction: "Shut them, *altogether!*" Loosen the pronunciation, let "altogether" serve as the plural article, and you have the modern Bislama: "*Sarem olgeta doa.*"

Bislama can be poetic in its literalness. *A pijin blong solwata* is the bird we all associate with salt water: a seagull. A telescope is a *glas blong looklook big.* A condom is a *rubba blong fakfak.*

French words have also slipped into the language. To know is to *savve* (from the third-person singular *save* of the verb *savoir*). There are Polynesian words: Food is *kai-kai*. Children are *pikinini* (though some say that word originated with the English label for black children, or the Spanish *pequeño*). Now phrases are being traded back and forth between various pidgin-speaking countries. The Ni-Vanuatu borrow from Papua New Guinea when they tell you good-bye: *lookim yu bakagen*. But the strongest word of all is pan-Oceanic. If something or someplace is *tabu*, it is forbidden. You stay away from it.

The stars faded, and Tanna appeared like an ink stain across the horizon. The silhouette gradually grew into a series of folded mountainsides. Blue smoke curled from thatched roofs. Surf fringed the shoreline, exploding occasionally into bouquets of white spray. Sunlight broke across a ridge serrated by rows of palms. There was no harbor. We maneuvered past a reef and eased alongside a cement jetty that jutted out from a tongue of coral stone at Lenakel, Tanna's only town.

I tossed my pack on the grass and waited. I had sent a message ahead to Port Resolution, which was within striking distance of the fabled John Frum stronghold at Sulphur Bay. The villagers at Port Resolution knew someone with a truck. They would come and fetch me.

"Port Resolution? They will certainly not come to collect you. They are rubbish men," advised a stern Tannese man who installed himself on the grass next to me. His name was Kelsen. He had come to claim his new wheelbarrow from the *Havanna*. It shone. Kelsen had an untidy beard, which he tugged on constantly, and a ponderous brow, which at first I mistook for a mark of wisdom. He sat with me as I waited by the sea. I told him I was looking for former John Frum cult members.

"The John Frum people are all going to hell, that much is certain," said Kelsen.

I was heartened. "So then some people here still believe in John Frum?"

"Yes, the fools believe. But *nogud yu stap long* John Frum people. They are dirty. They have nothing to eat. They are fighting each other."

Kelsen said he lived at the base of the Yasur volcano. He promised to tell me a magic story about the volcano that I would never forget. Nobody else could tell me the story. Just Kelsen. He owned it. The story had been passed down for generations. He was considering writing it down and selling it.

"I can tell it to you," he said.

"I'm listening," I said.

Kelsen's eyes narrowed. He had a better plan. It was best to tell the story at his home. If I wanted to hear it, I would have to forget about the sinners at Port Resolution and Sulphur Bay and come stay with him. Kelsen had built a hotel of his own at the base of the volcano.

The day was getting on. I didn't have much choice. Kelsen threw my pack in his new wheelbarrow and led me along a row of tin-roofed stores. The road was lined with cement poles. Electric power had come to Lenakel three months before my arrival—just in time for World Cup soccer, said Kelsen. We lay in the grass at a road junction. After an hour, a pickup truck appeared. Kelsen flagged it down. We climbed in the box and rumbled east on a dirt road, up through the palms into the mountains.

Tanna was so thick with life, it was a caricature of paradise: the black volcanic soil exploded with banana, taro, manioc, flowering poinsettia, orange groves, and tree ferns. Melon-sized papaya hung from house-high stems. Banyan trees cast shadows the size of baseball diamonds, their canopies balanced atop hundreds of roots that twisted down from the branches like strands of macramé.

As we passed in and out of the shadows, Kelsen explained to me that it wasn't just the John Frummers who were going to hell.

It was most of the people on Tanna, including many of the Christians. "These people disobey the Bible every day," he grumbled. "They break the rules that Moses wrote down in Leviticus. They eat unclean food: pigs, flying foxes, sharks, crabs. They smoke. They drink kava. All forbidden! Worst of all, they go to church on Sunday, when we know that Saturday is the true Sabbath. They will be punished in time."

Kelsen knew these rules because his family had converted to Seventh-day Adventism in 1922. They had never fallen for the John Frum message or any other false teaching, he assured me proudly.

The forest on the east side of Tanna was caked in gray dust, and the trees began to resemble stone carvings. We rounded a bend and entered the devastation. It was as though the jungle had been buried and sealed under a layer of scoured earth. Bucket-sized boulders were strewn across the ash plain like spilled marbles. The volcano rose directly in front of us like a great Saharan dune, a perfect, pristine, and not particularly threatening heap of sand. This was Yasur, the volcano whose fireworks had guided Captain James Cook into Port Resolution—named for his ship—in 1774. Yasur was sacred in those days. Each time Cook attempted to climb it, his Tannese guides led him in circles back to the sea.

Our driver didn't slow for the view. He sped over a spur of the volcano toward a gap in the forest on the far side of the plain. We were halfway there when the afternoon was shattered by a deafening explosion. The driver swerved for a moment, then continued, even as a salvo of rocks exploded from the peak like pebbles thrown up by some giant hand. I dove to the floor. Kelsen laughed. The mountain belched a black mushroom cloud of smoke, then fell quiet.

We entered the forest again and followed a rutted track to a clearing and a collection of thatch huts on stilts. This was Kelsen's grand hotel. It was crude and beautiful. There were flowering trees and dozens of potted plants. Chickens clucked. Children dashed back and forth. Somewhere in the forest, a pan flute played "Amazing Grace." It reminded me of the postapocalyptic idyll depicted in the pamphlets that Jehovah's Witnesses hand out on street corners. Nothing bad ever happens here, I thought. But then a terrific sucking noise ripped through the valley—like a tsunami rolling across a pebble beach—then another appalling roar, and then a momentary vibration, not of the earth but of the air, which caused the huts to tremble and pressed my shirt against my skin. More smoke boiled above the treetops. I noticed there was no grass in Kelsen's village, only a thick layer of ash on the ground. The garden, the huts, the trees, they could all be burned and buried in an afternoon.

Kelsen's wife was too shy to look at me, but she brought me a plate of *laplap,* a root vegetable pudding baked and served in coconut leaves. The pudding was cold and rubbery. It had been cooked on Friday. Today was Saturday, the true Sabbath, and work was forbidden.

Kelsen failed to tell me his volcano story that day or the next. He took me for walks instead. We tramped through the jungle, following scant trails from village to village. The forest floor was punctuated by crude holes and littered with coconut husks: the work of wild pigs. At one village I heard the banging of coconut shells and singing, coming from a tiny lean-to. There was an old woman inside, surrounded by children.

"What are they singing about?" I asked.

"The grandmother has her own religion. She teaches it to all the little kids," said Kelsen.

"Can we talk to her?"

"No, no, of course not. She's a woman."

"Yes, I can see that. Let's talk with her."

"No!" Kelsen said. "*Kastom.*"

"*Kastom?* Wha—"

But Kelsen was already stomping back into the forest. He moved with an inexplicable urgency.

At the edge of the next village, Kelsen led me into a clearing where a lone man stood beneath a banyan tree. He wore a *lavalava*, a light scarf, wrapped around his waist. He dropped the *lavalava* the moment he saw me. I was embarrassed for us all, until I realized he had done it on purpose. Kelsen called to him, encouragingly. The man approached, and I saw that he wasn't quite naked. His penis was wrapped in what looked like hundreds of strands of grass or bark, the ends of which dangled artfully about his bare testicles. The bulk of the contraption, the penis part, was held erect by a grass belt wrapped around his waist. This, I realized, was a *nambas*, which was the only thing most men in the region had worn for centuries. (The first Europeans to see *nambas* were scandalized by them. E. Vigors, an early visitor, cloaked his horror in Latin, proclaiming that the men were "destitute of all clothing *si excepias penem quem decorant modo dissimilis indigenes Tannae ube membrum virile semper erectum tenent, sub singulo ligatum.*")

The *nambas* man beamed at me. Kelsen barked at him in a language I did not understand, and the man performed something like a slow pirouette, as if to prove to me that yes, indeed, his behind was bare. They spoke some more, then the man charged off into the forest.

We marched through two more villages. At each of them, Kelsen issued more orders and pointed at me, now with a growing tone of urgency and irritation. I was beginning to dislike Kelsen when we entered a clearing, grander than all the rest and flanked by two banyan so huge they made the space feel like an auditorium. Kelsen sat me down on a little bench.

"You want to see the heathens dance?" asked Kelsen.

"Maybe," I said, baffled.

"You will pay them, of course."

After a few minutes I heard chatter in the shadows, and then chanting. One by one, a troop of familiar faces emerged from a gap in the roots of the biggest banyan: an old man with a patchy beard, then a sculpted young version of himself, another fellow with tidy dreadlocks, three giggling teenage boys, and finally our friend from the first village. They had all shed their town clothes and were naked except for their *nambas*. They formed a circle and began to dance. They clapped their hands and stamped the earth, peering over their shoulders to see if I was taking pictures. I was, of course, but mostly out of politeness, since it was no more inspiring than the dinner-hour dances staged for package tourists back at Le Meridien Resort in Port Vila. Kelsen, heathenism's greatest detractor, had managed to transform the old ways into a meal ticket. The *nambas* gang was bored. I squirmed on my bench, trapped, despising Kelsen more every minute. But I thought if I was polite I might at least be able to talk to the old man when they finished.

"You are Christians like Kelsen," I said to the chief when the dust settled.

He shook his head. "Ha ha! No, we don't believe in church," he said in Bislama. "We believe in kava and pigs."

"But didn't the missionaries ever come and talk to you, to change you?"

"Yes, they have heard the good news," interjected Kelsen in English. "But they don't want to listen. They are going to hell."

"The missionaries came," said the chief. "They told us not to make our *kastom*"—that word again—"but we were born with *kastom* and we won't forget it. My grandfather and my great-grandfather, they followed *kastom*. So I will, too. My life is easy. We eat, sleep, and drink kava for free. Christians have to work so hard. They have to pay for everything," he said, eyeing Kelsen slyly.

Kastom. I would learn that the word means many things to Melanesians. To translate *kastom* as "culture" is to chart only a part of its power. *Kastom* is Melanesian history, religion, ritual, and magic, but it also refers to traditional systems of economics, social organization, politics, and medicine. If you say something is *kastom*, you are attaching it to the traditions of the ancestors. You are sanctifying it. But sometimes the word is simply used to excuse a practice from scrutiny. (Why aren't women allowed to drink kava? *Kastom*. Why can't women be pastors? *Kastom*. Why don't kava bowls get washed between servings? *"Hem i kastom blong mifala nomo."*)

"We solve every problem we have using *pik-pik* and kava," the chief said. "For example, when we make a fight with another village, we can kill a *pik-pik* to make it better. If we have other kinds of problems, we drink kava, then ask the spirits for help. A spirit could be in the hollow of the banyan tree. It could be somewhere else, too, but it comes when we ask."

Kelsen nodded approvingly, but mumbled in English, "Idolatry."

"Friend, let me ask you a question," said the chief. "Suppose Kelsen goes to church and asks his Jesus for rain. Will it rain? No. Ha! But if I want rain I go to the banyan, drink my kava, and make a prayer to my papa or my mama. They are dead, but if I need rain they will bring it. If I have lost a *pik-pik* in the forest, they will bring that back to me, too."

"Foolish heathens," said Kelsen. "Jesus can make it rain harder."

It was impossible to talk to the chief about religion without running the gauntlet of Kelsen's commentary. I changed the subject.

"Your *nambas*. Does it hurt?"

"No, not at all," said the chief. "We have been circumcised. Our penises are very strong."

Kelsen jumped in again to explain that all Tannese boys were ritually circumcised before adulthood. Even his own boys would be circumcised amid much feasting and celebration.

"But why would you do it, Kelsen?" I asked.

"Because it's *kastom*."

"But Kelsen, you are Christian!"

It seemed a baffling contradiction. It appeared as though even Tanna's staunchest Seventh-day Adventist could not wrest himself completely from the ways of the ancestors.

"*Kastom* doesn't mean not Christian," Kelsen said gruffly, but before he could continue, the chief touched my hand to get my attention, then made a fist and punched the air.

"We have strong, strong penises! Even very old men on Tanna can make children. Friend, suppose you ever have a problem making babies on your own island, you just come back here and our *kastom* doctor can give you medicine for your penis."

I thanked him and asked about John Frum.

"Don't worry about John Frum," Kelsen said. "John Frum is for crazy people. John Frum has no power—"

"You must go to Sulphur Bay," interrupted the chief. "On Friday night they will dance for John Frum."

This agitated Kelsen no end. "Time for go now," he said, then asked me for five hundred vatu so he could pay the chief.

We retreated through the forest, me feeling like a tourist, knowing the chief and his boys would be climbing back into their regular clothes as soon as we disappeared.

"Five hundred vatu: a very good deal," Kelsen explained. "That's how much they charge tourists over in Yakel village. And those heathens wear grass skirts, not *nambas*. Sometimes you can even see they have shorts on under their skirts. More naked should mean more money, yes?"

Kelsen was skipping now.

"You see," he said, "I know the heathens. I am your best guide. You are very lucky to have found me."

Kelsen was a tragic case. He ridiculed pagan *kastom*, but he clearly suffered without it. For one thing, he was fighting with his brother over the money that guests paid to stay in their village. They couldn't hold a *kastom* pig-killing ceremony to settle the dispute, since pork was *tabu* for Adventists. The brothers could not rely on their ancestors or island myths to guide them. They would be parted like Cain and Abel, Kelsen had told me—though he would be the one to keep the money. He quivered with an obsessive, greedy longing. It was my first taste of the spiritual confusion that had metastasized into an all-out civil war up in the Solomon Islands.

Kelsen begged me not to go to Sulphur Bay. There was nowhere to stay, he said. John Frum's followers had left the stronghold of their faith and run off into the hills where I would never find them. He assured me that if I stayed with him just one more night, he would tell me his volcano story. But he had been promising that for three days.

I followed the cart track back toward Yasur, this time on foot. At midday, I reached the ash plain, where I spotted a trio of Mormon missionaries. Their white shirts blazed in the sunlight. Their ties flapped in the wind. We shook hands. I told them I thought they deserved great credit for keeping their shirts clean no matter how rough the mission field might be. They told me I shouldn't be so cheery, especially if I was going to hike down to Sulphur Bay.

"There is a false prophet on this end of the island," one said gravely. "He has led hundreds of people astray."

"John Frum," I said.

"No. The false prophet's name is Fred. He is very dangerous. He has been throwing babies into the volcano."

They gave me directions to Sulphur Bay anyway. I crossed the ash plain, mesmerized by the black mushroom clouds that periodically issued from the summit of Yasur. There was a single set of footprints in the ash, zigzagging up a spur to the summit ridge.

Babies in the volcano. Honestly.

But Fred . . . that name was familiar. Then I remembered.

Back in Port Vila I had met a Canadian man who had just served a six-month stint as Tanna's only doctor. Fockler was his name. He told me that the island had intrigued and baffled him. Like the time the national police had summoned him to Sulphur Bay to check on a man who had established a new village on a shoulder of the volcano.

"Rumor had it that this guy had gone off the deep end," the doctor said. "He was having all kinds of visions and he had been accused of all sorts of crimes—you know, ritual child abuse, or something like that. Oh, they also said that he had leprosy."

Fockler had dutifully trucked across the island with his rubber gloves and a bag full of antipsychotic drugs. He had barely begun to hike up the mountain when he came face-to-face with the infamous Fred, who was a big man with messy hair. It was clear that Fred had indeed suffered from leprosy. His eyebrows and hands were slightly misshapen. But it was also clear to the doctor that the condition was inactive and not contagious. Fockler pretended to examine the prophet's skin while actually conducting a quick mental status assessment.

"I asked him if he saw visions, you know, or heard any messages, and he said, 'I can't tell you that, it's the source of my power.' Well, that pretty much shut down my psychological assessment. But he didn't seem overtly psychotic."

Fockler figured that the police were looking for an excuse to lock Fred up, but he decided it was not his job to do their dirty work. He announced to Fred's followers—there were hundreds—that he would let them keep their prophet. They cheered. The doctor returned to the hospital in Lenakel, and Fred remained on the mountain with his visions.

I followed a track into the forest and down along a ravine. The slopes on either side of the ravine had been scoured right down to bare rock. That puzzled me: the creek that trickled through the gorge could never have done such damage. The devastation

widened to several hundred yards as I neared the sea. Then the
track veered away from the creek and ended in a wide field surrounded by huts. This was Sulphur Bay, but the village was empty
and the field had been thoroughly excavated by pigs, two of which
watched me silently from their craters. There was an old cement
cistern. Its tap yielded only dust.

I heard the sound of voices coming from the creek. I followed
them and found dozens of women bathing, singing, and slapping
their laundry, which steamed in the afternoon heat. Some of them
were topless, which was not exactly in keeping with the teachings
of the Presbyterians who first evangelized the island. I walked on
to talk to their husbands, who were bathing upstream.

I had scarcely mentioned the name Isaac One when a young
man leaped forward, grabbed my hand, and tugged me away
from the creek.

"Not here," he said adamantly. "Not Sulphur Bay."

He pulled my pack from my back and strode off with it, heading farther upstream. I had little choice but to follow him. After a
few minutes, we entered a clearing much like the ones I had seen
on my walks with Kelsen: an oval of earth pounded hard by bare
feet, this one shaded by a grove of breadfruit trees. Spiny fruit
hung from the branches like green piñatas. The clearing was full
of people: old men in filthy *lavalavas* and ski jackets, young men in
surf shorts. Boys and mongrels lurked shyly around their heels.
The men were tending little fires and puttering with great dirty
clumps of roots. They turned to gaze at me silently.

"Isaac One," I said. An old man stepped forward.

I pulled a bag of rice and three tins of tuna from my pack, in-
tending to hand them to the chief, but thought better of it when he
scowled and turned away. I placed them on a grass mat instead.
The chief did not acknowledge my gifts. He murmured something to my guide, who took my pack and disappeared into the
forest. I was nervous. The sky turned purple over the volcano.

Dusk settled on the *nakamal*—for that is where I had arrived: the traditional kava-drinking ground beside almost every village on Tanna.

"The chief is very drunk," said the man who brought me. "Kava."

Isag Wan (as I learned his name was really spelled) was beguiling. He was as thin and bent as the smoldering twig he clutched in one hand, at the ready to relight the cigarette that never left his mouth. He had the bloodshot eyes of a kava addict. But those eyes were still quick. His beard was peppered gray, and he wore a khaki jacket with "U.S. Army" stamped on the chest. He was forever kicking the mongrels that followed him around the *nakamal*.

I tried to introduce myself, to explain why I had come, but the chief just waved me silent with a bony hand, then proceeded to fuss over a grass mat, which he spread on the dirt for me.

"*Long moning yu kam long ofis blong mi,*" he said, then turned away.

Come to his office in the morning? An office, here? I hadn't seen so much as a tin roof in a week.

The night's kava session had already begun, and the chief would not be distracted. The scene was familiar—I had read accounts of the ritual by the earliest Presbyterian missionaries, who noted that the Tannese followed each gulp of the drink with an invocation of a spirit or a prayer meant to activate the power of a magic stone. The missionaries did not like that at all. They banned kava consumption for several decades before John Frum came to challenge them.

No women were permitted in the *nakamal*. I watched the men whittling away at clumps of kava. They halfheartedly scraped off the dirt and woodiest skin from the root, which looked like ginger, only fatter. Then they cut it up into bite-sized portions and handed them to teenage boys, who waited like dogs for table scraps. The boys chewed and the men fed them more bits of root, until their cheeks ballooned like singing frogs. Then one of the boys spat the contents of his mouth onto what looked like a hankie (which seemed appropriate, given the way he cleared his nose and horked once his chewing was done). The blob of masticated root looked like a cow pie. Isag Wan held the cloth and chewed root over a coconut-shell bowl. Someone poured water over the fibrous mass, then the chief wrapped the cloth around it and squeezed until the juice dripped into the bowl. They kept pouring and squeezing until the bowl was full of mud-gray slurry.

The chief drank his shell in three quick gulps. Then he turned and spat a great bouquet of spray toward the forest. As he was spitting, he made a sound somewhere between a groan and a yawn.

"The chief is saying his *tamavha:* he is praying," whispered a young man who had settled in next to me. His name was Stanley. A single knot of dreadlocks sprang from the back of Stanley's head. He wore a T-shirt with a cartoon mouse on it. The mouse was drinking tequila.

"And now it is your turn," Stanley said, smiling encouragingly. Everyone in the *nakamal* turned to watch me. I rose and was approached by a lad with red paint smeared across his face. He looked like one of the castaways from *The Lord of the Flies*. Snot oozed from his nostrils in vibrant shades of green and yellow. He cleared his nose and swallowed, then he handed me what I considered to be an unfairly large coconut shell that was close to over-flowing with the muddy brew.

"Just like the chief did," said Stanley. "All in one go, and then you say your *tamavha.*"

The kava looked like dirty dishwater, tasted of mud and cloves, and acted like anaesthetic. My tongue went numb even as I chugged my shell. I spat into the forest, barked "God help me," then peered into the shadows. After two more shells, the numbness spread to my stomach and my head. All was well. The world hummed quietly, and I tried to place the source of this newfound feeling of transcendence.

Scientists have been researching the pharmacology of the *Piper methysticum* shrub for more than a hundred years. Researchers in the 1980s found that the pepper's root contains compounds with anticonvulsant, muscle relaxant, and local anaesthetic effects. There may also be psychoactive constituents, but nobody seems to agree on whether or not kava contains enough to get drinkers good and high, in the clinical sense.

Kava is consumed in pockets right across the South Pacific. But nowhere is the drink said to be as powerful as on Tanna. That could be because Tanna is the only place where the root is prepared by chewing, rather than pounding or grating. Researchers have suggested that the root's active ingredients, whatever they are, have low rates of water solubility. Saliva might act as an emulsifying agent. In other words, all that chewing by all those snot-nosed virgins might actually release the kava's true power.

The night air was wrapping itself around me like strands of gauze. I sat on my grass mat and proclaimed the goodness of it all to Stanley. It dawned on me that he was a dear, dear friend of mine. "Everything is purple. Life is purple, really," I told him. "Don't you think?"

Stanley glanced around the clearing and shook his head sternly. "Quiet, quiet. Only whisper now." The *nakamal* was not like a bar where you could yell at your neighbor, he said.

So I whispered: "Do you believe in John Frum?"

"I believe," Stanley said.

Bingo.

"But who is he? What is he? Is he your god? Where did he come from?"

"Shhh," he said, and then he mumbled his answer into the dirt between us. "There is only one God but different messiahs. Your messiah is Jesus. Ours is John Frum. He is our best ancestor."

Stanley's voice began to trail off. I tapped his knee gently. It was like kicking a jukebox back to life.

"Back in darkness time we only had *kastom* on Tanna," he said. "The grandfathers drank the kava and did the dances. They had magic stones, and the stones would help them make the ocean rough or calm. They could make sun and rain, too. But then the missionaries came and told the grandfathers: 'You come to church. God will give you everything.' And they made a law to stop the grandfathers from using their magic stones. They said all *kastom* was bad—even kava.

"That's when John Frum came to us—as a spirit. He told the grandfathers, 'The white man has a light, the light of his Church, but he wants to use it to destroy your *kastom*. Go back to *kastom*, hold tight to it, because God created *kastom* for us to live by.'"

And then Stanley fixed his gaze on the fire, and he did not acknowledge my prodding, and he was silent for a long time.

I wanted more, but I had already constructed a collage of Frum history from European reports I discovered in the Port Vila library. According to these, the prophet John Frum was a direct by-product of Christian zeal. Presbyterian missionaries had established what amounted to a theocracy on Tanna by the time the French and British set up their joint administration of the islands. The church subjected the island to Presbyterian law enforced by roving bands of native enforcers. Anyone suspected of drinking kava, singing, or dancing could expect to be arrested and taken to a church court.

All that began to change in 1940. That's when the British district agent James Nicol heard rumors that a mysterious stranger had been calling the island chiefs together for secret meetings. The stranger wore a broad-brimmed hat and a white sports jacket with silver buttons. No one ever saw the stranger's face in the shadows, but they imagined by his high-pitched voice that he was a white man. He berated them for following other white men's laws. John Frum was his name—though some insisted it was John With a Broom (for sweeping away sadness). Regardless, it was his message that counted. He said the Tannese should turn their backs on the Presbyterian missionaries who had banned the things that made them whole. They should return to the *kastom* Stanley had told me about: extravagant dances, rainmaking magic, circumcision ceremonies, and polygyny. They should throw their European money in the sea and get back in touch with their ancestors. If the Tannese did all these things, the colonial police and the strict Presbyterian missionaries would miraculously disappear. And then the prophet would return on a big white ship, and that ship would be loaded with riches from America. Refrigerators, cooking ware, and Spam would be as plentiful as coconuts.

Some islanders said that John Frum was the king of America, or perhaps the son of God: like Jesus, only older. Others insisted thousands of his soldiers were inside the volcano, waiting for the right moment to charge out and chase the British and French away. Several chiefs claimed to be Frum himself.

The prophet's followers exploded into action in 1941. They slaughtered cattle and pigs and turned in their European currency in preparation for Frum's golden age. Hundreds gathered to swill kava and dance all night on the south end of Tanna. One Sunday that May, the Presbyterian ministers found their churches completely empty for the first time in decades.

Nicol had had enough. He called in reinforcements from Port Vila and arrested dozens of Frum's most adamant followers.

The movement might have died had Frum's prophecies not come true. In December 1941, the Japanese bombed Pearl Harbor. The American fleet reached the New Hebrides the following March. More than half a million soldiers passed through the islands during the war. The U.S. soldiers were spectacularly generous, handing out pots, pans, cigarettes, and tinned meat. One black GI, hearing of the Tannese struggle, reportedly gave them a flag. (Some say it was red; others insist it was the Stars and Stripes.) He told the Frummers that America would always be there to protect them from their colonial masters. Now the Tannese were even more sure of their prophet's connection with America. They raised that flag at Sulphur Bay on February 15, 1957. They built a cross and painted it red, to match the crosses they had seen on U.S. Army ambulances. They carved wooden "rifles" and gathered U.S. Army surplus clothing. To honor the day of their redemption, the Frummers don those fatigues, take up those rifles, and perform marching drills around their Sulphur Bay parade ground on each February 15.

But Tanna is hardly unique in the messiah department. Melanesia produced dozens of cargo cults in the last century. Across the archipelago, a generation of messiahs promised the arrival of shiploads and planeloads of untold riches, but only for those who obeyed their edicts. The cults emerged independently on at least a dozen islands, and they all revolved around the manipulation of supernatural forces to bring about an age of prosperity and freedom. Most advocated giving up foreign goods and customs while at the same time promising the spontaneous arrival of consumer goods. People built wharves, warehouses, and even airstrips to facilitate the cargo magic. The cults that emerged before World War II relied on returning ancestors to bring wealth. But after the war, that changed: the magic cargo would come from America. After U.S. soldiers left Espiritu Santo, three hundred miles north of Tanna, leaders of what became known as the Naked Cult told villagers to cast off their clothes and conduct all their sexual intercourse in public, "like dogs and fowls." Doing so would bring the Americans back and usher in a golden age of prosperity and everlasting life.

There were so many cults in Melanesia that church leaders

created guidelines for the missionaries who battled them. A 1971 paper advised Christian pastors to be patient. They should try to ignore the villagers' use of Christian crosses in pagan rituals, and divert the cultists' attention with movies and sports events.

A few anthropologists have suggested that the cargo cult phenomenon was a response by primitive cultures to the seemingly supernatural levels of material wealth possessed by Europeans and Americans. The theory goes like this: The industrial products white men used were so shockingly different that islanders thought they must have come from the spirit realm. Guns, Jeeps, and tinned food were also seen as evidence of the white man's mastery over Melanesians. The possession of those things would bring to islanders a kind of material and spiritual emancipation. There was a secret to white men's good fortune. Discover that secret, grab the cargo magic, and the days of slavery would be over.

So why would a regular guy like Stanley buy into such an outrageous myth? There was no doubt about his allegiance. Stanley lived in Port Resolution, but he had hiked over the mountain to celebrate tomorrow's John Frum Sabbath with Chief Wan. But was he really desperate for Spam? And if Sulphur Bay was the epicenter of the Frum movement, why had I found that village empty? There were many questions, but the chief had forced two more shells of kava on us both, and it had simplified us, and perhaps only that one last question actually left my mouth. Anyway, it was the only one Stanley heard.

"Sulphur Bay is dead because of Fred," he said. The leper prophet. "Didn't you see what Fred did over by the volcano? There was once *wan bigfala* lake on the ash plain. Fred used magic to drain it. He made a flood. It destroyed the river and killed some houses in Sulphur Bay. Fred told everyone that God did this, but we know it was Fred using *kastom* magic. Isag Wan had to protect the people from Fred. That's why he moved out of Sulphur Bay to this village, Namakara."

"Yes, Fred is a bad man," I said, now wishing Stanley's words would match the rhythm of his lips, which seemed to be moving in slow motion. His voice was like mud. Now it was trailing off into an incomprehensible mumble. Stanley was sitting next to me, but the words seemed to issue from far beyond the edge of the clearing, where they mingled with the whirring of thousands of cicadas and the murmuring of the forest. The stars, however, looked close enough to touch. So did the fires that glowed like jewels in the dirt, and the ends of cigarettes that moved like fireflies, and the eyes of the pigs and dogs that flashed in the shadows. Tranquillity settled like a fog on my thoughts. My knee rested against Stanley's knee, and it was warm and good.

A boy took my hand and led me through the trees into a hamlet of darkened huts. A warm light shone from one of them. The boy removed a thatch screen, and I stepped inside to find my pack, an oil lamp, and a plate of steaming food. It was the rice and tuna I had given the chief. I ate, then fell into a deep sleep.

I awoke well after dawn with the gray sponge of kava still hanging in my head and a hint of diarrhea stirring in my gut. Isag Wan was squatting in the dirt outside my hut, agitated. At his heel, two piglets fought over a banana peel. The chief had a watch, which he checked three times before losing patience and calling me out. He led me to a dirt plaza in the middle of the village, and then we stood at attention together. After an uncomfortable minute, the chief consulted his watch again and coughed loudly. It was eight o'clock. Women stopped their sweeping. Pigs ceased rooting. The village fell silent. Even the volcano seemed to stop rumbling for a few solemn moments. Then a whistle sounded, and on a hillock in front of us, the Stars and Stripes was hauled up a bamboo flagpole. The cult of John Frum was alive and well.

The chief led me to his "office," a broad hut decked with grass mats and filled with bric-a-brac. There were wooden clubs and woven baskets, an airbrushed poster of frolicking cats and lions, a picture of a white Jesus, and a calendar with scenes from the coast of France. A carved wooden eagle stood on the table. Dominating it all was a crude painting of Yasur, with slogans painted across its slopes in a mix of Bislama and English. I remember one of them:

MANI HEM GUD LAIF

BUT MANI I MEKEM MAN I STAP

RAPEM BROTHA MO SISTA BLONG HEM

Money is good life, but money makes a man exist to rape his brother and sister. It didn't quite seem like a plea for cargo. Isag Wan cleared his throat, tossed his cigarette to a lad sitting on the floor, and, with the boy translating, told me his version of Tannese history. It paralleled those I had read in Port Vila, though in Isag Wan's version, his own grandfather had been the first to champion John Frum's pro-*kastom* ideas. The chief was the heir to a spiritual dynasty.

"So has John Frum returned, or are you still waiting for him to come back from America with his ship full of cargo?" I asked.

"John Frum speaks to me often."

"So he *has* returned," I said, remembering my afternoon of ice cream back at the Joy Bible College in Port Vila. The missionaries had insisted that their friend, John Rush, had converted the chief. "John Frum. John Rush. John Frum is John Rush!" I said. "Right?"

"No! I remember John Rush. He came and told us John Frum was inside of him, but I never believed it. John Rush is only *wan man blong* church. We don't need church. We need to stay together and follow John Frum."

"So where is John Frum?"

"Away."

"Then how can you talk to him?"

"He sends others to talk with me. Spirit men. They come through the volcano. There's a road underneath the fire, it goes all the way to 'Merica."

We were speeding into fantastical terrain. I certainly didn't want to break the momentum by questioning the physics of the chief's assertions. I encouraged him:

"Maybe you have been to America . . ."

"Yes, I have!"

"How did you get there? Through the volcano? Did John Frum take you?"

Isag Wan glared at me, eyes narrowing with irritation. Of course not, he said. A visitor to Tanna had paid for him to fly to America on a plane. How? With his Visa card, of course.

"I have seen Atlanta, Dallas, and Washington," said the chief. "I went to the White House and I spoke to President Clinton's general secretary. He was happy to talk to me because he knew that Tanna has flown the U.S. flag for so many years. But 'Merica made me very sad. Too many trucks, too many poor people. Did you know that some men there have no land at all? I met them on the road. I gave them all the money I had in my pockets."

It was too mundane a story to doubt, though I wished the chief would get back to miracle talk.

"I thought John Frum promised to make you all rich, like Americans."

"We will not follow 'Merica. 'Merica should follow us. Look," said Isag Wan, doodling in the sand with a stick. " 'Merica has lost the road. They think money is Jesus. 'Merica must remember the promise of John. Remember the true path."

I took a deep breath and closed my eyes. I could feel the dregs of the previous night's kava pulsing behind my temples. "The true path—"

"The life way. Don't follow government. Don't follow church. Don't follow money. Follow *kastom* and peace. That's what Jesus and John Frum say."

"But you don't have peace here. You've abandoned Sulphur Bay. You are fighting your old neighbors. Stanley told me you are fighting with this man—this prophet—Fred."

"Fred is not a prophet. He is an evil man. He tells people he has the spirit of John Frum, but it's a lie. I know where Fred's power comes from. He is using the power of the black sea snake to trick us all."

The whole Fred business had started two years before, said Isag Wan. "Fred made bad talk. He told the old men in Sulphur Bay to kill nineteen pigs and drink nineteen shells of kava in order to wash away their sins, but look what happened instead: he broke the lake and he washed away half the village. Fred promised to turn all the old men in Sulphur Bay into children again. But the old men are still old! Fred promised that if people followed him to the top of the mountain, Jesus would come and take them all to heaven. Jesus didn't come! He said he would stop the sun from setting, but look at the sky. Night still comes. Fred lies!" The chief paused to swipe at a dog that had poked its head through the door of his shack. Embers flew from the end of his stick. "Worst of all, Fred told people to destroy the last of the *kastom* stones, and now he is trying to make everyone go back to the church. That's why we had to leave Sulphur Bay. It belongs to the church again. Namakara is the new home for John Frum."

"So Fred lives in Sulphur Bay."

"No! He has taken the people to live on the volcano. He told everyone he is the Messiah and he would take them to heaven if they followed him. But they still haven't gone to heaven. Lies!"

I spent the afternoon lounging in the bathtub-warm waters of the creek and trying to clear the kava from my head. At dusk a drum sounded, and I followed it back to the plaza in the middle of the village. The John Frum Sabbath was beginning. Boys poked at a bonfire. The pilgrims from Port Resolution shuffled quietly across the dirt, carrying four guitars, a homemade banjo, and a couple of bongo drums. Stanley was with them, still wearing his tequila T-shirt. The people settled onto palm mats. The women made a circle around the men. Then the band started to play, slowly at first, softly; then the women joined in and sang a song tinged with an autumnal sadness that made me homesick. The night sped on, and Stanley's band gave way to three others. The rhythm quickened until the chorus rose in great triumphant arcs, suggesting a time of flowers and love and smiles and cumulonimbus clouds touched with sunset gold. "Namakara! Namakara! Namakara!" The people chanted the name of the village over and over again to the stars.

Now more than a hundred figures had emerged from the shadows: men, women, and children, all swaying in loose formation around the band. The women had glitter paint around their eyes and wore rainbow-painted grass skirts. Some of the men wore skirts, too, over their rolled-up trousers. As the music rose toward a crescendo, those grass-skirted bums began to shake. Boys jumped and writhed. The air filled with whoops, chirps, and rhythmic hissing. Stanley bobbed beside me, smiling broadly and touching my elbow: "Come on! Come on! Sssst! Sssst!"

I saw Isag Wan in his grass skirt and camouflage T-shirt, cigarette burning in the corner of his mouth, his frail frame shaking, his eyes rolling ecstatically. I was struck by the thought that there was nothing very strange going on in Namakara. Whatever its beginnings, the John Frum movement was no more audacious now than any church. The cult had gone mainstream. Frummers have been elected to Vanuatu's national parliament, and government ministers have attended the annual Frum marches at Sulphur Bay. Ralph Regenvanu, the director of Vanuatu's National Cultural Center, told me that John Frum was not a ghost or a foreigner or a crazy man. Frum knew exactly what he was doing, and so did the chiefs who have invoked his name—and changed his story—for sixty years: their promises of cargo are simply window dressing for a sophisticated attempt to halt the spiritual disintegration that they feel Christianity causes.

If that was so, it was almost beside the point that Isag Wan claimed to receive the occasional dispatch through the fiery gullet of the volcano. The chief didn't pray for the diversion of the white man's wealth. He wasn't asking for anything particularly radical from his people. His cargo was the spiritual riches the world would share when churches and governments stopped fighting each other. Or something like that. This, I thought, is what happens to cults when they mellow over time. They become religion.

Isag Wan didn't claim to be a prophet. He wasn't the chosen one. Not like the mysterious Fred, who, depending on whom you asked, was either in direct communication with God or was working a terrible kind of black magic on all who opposed him.

Above Namakara's huts and flagpoles, past the darkened folds of jungle, flecks of magma arced like ocher fireworks through the night sky. The mountainside was illuminated, and for just a moment, I was sure I could make out a hint of campfire smoke rising from a distant ridge.

4

The Prophet Raises
His Hands to the Sky

The mountain is awake, with utterance
Of flame and burning rock and thunderous sound—
Abode of the ancestral spirits who dance
In blissful fire! Tremors run through the ground
And through men's hearts. The people stand dismayed
By prophecies as mantic ghosts invade
With alien voice the soothsayers in their trance.
—JAMES McAULEY, Captain Quiros

The nearest village to Fred's mountain camp was Port Resolution, on the south side of the volcano. I followed Stanley there and found the village chief on the dirt floor of his hut, holding his stomach. There wasn't much to him. Flies gathered at the edge of his eyes, which had sunk deeply into his skull. Skin hung from his face like soggy paper. A doctor had told the chief that his liver had simply given up trying to process all that kava, but the chief and everyone else in Port Resolution knew that grog wasn't the problem.

"It's Fred," Stanley told me as we retreated from the hut. "He has poisoned the chief with his magic."

Port Resolution was a perfect teardrop of glowing aquamarine nestled against a long sweep of black sand. Palms hung languidly over the beach. Men threw fishnets from outrigger canoes. Steam curled from vents on the forested ridges that led to Yasur. The bay once served as the base for Tanna's first Presbyterians, but now its two hundred villagers were served by no less than four churches: Presbyterian, Seventh-day Adventist, Assemblies of God, and an outpost of the Neil Thomas Ministries, an evangelical outfit from Australia. The residents drifted back and forth between faiths like butterflies on flowers. There was a Seventh-day Adventist school, which meant that children born to pagan families learned the Bible early on, then switched back to *kastom*, pigs, and kava when they hit puberty. Church bells rang each morning, but Stanley's John Frum string band practiced on the soccer field each afternoon, after which we retired to the *nakamal* for our kava. If a boy was Adventist he couldn't drink kava, but he was still expected to chew it for his father's nightly brew. The chief of Port Resolution was pagan, but his son, Wari, was Adventist. That caused a slight problem, since Wari was responsible for the village's shark stone, a magic rock that could be used to manipulate the habits of sharks and mackerel. He wouldn't show me the shark stone, but he told me how it worked.

"If you want to attract fish," said Wari, "you get some *kastom* leaves and rub them on the stone and leave it in a special *tabu* place."

"But you are Adventist. You can't eat fish without scales. You can't eat shark."

"True, but if I am the keeper of the shark stone, it's *tabu* to eat the shark anyway. I must treat it like a god. And besides, the ancestors didn't use the shark stone for catching fish. They used it to make the sharks eat our enemies."

Thus Wari dispatched any ideological conflict.

The villagers had built a kitchen and a clutch of rough bunga-lows on a bluff above the bay and erected a sign: Port Resolution Yacht Club. There was no dock, but the yacht club had a com-modore who went to great lengths to take care of visiting yachties: for example, if the radio forecast a cyclone, it was his job to put special leaves in the ocean in order to calm the wind and waves.

Nobody wanted to help me track down Fred. No wonder. People were terrified of him. The prophet had eclipsed John Frum as the source of gossip and myth on Tanna. Everyone had a Fred rumor to pass on. Some accused Fred of cursing people. Others said that Fred was a pervert: according to one story, he enjoyed sitting in a pit above which were placed two thin boards; women were forced to step across those boards so Fred could peer up their skirts. Then of course there was the one about Fred throwing babies into the volcano.

Those were rumors. What seemed more alarming to me was the effect the prophet was having on human geography. Families from all over Tanna had abandoned their gardens in order to join Fred on the volcano. Farmland was going fallow. Pigs were disap-pearing. Things were falling apart. While Fred's followers waited for their ride to heaven, they pilfered the gardens of the villages at the base of their mountain. It was whispered that a handful of old folks and children had already died up at Fred's camp.

My chance came on my second night in Port Resolution.

We were crouched on a log at the *nakamal*, and well into the kava. I asked Stanley if he had a girlfriend.

"No," he said. "I'm waiting for a girl with blond hair, like yours."

We stared together into the fire, knees touching again. I saw my window.

"Please, Stanley, if you are my true friend, you will take me to Fred."

He smiled broadly, my favorite smile, and he agreed. At least,

I thought he agreed. The next morning we started along the beach toward the mountain, Stanley dawdling all the way, scratching his head, pulling at his clump of dreadlocks. He wanted to sit by the water and philosophize about John Frum.

He mused that John Frum's prophesied return from across the water was something like a metaphor, though he didn't use that word.

"John Frum told us he would return on the ocean, in a ship. But you know, for us, the sea is wealth. When someone says *solwota*, they mean wealth."

"It's a symbol—"

"Yes! So now when good things happen, when foreigners come with money, we know it is John Frum coming home to us."

In other words, the golden age that Frum had promised had already arrived, in the form of foreign tourists and international aid.

"Look at the solar telephone in our village," Stanley said. "It came from across the water, just like John Frum promised."

This seemed a fairly liberal and reasonable interpretation. I liked it, even if the solar phone happened to be a donation from Australia rather than America. Stanley was a postmodernist! He was also full of contradictions. When we reached the end of the beach and started up a faint trail, he slowed to a shuffle. At the edge of the last coconut grove, he stopped.

"I can't go up there," he said.

"But why? I'm with you. Nothing will happen."

"I want to help you, but I can't. If I see Fred, if I even look at him, I know I will get sick."

So much for metaphors. It was apparently easier to massage contemporary meaning into an old myth than it was to confront the potential horrors of the new. Stanley traced me a map in the dirt, and I continued on alone up a series of braided trails. I passed two abandoned villages. The forest changed. The benevolent jun-

gle of Port Resolution gave way to a ragged and desperate landscape of stumps, cracked coconut palms, and clinging brambles. I
heard screams and hoots in the forest. As I climbed away from the
bay, I began to encounter people. Children with machetes hacked
branches from breadfruit trees. When they saw me they screamed,
"*Waet man!*" They called back and forth in Bislama, which meant
they didn't share a common tongue. Of course: Fred's followers
came from all over Tanna, and there were at least six distinct languages on the island. I saw adults, too, all coming down from the
mountain with empty baskets and water jugs. One old man
grabbed me by the sleeve and pulled me close. "Go on," he hissed
in my ear. "He is waiting for you."

I followed the trail through a great maze of vines and spiraling
banyan roots, up through a series of cliffs and onto a ridge pock-
marked with vents that steamed and oozed iron-red mud. From
there, I could see over the forest and coconut plantations to the Pacific. Storms seemed to be coming from all directions. Shadows
raced across the ocean. Then the rain swept across the mountain
and hit just as I entered a village, making it seem especially squalid.
Hundreds of grass huts jostled for space on a small plateau and
spilled down a series of mud ravines. The huts were new, judging
by the pale jade of their thatch, but they were not like the quaint
bungalows I had seen elsewhere on Tanna. These were makeshift
lean-tos and A-frames, all of them ill-proportioned and too low to
stand in. Children shrieked and rolled in the muck. Sores glistened
on their ankles and on their heads. There was a dirt parade ground,
too, with a bamboo pole planted dead center. Dangling limply from
it was the U.S. flag.

A man stepped forward.

"Fred?" I asked.

"No, I'm Alfred. Come with me."

I followed him toward a broad, open-air shelter. Trailing behind us was what appeared to be the village idiot: a quiet fellow

with an abnormally large and slightly misshapen head. He made me nervous. He walked so close I could see the patches of hair missing between his dreadlocks and the tears that streamed constantly from his left eye. He had an untidy beard and wore a filthy ski parka that had once been green and pink. But it was the man's head that captivated me. It looked as though it had been fashioned from rubber and then squeezed at the temples, or melted, so that his forehead seemed on the verge of collapsing around his eyes. He had no eyebrows. Of course. Leprosy. This was Fred, the prophet.

We sat on a bench under the shelter. Rain dripped through the thatch roof. I explained that I was here to help Fred spread his message around the world. Fred mumbled like a child in his own language and dabbed at his teary eye with a pair of torn bikini briefs. Alfred interpreted. This, he said, was the prophet's true story:

Fred was born in Sulphur Bay but had spent a decade working on a Taiwanese fishing boat. In his last year at sea, he began having visions. They came to him as lights from the sky, like stars, only they shot straight at him. Fred wasn't afraid when the lights came. He would just close his eyes and go to sleep. That's when he would hear the voice. It reassured him. It gave him clues about the future. Fred knew the voice was God talking to him. One day, the voice told him he should return to his own island to bring the people together in peace, so Fred came home to Sulphur Bay and began sharing his predictions with his neighbors.

In one vision, Fred saw the lake at the base of the volcano, Lake Siwi. He saw that the water in the lake was not good. The volcano was polluting it with ash. The voice advised Fred to pray to make the water run out of the lake. He did. It worked. And now, said Fred—through Alfred—the water in the creek at Sulphur Bay was much better for drinking. Fred gained credibility, at least with those whose homes hadn't been destroyed by the flood.

Then Fred predicted the bombing of the World Trade Center

in New York. When the prophecy came true, his followers paraded in Port Vila to show their sympathy for 'Merica. That's when an American gave Fred the flag that now flew above his village.

"Any other miracles?" I asked.

Fred gave a long, slurred reply. Alfred gave me the *Reader's Digest* version: "Before Fred came back, the volcano used to explode and kill many people. But Fred asked God to make it stop. It did. Oh, and the hurricanes. There will be no hurricanes on Tanna for five years."

I asked politely about Fred's alleged dark side. "Some people say you are working black magic here to trick people and make them sick."

Fred rolled his eyes back into his skull, then leveled them at me. *"Hem i no tru. Hem i rubbish toktok,"* he said. *"Disfala power, hem i power blong God."*

Black magic and prophecy are not covered by Vanuatu criminal law. That must have been why the police had tried to use the Canadian doctor to oust Fred. I told Fred what the doctor had told me: that he was not crazy. He nodded his appreciation.

"But what are you doing up here on the mountain?" I asked.

Fred returned to his mumbling.

"God told Fred to bring the people together in Unity," translated Alfred. "All the churches, John Frum people, and *kastom* people, must come together and follow one way. One people in Unity. So we sing John Frum songs on Wednesday beneath the flag. And on Sunday we go to the church. Unity! See?"

Perhaps, but the truth was that the rest of the days, Fred's hungry followers stole food from surrounding villages. I didn't say that.

"How long will you stay up here?"

"Fred had a vision about that, too," said Alfred. "He saw that twelve virgin boys would be circumcised. Only then will God tell us what we should do next."

"I thought all boys on Tanna were circumcised."

"Yes, but these boys would be circumcised by God." Alfred paused for effect. "And the miracle has already begun. The first boy has been cut. Nobody touched him. His parents simply found him circumcised one morning last week."

"Can I see it?"

"The boy?"

"Well, yes, but really, it's his miracle penis that counts."

"No. But you come back tomorrow. Tomorrow we bring John Frum together with Jesus."

I wasn't sure exactly what he meant, but it sounded like just the kind of spectacle I had been hoping for all week. Alfred patted my shoulder encouragingly. Fred offered me his hand, which was as soft and cold as an oyster, then wandered off to gaze at the clouds. Fred might not have been crazy, but he certainly didn't seem to have enough of a grip on reality to be in charge of this operation. Who was? And who was in charge of Fred? Before I left, Alfred made me promise to return the next day with my camera so the world would have proof of Fred's religion, Unity.

I trotted down to Port Resolution and searched the village for Stanley, to let him know I was alive. I saw him, once, across the soccer field, and I waved. Stanley didn't wave back. He turned and fled into the woods, and I never saw him again. In fact nobody in Port Resolution was so keen to talk with me after my visit with Fred.

The next morning Fred preached to a rapt crowd of four hundred up on the mountain. I couldn't understand any of it, other than the words *New Jerusalem,* which he shouted over and over. Encouraged by Alfred, I climbed through the brambles at the edge of the clearing and took photos. That's where I learned there was no toilet in New Jerusalem.

Most of the congregation wore rags, but there were two men in white shirts and ties. They sat on a bench behind Fred, beaming and nodding with approval as he spoke. The younger one waved to me as I attempted to wipe the shit from my sandals. He motioned for me to come sit with him on the VIP bench.

"You must take many photos," he said, straightening his tie. "Fred is a very important man. Take many photos and send me copies of them. I want to present them to the Presbyterian Congress on Makira, to show them our work here."

The man's name was Pastor Maliwan Taruei. He was the grandson of the Presbyterian minister who had battled it out with the John Frummers back in the 1940s. Isag Wan's grandfather had driven Taruei's grandfather out of Sulphur Bay, then torn down his church. Now Maliwan Taruei had rebuilt it. The family feud was still on.

"Isag Wan is destroying this island with his idol worship," the pastor whispered to me as Fred preached.

"Don't be ridiculous. Isag Wan is a sweet old man," I said.

"Well, anyway, Fred is much better. Look at him, he is just like Moses. He led four thousand, four hundred sixty-six people up this hill, just like Moses led the Israelites out of Egypt to the promised land. And best of all, Fred invited the Presbyterian Church."

Wasn't it strange, I asked, for the church to support a man who championed both God and *kastom* magic? It didn't fit with any version of Christianity I had ever heard of. "Aha, you don't understand Tanna, do you? Our *kastom* stories are just like the Bible stories. Don't you know the real name of our volcano? It's not Yasur. It's Yahweh, the Hebrew name for God. The Bible tells us that one day the world will become paradise. But *kastom* tells us that one day Tanna will become a paradise, a new Jerusalem. Tanna people know we have two choices. We pray for both of them."

"But is your savior Jesus or John Frum?"

"My friend, God will give us the answer, and it will be one of them. Either way, I assure you that the church has returned to Sulphur Bay, and all these people will be there on Sunday."

Taruei was facing the same dilemma the first missionaries had faced on Tanna: Was winning people's allegiance more important than the shape of faith itself? For Taruei, getting bums into church pews was clearly more important than preserving the purity of Presbyterian doctrine.

The crowd had disappeared. Now they were back, filing onto the dirt plaza by the hundreds. They had changed out of their rags. The men came first, banana leaves tied around their heads and bare chests shining in the sun. Women followed, their faces painted yellow and orange like hornets. They wore feathers in their hair and grass skirts dyed with rainbow checkers. Wreaths of Christmas tinsel dangled from their necks. Their dance was not the dead-eyed shake of Kelsen's *nambas*-clad friends, nor was it the cheery campfire rumba I had joined in in Namakara. It was like a war dance. The men stamped the earth, grunting and exhaling simultaneously in great stormy whooshes. The women gathered around them in loose whorls, wailing and waving tree branches toward the Stars and Stripes. They charged the flag, jumped back again, and raced in circles until the plaza became a maelstrom of dust and leaping bodies. The Presbyterian Congress, I thought, would be mortified.

The pastors shifted nervously on the grass mats where they now sat. The older one adjusted his glasses. He looked like the square kid in a room full of marijuana smoke. Taruei reached for my hand, but I couldn't sit still. Shaking with excitement, I dashed across the clearing, climbed to the roof of a hut, and pulled out my camera. There was Fred, sitting alone on a footstool, watching the dance with one eye and me with the other. He nodded when I pointed my camera at him. Taruei shouted to the dancers, who quickened their pace. I raised the camera to my eye, and the frame was filled with dust, flashing color, and shining skin. The crowd had spread across the plaza: the frame couldn't contain them all. I stood up, straddling the gable of the hut, raised my arms above my head, motioned like Jesus on the mount. Closer together. Move closer together. The crowd responded.

"Closer!" I shouted when the dance ended. The crowd moved closer still. Adrenaline rushed through my veins.

"Raise your arms to the sky," I shouted when the dance ended. "Not Fred, just the rest of you!" They did as they were told, sweat-drenched men, dust-caked women, naked children, all four hundred of them; even the Presbyterian pastors stretched their arms in the air. It felt wonderful to see them obey. The dancers all looked up at me, knowing that they had done good work, knowing they were among the first to proclaim a message of peace and unity that would certainly sweep across Tanna and, with my help, around the world.

I gazed down at Fred, standing serenely among his followers. It would be easy to be a messiah here. You have your visions. You make your prophecies. You lead your people to the mountain. You tell them a new story. Then, if you are lucky, you are martyred like Jesus or you disappear like John Frum. If you are unlucky, you just go on living while your aura fades and you become ordinary again. But the key to success is your own faith. It must be rock solid. In other words, you either possess supernatural powers or you are nuts. There is no middle ground.

It was one thing to believe in yourself. But the faith of the people, where did it come from? The Tannese seemed to have the capacity to accept any prophet, any myth. They were more than just tolerant. They had sponges for souls. *Kastom* traditionalists sacrificed to the spirits and waited for John Frum. John Frummers waited for Jesus and John. Christians hedged their bets. Nobody was interested in discussing the contradictions.

I had always traced the impulses of faith to environment. In the years after I abandoned my family's church, I found that the universe spoke to me most loudly in the fullness of mountains, the endlessness of the sea, the fury of storms, the boom and crack of living physics . . . that's when the world itself seemed to offer a voice and a breath that felt something like *mana*, and which begged to be given a name and a shape and a myth to explain it all. Tanna was a nexus of such signals. The landscape was as powerful, as crowded, as sharply schizophrenic, as the island's apparent train wreck of faiths. The island was a confluence of primal signals. The vibrating jungle. The dusty stillness of the ash plain. The torrential rains. The fires of Yasur. Yes, the volcano, which had not ceased bellowing since my arrival, declaring its power, demanding attention.

I slid back down the thatch roof, shook two hundred hands, then jogged to Port Resolution. I caught a lift on a Land Cruiser headed for Lenakel but jumped out when we reached the ash plain.

I stood for an hour there at the foot of the volcano. The mountain didn't make a sound. In the last few years, tourists had begun to fly down to Tanna from Port Vila, drawn by the spectacle of Yasur's eruptions like moths to a giant flame. A handful had been struck and killed by flying rocks. Two weeks before my arrival, a woman had ventured onto the mountain and was hit by a rock that melted a hole in her leg. Kelsen had advised me that the bombs only flew north. Or was it east?

Almost without thinking, I started up through the ash, slowly at first, pausing to gaze at the crest of the cinder cone with each tentative step. I sank up to my ankles in the rubble, sliding a step back for every two forward. Sand gathered between my toes. I cursed my sandals. I stumbled over bucket-sized pockmarks and yard-wide craters. They all cradled stones: some were as delicate and light as pumice, others looked like pieces of flesh ripped from a burned corpse. Some were all bubble and froth, the texture of water frozen in midboil. Some were as big as bathtubs. Some had settled into the earth, as though they had been spit from the volcano decades before. Others were young: the sand around them had been heat-seared into a frosty white ring still undisturbed by rain. But hadn't it rained just that morning?

I was three-quarters of the way up the mountain when it made the most terrifying sound. I could tell you it went *boom*, but that wouldn't be enough. Roared? Not enough. Thundered? Perhaps. It was the kind of sound that assures you that you are a fool, and that if you die, everyone will know you were a fool. A fool, a fool, I thought as the ground trembled and the sand trickled around my feet. I couldn't see past the crest of the cone. I remembered what Kelsen had told me. Don't run away when the mountain explodes. Don't turn your back. Face it, so that you can sidestep the bombs when they come at you. Ridiculous. The mountain shook again, hollering at me to turn back. I did think of turning back. But sometimes a journey takes on a momentum that won't listen to logic.

I carried on, pulling at the sand and ash, my knees grinding into the scree. My feet bled under the straps of my sandals. I didn't decide to beg: the words just seemed to form themselves amid the moans each time I exhaled. *Please don't kill me. If you spare me, I promise not to point my camera into your crater.* It was all I could think of to offer. I know it sounds absurd, begging to a mountain. I knew it at the time. Mountains cannot hear. But if you were there, you would have done the same thing, even as you reminded yourself that the unthinking forces of gravity and physics and geology were never meant to be anthropomorphized.

I reached a cornice of fractured rock and peered over it into the crater, which was the size of a soccer stadium. There were three pits at the bottom. One glowed faintly orange. Another smoked like a bonfire of wet leaves. Occasionally it sucked at the late-afternoon air like a steam engine. The third had no bottom. I gazed into that crater, and I didn't see John Frum's armies or a fiery spirit or the power of a heavenly God. I knew the rumbling, the explosions, the tremendous heaving power, all of it came from the earth. The mountain did not have feelings. It would not respond to my prayers any more than it would to Fred's commands. I was certain about these things. So why did I leave my camera in its case? Why did I reach instead into my pocket, pull out a five-hundred-vatu note, and slip it under a rock? I did not ask these questions at the time. I didn't allow myself a moment to feel foolish about keeping my promise to the volcano.

The sun was setting. I scrambled along the south edge of the crater until I reached a fence made from bamboo sticks. Someone had built a makeshift lookout on the lip of the precipice. This would be the pristine side of the volcano. I followed a trail that led down from the lookout toward a plateau a few hundred yards away. There was a truck there, and someone waving. As I waved back, the mountain boomed like a cannon, then boomed again behind me. I turned and froze. Magma sprayed into the purpling sky: great gobs of red-and-black-mottled jelly spiraled, spun, broke apart in the heavens before finding their weight, losing momentum, and falling back down toward the earth. The igneous rain exploded across the slope I had just crossed.

I ran-stumbled down toward the truck. It contained four men, volcanologists who had flown down from Vila for a night of fireworks. The men toasted my arrival with tin cups of instant coffee. They said they had been sprinting back and forth to the crater's edge all afternoon. It was the coffee that kept them going, one said, laughing. As if on cue, a bearded fellow with a heavy brow appeared to refill their cups. I should have known. Kelsen. If Yasur was Tanna's real temple, then Kelsen was its money changer. He had lugged a kettle up from his village and lit a little fire at the edge of the plateau. Coffee was one hundred vatu a shot.

"If you come back and stay at my hotel," Kelsen was saying to them, "I'll tell you the legend behind the volcano."

5

Ninety Hours on the MV *Brisk*

The religious life, then, begins with a call to this sleeping God to awake.

—NORTHROP FRYE, *Notebooks and Lectures on the Bible and Other Religious Texts*

It was impossible to say just how Tanna had been transformed into such a psychospiritual Disneyland, such a breeding ground for prophets and wide-eyed, contradictory faith. Perhaps it all went back to the clash between *kastom* and the Old Testament absolutism the Presbyterians brought to the island.

Take the Reverend John G. Paton, the firebrand who landed in Port Resolution with his wife in 1858. Paton had a taste for confrontation, retribution, and high drama. His autobiography reads like the screen treatment for the Melanesia of my boyhood dreams. He describes how he dueled with pagan warriors and sorcerers; how they burned his house to the ground and stole all his possessions; how his wife, his child, and a colleague all died within three years of their arrival; how he sat for ten days, gun in hand, guarding his dead wife's grave to prevent islanders from getting their hands on her putrefying remains. The heathens, he insisted, were voracious cannibals who "gloried in bloodshedding" and delighted in the taste of human flesh. After one tribal battle, Paton recalled that the bodies of half a dozen men had been stewed in the hot spring near the head of the bay. This presented a unique problem: "At the boiling spring they have cooked and feasted upon the slain," Paton's cook allegedly reported to him. "They have washed the blood into the stream; they have bathed there till all the waters are red. I cannot get water to make your tea. What shall I do?"

Paton fled on a passing ship in 1862. His story was so captivating, he managed to wring £5,000 from church audiences during a speaking tour of Australia. It was years before anyone realized that Paton had fabricated the juiciest bits of his story. (His claims of widespread cannibalism, for example, were exaggerated. Anthropologists who bothered to ask were told that enemies were eaten not because they tasted good but as a means of capturing *mana* and honoring one's own ancestors. A single corpse might be passed from village to village as a means of solidifying alliances. And cannibalism was restricted by rules of *kastom* and kinship. There were never more than twenty-eight families on Tanna whose members had the right to consume human flesh.) Still, Paton had no problem with violence if it was carried out in the name of his own god. He returned to Port Resolution on the warship HMS *Curaçoa* four years after his departure. The ship shelled the villages along the bay, then its men landed to smash canoes, burn houses, and destroy crops. Paton claimed that the attack, which killed a handful of Tannese, did wonders for the Presbyterian mission. His successors ruled the Tannese as if they were children.

Henry Montgomery shared Paton's sense of mission and some of his sentiments about race. He was confident of Anglo-Saxon superiority. But with greatness came responsibility: "Englishmen would do well to remember that their wonderful supremacy throughout the world is due in great measure to the existence of races inferior to their own." The point, which he made often, was that it was England's God-given duty to nurture the lesser races, who were not quite up to the task of leading themselves.

"It would appear that among certain child races independence is for centuries impossible," he wrote years after his journey. "The power to transmit orders is not lightly to be put into hands that are not fit to wield such privileges."

Unlike Paton, Montgomery was fond of Melanesians, but preferred to portray them as children rather than savages. Like boys and girls, islanders required education in manners and character as well as religion. He was thrilled to discover that his heroes, Selwyn, Patteson, and Codrington, had not forgotten the lessons of Eton: "The wise founders of this mission saw that the education of their charges lay more directly in their passage from idleness and dirt to cleanliness and diligence and method than by learning to read and write. . . . Improvement in diligence and orderliness went hand in hand with knowledge of the Heavenly Father."

Everyone agreed that Melanesians needed guidance. Yet there was fierce rivalry among Anglicans, Presbyterians, and Roman Catholics as to just who would do the guiding. When the Presbyterian reverend John Geddie spotted white men wearing the telltale robes of Catholic priests on the shore of Aneityum, near Tanna, in 1848, he despaired: "In this we recognized at once the mark of the beast."

The Anglicans of Selwyn's Melanesian Mission were as fond of gilded finery and High Church ritual as Roman Catholics—in fact they considered their church to offer a purer, even more traditional version of the Catholic faith—but they disdained the French missionaries who dropped in on their islands uninvited. Henry Montgomery warned that the work of Roman Catholic missionaries was almost always fostered by the French government, "in order to counteract the influence of England." A mission conducted for such unworthy motives could hardly have a noble and lasting effect. Therefore the Anglican mission had to do everything in its power to "protect native Christians from unscrupulous and ruthless [Roman Catholic] propagandists."

The rivalry was just as fierce between English churches. Selwyn, Patteson, and Codrington were graduates of Britain's most prestigious public schools and universities. They were of a different class than the members of grassroots mission societies, and both sides knew it. The Anglicans felt that their protestant competition—lowbrows who, like Paton, were forever waving their Bibles in the air and screaming warnings of eternal damnation—lacked the necessary intellect and temper for the task at hand.

"Well-meaning Englishmen who have been brought up in a somewhat narrow circle of thought and opinion are apt to make non-essentials into essentials, to the grievous hurt of the great cause," opined my great-grandfather—himself a Harrow and Cambridge man.

The Anglicans thought themselves so different from their Protestant peers that one mission historian dubbed them "God's Gentlemen." They endeavored to remain polite and unfailingly reasonable in the face of defiant heathenism, but they also adapted a tenuously tolerant stance toward *kastom*. Dancing, smoking, drinking kava, the payment of bride price, none of the traditions the Presbyterians banned on Tanna was seen necessarily as a barrier to Christian salvation. Bishop Patteson told converts they should make up their own minds about them. As long as they pledged allegiance to the One True God, as long as their *kastom* didn't break the Ten Commandments, then islanders weren't necessarily against Christianity, even if they weren't altogether for it just yet. The Anglicans delighted in traditional dances and costumes. Some gained a fondness for kava. They prided themselves on their tolerance, and they pooh-poohed the Presbyterians, who had a habit of outlawing any practice that reminded them even faintly of paganism.

For decades, the doctrine of "Christianity with civilization" had been an axiom for English missionaries around the world. The gospel was just one part of a curriculum that included aesthetic "improvements" such as the introduction of clothing, homes with separate bedrooms, and encouragement to enter the market economy. But here in the South Seas, the Anglicans were concluding—at least on paper—that some Melanesian social and cultural traditions could provide a cornerstone of a strong church.

R. H. Codrington, who was the first among Anglicans to write down the Melanesians' stories, was the most sympathetic to *kastom*. After years as Patteson's school headmaster, he ventured that *kastom* had already equipped Melanesians with a sense of right and wrong, a belief in life after death, and a concept of something like a human soul. In other words, there was already some light in Melanesia before the missionaries arrived. *Kastom* had in fact provided the heathens with a good foundation for Christian teaching.

By the end of the century, many Anglicans had even dismissed the notion that "civilization" was a necessary companion to Christianity. They encouraged islanders not to adopt heavy clothing and not to become "imitation Europeans." While the Presbyterians were arresting Tannese dance troupes, the Anglicans were romancing *kastom*.

The Anglicans were determined to avoid the ungentlemanly squabbling that saw mission societies battling over various islands throughout the New Hebrides. As Henry Montgomery put it: "Ours is rather a godly rivalry; not to pull others behind us, but to be first honourably and fairly in the great cause." So after a few years of haggling, they agreed to leave the Loyalty Islands near New Caledonia to the London Missionary Society, and to let the Presbyterians and Roman Catholics fight over the southern islands of the New Hebrides—including Tanna and Efate. Selwyn and Patteson promised to concentrate their efforts north of Espiritu Santo, at the top end of the New Hebrides.

After ten days on Tanna I flew back to Port Vila—of course I flew: VanAir offered daily, air-conditioned flights between Tanna and the capital—and I waited for a passage north to Espiritu Santo, the gateway to Anglican Melanesia. The Anglican islands would be different, I thought. The Presbyterians had allowed no middle ground on Tanna, no compromise between *kastom* and Christianity. The collision of the two systems had buried the island's soul in an avalanche of discordant cosmology. If Presbyterian ferocity had produced Tanna's spiritual chaos, then surely Anglicanism would have fostered a more stable, reasonable cosmology. God's Gentlemen would have eased their converts away from ghosts and magic while ever so politely applauding their quaint dances. Part of me hoped to find a pastoral, Victorian paradise. That was the part that was weary. Most of me wanted more sparks, more rumors, more magic. I had touched the edge of a mystery. I wanted to fall into it.

I found the MV *Brisk* at sunset, docked—or rather, run up like a World War II troop transport—against a grassy wharf on Vila Bay. She made the *Havanna* look like the *Love Boat*. She was more barge than ship; a shallow tub with all the crude geometry and elegance of a sheep dip. I couldn't imagine her navigating the house-high swells that we would surely hit on our four-day journey north to Espiritu Santo. But I no longer feared the sea. I had acquired a supply of motion-sickness pills.

We set sail after dusk. The two dozen passengers on the open cargo deck had built mounds of pallets and luggage on which they huddled like penguins on bergs. As we left the refuge of the harbor, I saw why. The *Brisk* rolled pleasantly enough in the swell, but waves spilled over her bow anyway. Gradually, the cargo deck filled with water until it was as deep as a wading pool. I climbed up to a makeshift roof of corrugated iron in front of the wheelhouse. A thin layer of cloud spread across the sky, like a veil thrown up to protect the moon from the sparkle and glare of the sea. A warm breeze ran over me. I dozed off to the murmurs of the crew, the rumbling of the engine, the whoosh of the waves, and the rhythmic click and bang of the wheelhouse door, which opened and shut with each roll of the ship.

My dreams were peaceful at first. But then I drifted away from the *Brisk* and a forest grew up around me, and the knocking became the sound of tree branches jostling in the wind. I peered through the forest, through shadows that shifted across the moonlit earth, and there was the prophet Fred, sitting cross-legged, mumbling indecipherably and cradling a baby wrapped in gauze. A bloodstain appeared on the cloth and spread across it. I knew that Fred was performing another spontaneous circumcision. He raised his head and scowled at me. He had known all along I would betray him. The stain turned black and broke apart into a thousand tiny wings that rose from the cloth, swarming around me, droning in my ears, dancing around my eyes, landing on my neck. The mosquitoes prodded, poked, tested the surface with their invisible probosces, and then, one by one, they injected their poison into me.

Dreams are manifestations of unconscious fears and delusions. That's what Freud taught us. I have always sought to return to this refrain, to see my dreams as the contents of the cluttered attic of my mind, so much bric-a-brac to be considered, yes, but then filed and packed away so that I might see each new day with clear eyes.

But this dream reached past the veil of sleep. It did not evaporate in the light of dawn. My skin began to itch even before I had awoken. Spots rose like tiny red kisses on the soft flesh of my arms and torso.

I dozed on the roof for three days as the *Brisk* bounced from island to island, threading together villages, mission stations, and coconut plantations, running into dozens of sandy shores, dumping cement mixers, rice, and rebar, collecting sack after sack of yam, taro, and sweet potato. We headed north, following the protected lee sides of Efate and low-lying Epi. When we rounded the northern tip of Epi, we were broadsided by the southeast swell. The *Brisk* did not cut through the waves like the *Havanna*. It was lifted by them, carried up over their shivering crests and swept down again into canyonlike troughs. Those waves were unnaturally blue, the color of transmission fluid. They lumbered. They were not violent. But they carried smaller waves that jostled, broke, and exploded over the ship's bow until the cargo deck frothed and churned like a river in flood. We passed a volcanic cone that rose steeply into the clouds. That was Lopevi. We made three stops on a dark fin of black rock and jungle in Lopevi's shadow.

My skin burned. The dream spots on my arm had multiplied, joined, and grew into an angry rash. I wanted to leap into the ocean.

"You cannot swim at this island," the ship's engineer told me. His name was Edwin. He was a rough man with cunning eyes and sores on his neck. "You will be eaten by the shark."

"They have sharks here?"

"Just one shark. A *kastom* shark. We call him a *nakaimo*. He is the spirit of a dead man, and he likes white flesh. He ate his first white man fifty years ago. I can swim here, but you can't. Ha!"

We crossed from Paama to Ambrym, which, according to my map, was dominated by a twelve-mile-wide caldera of black ash and steaming vents. All that igneous action had imbued the island with a certain cachet. Ambrym, they told me in Port Vila, was the island of fire magic. People were uniformly terrified of Ambrymese sorcerers, whose most infamous trick was to float into the homes of sleeping enemies, cut them open and pull out their guts, then replace them with leaves and sticks. The victims showed no scarring, but they tended to cough up plenty of leaf mulch before their deaths, which usually occurred within a few days. In 1997, Prime Minister Fidel Soksok told the *Vanuatu Trading Post* that black magic and poison were the biggest obstacles to economic development in the country. Everyone knew he was talking about the influence of Ambrymese sorcerers, who could not abide the successes of others.

The rim of the caldera was obscured by a great mushroom of dark clouds. We slid through a gap in the reef that guarded the island's west coast and stopped to pick up a couple of red-eyed men at a Catholic mission station. The passengers on deck stepped back—or rather, recoiled—to make room for the Ambrymese, who chuckled and cooed menacingly.

Another night. The *Brisk* chugged toward specks of light on the horizon that grew into shoreside bonfires as we approached. The fires, which had been lit by people who hoped to send or receive cargo, marked passages through unseen reefs. I was not permitted to read or sleep. Men gathered around to eat my cookies and do what Melanesians like best, which is *storian* ("story-on"). Edwin, the engineer, was the bravest. He asked me if I liked island pussy. I sidestepped by asking him the first question most Melanesians usually ask strangers: "To which church do you belong?" He was a Seventh-day Adventist. In other words, no kava, no alcohol, no promiscuity, no dirty talk, I said. Edwin admitted he broke all those rules. He was *wanfala backslider*.

There was another backslider on deck. Graeme was a handsome, neatly dressed man who cradled a young boy in his arms. He shook my hand and asked me what my business was. I told him I was following the route my great-grandfather had taken aboard the *Southern Cross*. His eyes narrowed.

"So that means your granddaddy stole my granddaddy, doesn't it?" Graeme asked in English.

"I suppose, um, yes."

"Yes, that is exactly what happened. I know the story. They took our granddaddies to New Zealand and taught them the *kastom* stories of Israel. Then our granddaddies came back to our island and convinced everyone to join the church. It was easy to do, because the teachers had knives and axes and tobacco, all the good things that foreigners had."

The crowd laughed jovially, but Graeme was earnest and breathless in his monologue. His eyes reflected the flame of an approaching fire. "Most people have forgotten that we once had our own god on Pentecost. Taka was his name. He helped us work magic to bring rain and food. Only a few people can do the magic now, but I am learning it. I go to the old *kastom* chiefs. I drink kava with them. We *storian*. They teach me."

"Teach you what? Magic? Show me," I said, knowing he would not.

"I am just now learning magic. But I know how to make sweet mouth."

"Show me this sweet-mouth magic. I want to see it!"

The crowd exploded with shrieks of laughter.

"Sweet-mouth is magic for love," explained Graeme. "You rub a chicken feather on a special stone, and then you say the name of the girl four times. After four days, she will come to you. She will follow you like a puppy."

Graeme lived on Pentecost, which I know only by the embers of its beach fires and the clovelike taste of its kava. The *Brisk* ran up against a soft beach, and I followed Graeme to shore while men heaved sacks of copra across the beam of the ship's searchlight. There was a shack selling kava, but only time for one shell.

"What about flying?" I asked Graeme, licking the kava scum from my lips. "Can you turn yourself into an owl or a flying fox?"

This was not such an absurd question. The first Anglican I met in Vanuatu, a sales executive for Le Meridien Hotel, had presented an equally fantastic notion to me several nights before. The exec was a modern woman. She had a business card, an e-mail address, and a diploma from a New Zealand business school. We had met to discuss the hotel's golf course. But after two glasses of complimentary Chilean merlot, she announced matter-of-factly that her uncle was a sorcerer. When she was just a little girl, the uncle would cross the ocean to visit her at her village on Pentecost. No, he didn't come by canoe. He changed himself into an owl, and he flew across the water. He had to be careful never to fly over a church while in his owl body, because every church had a column of energy, like a ray of light, shooting up into the sky from its roof. If he flew over that ray, he would crash. So the uncle flew carefully, but he flew often. When he reached Pentecost, he would sit in the breadfruit tree outside the girl's window to keep her company at night.

So Graeme was not at all surprised when I asked him if he could fly.

"Not yet. I haven't learned that yet," he said. "But I will. And I will also learn how to swim under the ocean like a fish."

"Graeme, you are clearly not a Christian," I said.

"Oh, yes, of course I am. All my family is Anglican."

If there was one thing I learned as a teenager in my Anglican confirmation classes, it was that you had to choose sides. You were either a Christian or an ancestor-worshipper, but you couldn't be both. God was jealous. So Graeme's brand of fusional cosmology was baffling, even though I knew it was hardly unique to Melanesian converts.

The Roman Catholic Church, in particular, has always excelled in overlooking the lingering heathen habits of its flock. Back in the seventeenth century, Catholic missionaries in the lower Congo Valley were compelled to turn a blind eye while their converts made offerings to their ancestors, particularly during the Christian holiday of All Souls' Day.

In the latter half of the twentieth century, a generation of jungle prophets combined African ritual, Christianity, and a powerful psychoactive tea to spawn at least three new proto-Christian churches in Brazil. The tea, known as *hoasca* in Brazil and *ayahuasca* elsewhere, was brewed from the bark of a rain-forest vine. It was once an essential tool of pre-Christian shamans, but it has now replaced wine as the new churches' sacrament. Church leaders say the tea catalyzes direct contact with the divine, though it almost always induces vomiting and cataclysmic diarrhea.

A similar kind of drug-fueled syncretism has occurred in the southwestern United States, where the Native American Church (which is not affiliated with any established Christian church) has adopted peyote—a small, spineless cactus also considered a tool in pre-Christian ritual—as its own sacrament. The group still combines its hallucinogenic pre-Christian ritual with biblical teachings and has been credited with reducing alcoholism in Native American communities.

Spiritual syncretism naturally bothers fundamentalist Christians. If theirs is the one true religion, then to water it down and distort it must certainly be blasphemous. Of course, some of these theological hard-liners also happen to be the most likely to cling to a version of Christianity that has created an image of a tall, pale, decidedly un-Jewish Jesus.

Modern Anglican theologians have adopted a more nuanced stance. Fergus King, an officer of the United Society for the Propagation of the Gospel (the modern incarnation of the mission society for which my great-grandfather was secretary) told me that even John, the writer of Revelation, practiced what he calls "inculturation." As he preached in Asia Minor, John never hesitated to adopt symbols from local pagan traditions to describe the holiness of Jesus. The evil eye, magic bowls, and the double throne of Zeus all served to strengthen John's evangelical message in Revelation.

The Anglican Communion seems to have followed John's lead. A black Christ? No problem. Rejigged pagan dances and grass skirts in church? Sure. Ancestor worship? Well . . . yes, as a matter of fact. While conducting research at the School of Mission at Selly Oak Colleges, Birmingham, I met a Nigerian Anglican priest and theology student who told me that he and his parishioners still worshipped their ancestors.

"But all that stuff is against the rules," I said.

"Rules?" he chortled. "Look, when the missionaries first came to Africa, they saw us worshipping our forefathers, and they called it idolatry. They condemned us for it. But we soon realized Jesus was an ancestor shared by all of us. That is the Christian message, isn't it? Jesus was human, and he was also divine. So now we do not feel at all bad about worshipping our ancestors along with Jesus in church. I trust you won't belittle this. After all, you are the one who has followed the ghost of your ancestor to England. Your great-grandfather has spoken, and now you are following him. Good for you. Listen to him."

My great-grandfather considered himself open-minded, but he warned Christians to guard against the infecting influence of other cultures. In a book of advice for clergy he condemned the idea that "all men can form their own conceptions of God, and that one of these is not much more true than another, forgetting that God has made a definite Revelation of Himself." He would have been bothered, for example, to hear what a teacher at Fiji's University of the South Pacific told me: that he gave one of his students several months' extension on an assignment so that the boy could return to Vanuatu to battle a band of sorcerers in his hometown. He would have been aghast at the Melanesian who offered to assist in an Australian woman's marital troubles by having his brother turn into a crocodile who would eat her problem boyfriend. After all, these people were supposed to be Christians.

I suppose I was bothered, too. I found it irrational enough to believe in one god, but here were educated, seemingly reasonable people, weaving together strands of clearly conflicting myths. They couldn't all be true. Were these people fools? Daydreamers? Liars? The anthropologist Ben Burt had told me in London that what impressed him most about Melanesians was their capacity to hold on to such apparently contradictory belief systems at the same time. It was not a sign of intellectual weakness, Burt had said. It required a sophisticated mind to perform such spiritual acrobatics.

Regardless, it was clear which religion was more powerful here. It wasn't Christianity that was being given credit for daily miracles.

I was disoriented but enthralled by my new friends' fantastical claims, and I was overtaken with a terrible regret as the fires of Pentecost receded behind the *Brisk*. I told myself I should have stayed onshore, I should have followed Graeme home to his village, I should have begged him to prove his magic. I wasn't out to change Graeme. He was the evangelist, not me, clouding my thoughts with all his fantastical claims. If I had put his magic to the test, we would see that his magic talk had flowed from his dream life and nothing more, and the frontier between truth and fantasy would be made clear again.

But when I closed my eyes and drifted toward something like sleep, the stars burned holes through my eyelids and I heard another voice, the dream part of myself, whispering, praying to the sky, asking to feel the *mana* that once and perhaps still surrounded these islands, seethed through their forests, flowed through the hands of their sorcerers, and made believers out of Melanesians and Irish bishops. The constellations turned in the clear sky above me, then broke apart. The stars fell, rained down on me like hot sparks. When the sun rose, my dreams were imprinted in my skin as they had been the previous morning, only multiplied: a thousand red stars scattered across my arm, my shoulder, my back, my abdomen. My bones ached, and my ears rang with the buzz of unseen mosquitoes, and although the dawn was blinding it felt not so much like a new day as a bleached continuation of uncertain night.

6

The Book of Espiritu Santo

The green and stagnant waters lick his feet,
And from their filmy, iridescent scum
Clouds of mosquitoes, gauzy in the heat,
Rise with His gifts: Death and Delirium.
—LAURENCE HOPE, "Malaria," in *India's Love Lyrics*

At dawn on the fourth morning, the MV *Brisk* tied up at Luganville, on the southern end of Espiritu Santo. This was the end of the run. Luganville was Vanuatu's preeminent port and a jumping-off point for the Banks and Torres islands, the Anglican stronghold on the country's northern frontier. After that, Nukapu, my grail, would only be a few days' sail north.

So I did not intend to stay long. But by the time the *Brisk* ground into shore at the edge of town, the rash that had begun as an artful smattering of stars on my arm had spread across my entire body. The stars had lost their form and blended into one another, and my skin was one vast welt. My body sizzled with fever. My head ached. I was dizzy. The sky had shattered into fluorescent pixels. The sun had drawn close to the earth and grown spines. I wanted help.

Luganville had hosted a hundred thousand American troops during World War II. It was supposed to be a bustling commercial hub, a capable place. I found a town anesthetized. There were a hundred broken hedgerows, a hundred empty lots, a hundred rusting Quonset huts collapsing in the grass. There was a boarded-up cinema. There was an empty park with an empty bandstand, from which a loudspeaker blared country gospel songs to no one in particular. The harbor was still but for the tide, which tugged at the skeletons of discarded war machinery.

Luganville's lethargy was so thorough that nobody I met could be bothered to wrap their lips around the town's full name, let alone the full name of the island. Both were reduced to a tired grunt. Santo.

I lurched along Santo's one paved avenue, which was as wide and empty as a prairie. Every now and then a beaten-up minibus sputtered down the cracked tarmac. None stopped. The horizons were punctuated by ramshackle monuments to the Chinese diaspora: Wong Store. Shing Yau Store. Ah Yuen & Company. Sun-bleached polyester bras and Bob Marley T-shirts hung in their windows.

I closed my eyes, shielding them from the blades of sunlight. When I opened them I saw a vision from the outskirts of Las Vegas, circa 1955, right across the street. A line of sculpted concrete buttresses supported an elegant two-story edifice, a collage of post-war modernism surreally out of place here amid the wilting palms. It was a proper hotel. I crossed the avenue, dropped my pack in the forgiving shade, and turned to regard the expatriates who regarded me from the bar. They were Australians. This was obvious because they were drinking beer for breakfast. They looked as though they had been hauled in from the outback:

leather boots and faces, sun-starched work shirts, wide-rimmed hats, strong hands.

There was one woman among them, a tall, middle-aged half-caste clad in a fitted white jumpsuit, gold earrings, and Liz Taylor frog glasses. She was as peculiar and anachronistic as the hotel itself. She raised a slender arm and ordered me closer with one bejeweled finger, introducing herself as Mary Jane Dinh. She had run the Hotel Santo by herself for decades. She had seen the French plantation owners kicked out after independence and the Aussie ranchers move in. Mary Jane was tough. She knew how life was. She also knew malaria when she saw it, and she saw it in my face.

"Of course the malariar's got 'im," bellowed one of the ranchers. "Lookitim! The boy can barely stand straight. Har! Get 'im a beer at once."

I was heartened by the diagnosis, and I knew what I required: I wanted Mary Jane to drive me to the hospital in her car, holding my hand, whispering reassurances all the way. I wanted a cup of hot chocolate. I wanted her to mother me. She did not.

"There's no need for hysteria," she said, hustling me out to a cab. "Malaria's as common as the flu."

The government of Vanuatu supported a small army of nurses whose sole task was to gaze through microscopes at drops of blood, looking for the tiny, threadlike plasmodium parasites that female mosquitoes are so good at injecting into humans. One such nurse determined that 5 percent of my red blood cells had been consumed by the parasite. If I were Melanesian, said my doctor, I would have built up a resistance to the disease, and I wouldn't have to worry about dying from the fever or the cranial swelling that the worst strains of malaria produced. But I was a white man, an autoimmune weakling. He insisted that I stay at the hospital. I gazed around at the peeling walls, the spit-smeared cement, the twittering cockroaches, the torn fly screens, the noses dripping with phlegm, the flickering fluorescent lights. I thanked him, then collected my plastic bag full of pills and retreated to the Hotel Santo.

It was afternoon. Mary Jane had changed into a floral print dress and pearls. She was taking tea with her ranchers. The avenue, the hedges, the town, the ranchers, had become a blur for me, but not Mary Jane. She was like her hotel: absolutely composed amid the malarial decay. I wanted to curl up at her feet. I'm not sure if I told her that.

"To bed!" she ordered, and turned back to her tea.

I shuffled off to my room, irritated by Mary Jane's casual approach to my possibly deadly malaise—and yet feeling vaguely heroic for having caught it. Hadn't malaria crippled empires, murdered conquistadors, and baffled healers for thousands of years? Hadn't it been blamed for killing half the people who ever walked the planet?

Malaria certainly killed many more traders and missionaries in Melanesia than did war clubs and poison arrows. It was malaria that claimed the life of the first European to discover the archipelago. The Spaniard Alvaro de Mendaña had tried to establish a Christian colony at Santa Cruz, near Nukapu, in 1595, but the fevers killed him within weeks and the survivors packed up and went home to Peru. Ironically, it was Peruvian Indians who would introduce the Spanish to a cure for tropical fevers half a century later. The cure resided in the bark of a shrub the Indians called quina quina, which grew high in the Andes. By the 1840s, exports of the bark to Europe were worth £1 million. Without that bark, and later its active component, the alkaloid quinine, the British Empire would never had held on to its possessions in India or Africa. By the end of the century, the British army was consuming 750 tons of the bark per year in India alone. No wonder tonic water laced with quinine—and gin, of course—emerged as the quintessential British drink.

In 1906, when the writer Jack London arrived in Melanesia on his attempt to sail around the world, the crew of his fifty-five-foot ketch were still debating whether or not to take quinine pills, even as they were struck helpless by fever, chills, and diarrhea. "Everybody had fever, everybody had dysentery, everybody had everything. Death was common," he wrote shortly before giving up his adventure. London had no fear of hyperbole, but he did take his quinine tablets.

I swallowed four tablets of chloroquine (quinine's synthetic descendant), turned on the ceiling fan, and lay down on my bed. I had nothing to read but the King James Bible, which a Mormon cousin had pushed into my backpack. ("So you can understand your great-grandfather," she had explained. Though I knew her motives were evangelical, I carried it out of duty, or guilt, or both, with no intention of opening it.)

It took an hour or so for the chloroquine to hit. When it did, it felt as though it was joining forces with the malaria rather than fighting it. It stole my sense of balance. It gave me cotton balls for fingertips and needles for nerve ends. It seeped into my brain like a yellowing fog, then wrapped itself tightly around my eyeballs until I could not focus on anything more than a couple of yards away.

The next four days passed in a series of grand hallucinations, interrupted only by the chattering of my teeth and the occasional lunge for the toilet. I opened that Bible. I turned pages with damp fingers. The Old Testament rose around me in a phantasmagoria of dream, delirium, and liquid vision, all spinning through my skull to the rhythmic hiss and click of the ceiling fan.

I saw the god make two great lights, one to rule the day and a lesser one to rule the night. The god gathered a handful of dust and pressed that dust into a shape with arms and legs. Then the god breathed life into that shape and called it man. I drifted through the garden, saw the oily glint of the serpent's scales and the shamed flight of man and woman. I saw the flaming sword, spinning in all directions to keep them out. I saw the face of Mary Jane in the blinding light of my window, a vision from a Kennedy cocktail party, flickering like a Super 8 angel. Somewhere a loudspeaker crackled and echoed a call to prayer.

Genesis. Exodus. Reggae from a distant bar. Abraham's knife, raised above the delicate throat of his son.

I didn't eat. I floated above Sinai, where the god opened a hole in the earth to swallow those who doubted its word. The god came to Moses as a cloud and then a firestorm. It thundered in his ears: *I will send my terror in front of you.*

This was a god of war. It told its followers to kill everyone in their path, and when they were not strong or merciless enough to kill, the god used its invisible hand to dash enemy armies to pieces, or to place unspeakable sores on their genitals, or to incinerate them with bolts of fire. The killing flooded my room. The fan turned above my head, spinning the years away. There were rivers of blood. The ashes of the dead fluttered in the wind. The blood flowed in rivers. It went on for centuries. And then, forty-two generations after the reign of Abraham, in the first book of the New Testament, in the first verse of the Gospel according to Saint Matthew, at dawn on the fourth morning of my convalescence, at the apex of my fever, the tide of violence turned.

The miracles became gentler. There was the man-god, calming the sea. There he was, turning water into wine. He spoke softly, but his voice was lifted and carried by the breeze. *Just love each other*, he said, and the idea somehow became the story's best miracle. It was as though the god of vengeance, favoritism, and thunderbolts had been replaced by another.

Dawn came as a faint glow through the curtains of my room. Then the piercing glare of day. Then, always in the afternoon, a tapping on the roof and the smell of rain. Then darkness again, and more dreams shot through with miracles and dust and blood, and in those dreams I recognized the god of my own family, the one who helped us smite our enemies yet claimed to love and forgive even those he cast into the wilderness. A god with two faces. My great-grandfather always said we were guided by the god of love, but from our stories I suspected we had always been fired by the god of war. We offered it thanks for every victory the clan ever won and for the spoils we enjoyed in peace. We wove this certainty into a story every bit as bloody as the Old Testament.

My ancestors once worshipped the moon and the sun, and fire, too. Our eyes were blue-gray and cold as the fjords of their Scandinavian homeland. Nearly a thousand years after the crucifixion of Jesus, we wandered south to the coast of France, and we were introduced to the god of war and love, whom we embraced.

We gave up our heathen names for ones that sounded better to Christian ears. The warrior-wanderer Biorn Dansk—the Danish Bear—became Bernard Danus and, from his hilltop fortress on Mons Gomerici, ruled over vast tracts of Normandy. The Montgomery clan honored the new god by founding the church of Troarn and providing for twelve monks, and that is why we prospered in an era of violence and feudal warfare.

In 1066, clan patriarch Roger de Montgomery sailed across the English Channel with William the Conqueror under a banner consecrated by the pope himself. Roger marched into the Battle of Hastings at William's right flank. At the height of the fighting, an English giant led a charge of one hundred men against the invading Normans. That English knight was as strong and swift as a stag. As he ran, he swung his great ax and slew himself a path of dead Normans with his foot-long blade. The Normans were ready to turn back until Roger galloped up on his own horse and drove his lance right through the English giant, knocking him down just as David had knocked down Goliath. Then he cried out: "Frenchmen, strike, the day is ours!" The English armies were humiliated, their king was sent to hell, and the Normans planted their holy flag on the bloodied earth. And so it was that God delivered England to William the Conqueror and to our clan.

Six hundred years later, after Henry VIII had cleaved the Church of England from the Roman Church, we fought our way into Ireland, where Protestant armies were being handed huge estates for their loyalty to the crown and the Church of England. James Montgomery, an Anglican curate, fought the Irish Catholics with a Bible in one hand and a sword in the other, and he won, because it was the god's will. We built a grand estate on the Inishowen Peninsula, where to this day a Montgomery collects rent from the Catholics.

When the British Empire spread to India, we followed, and brought our god with us. As commissioner of Lahore, Robert Montgomery built himself a sprawling stone villa in the Punjab. His servants were Muslim and Hindu. So were his troops, and so were his enemies. When rebellious Indian regiments of the Bengal Army captured Delhi in 1857, Robert tricked tens of thousands of his Indian troops into laying down their arms, then ordered his white officers to hunt down disloyal soldiers and blew them to pieces. The Delhi rebels were chased down and hanged, the white garrisons were saved, and the Punjab became the base for the Britain's reconquest of northern India.

"It was not policy, or soldiers, or officers that saved the Indian Empire to England, and saved England to India," wrote Robert. "The Lord our God, He it was who went before us and gave us the victory of our enemies, when they had well nigh overwhelmed us. To Him who holds all events in His own hand, and has so wondrously over-ruled all to our success, and to His own glory do I desire on behalf of myself and all whom I represent to express my devout and heartfelt thanks." It was just like the Old Testament. Our god was not detached from politics. The Lord stood for England and vice versa.

The fan clicked, forcing its way through the heavy air. Night.

Cicadas screeching. A scene: A shadowy sitting room behind the stone columns of that Punjabi villa. A palm in the corner, framed portraits of ancestors hanging on the walls. The voice of Mary Jane Dinh echoed in some distant hall, but the sitting room was as tranquil and grave as a church. There, kneeling on a woven carpet, was my great-great-grandfather Robert, and with him his eight-year-old son Henry. They prayed aloud together in the heavy air. Robert asked the god to keep Henry safe. They rose. The boy left the villa with his Muslim manservant, never to return.

Henry attended Miss Baker's Preparatory School in Brighton. Miss Baker was a Christian of the most fervent evangelical principles, who was determined to impart on her pupils the lessons of Revelation. The future bishop of Tasmania later noted: "I was brought up on almost undiluted hell fire. On the whole such diet has done me immense good, for it has left behind in me an awful sense of the Holy Will of God. The thunders of Sinai should not be forgotten by any Christian."

If the Old Testament taught Henry Montgomery about God's power and the New Testament taught him about God's love, then it was a life lived in the Victorian era that taught him that the English were the new chosen people. God clearly favored the British Empire above all others, granting Queen Victoria dominion over lands, seas, and peoples from Africa to the Americas to Australia. The way to repay the favor was to fight the spiritual battle with the same fervor with which England spread its commerce. "The clergy are officers in an imperial army," he wrote. "The language, indeed, of all the great men of the Old Testament is the true language of our army."

When he returned to England from the South Seas in 1901, Henry was named secretary of the Society for the Propagation of the Gospel in Foreign Parts. This made him a de facto foreign minister for the archbishop of Canterbury, and thus the most influential Anglican missionary in the world. He fought for years to formally bond the Empire and its church in one common evangelical mission. He failed—at least in the project of building a Christian theocracy—but his church did extend its reach to every continent. Henry served his god well, and his story would not have been complete without the acknowledgment, the personal visitation, the commendation from God and ancestors, that came to him that Easter morning so many years after he left the South Pacific.

The fan glided to a halt in the dead air of my room. The years converged in the stillness. The climax of my great-grandfather's story returned to me not as text but as an image so clear it should have been my own memory: A crystalline Irish dawn, a garden above the sparkling waters of Lough Foyle, the appearance of a procession of approving ghosts, then a blinding cloud and a voice pressing through the mist like soft thunder, asking Henry, "Lovest thou me?" so that the believer would know that the God of Love and the God of War were the same, and that He would be manifest to those who were ready, and that this gift of sight would be passed on to one's descendants.

7

The Word and
Its Meaning

Every day, every week, every month, every quarter,
the most widely read journals seem just now to vie
with each other in telling us that the time for religion
is past, that faith is a hallucination or an infantile
disease, that the gods have at last been found out and
exploded.

—MAX MULLER, *Lectures on the Origin*
and Growth of Religion, 1878

This being a story about myth, it would be wrong to continue without explaining what I mean when I use that word. Some people say "myth" when they mean fanciful and false. I do not, because I am learning how hard it can be to discern the frontiers between history, propaganda, dreams, and the terrain of miracles. And besides, the power of a myth always has more to do with its function than historic origin.

Here is my definition.

> **Myth:** A story, often involving the expression of supernatural
> power, that explains its believers' relationship with the world.

The definition will not alienate anthropologists, mythologists, or mystics because it omits the question about which men have argued since they first gathered to tell stories around campfires: *Which myths are historically true?*

When my great-grandfather was sailing through the South Pacific, his countrymen were digesting Sir James G. Frazer's *Golden Bough*, in which the Cambridge anthropologist reduced magic, myths, and religion to primitive and futile attempts to control the natural world. Charles Darwin's *Origin of Species* had already shaken the foundations of nineteenth-century British Christian thought. Now Frazer was taking the quite radical step of placing Christian texts under the same microscope as "primitive" religion. He assured readers that science and technology would inevitably extinguish the superstition inherent in all this mythology.

Most of the people who have studied and wrote about myth since then have focused on their function and structure, while generally assuming their falsity. Freud gave myths hell. He insisted they were "public dreams"—collective expressions of obsessional neuroses. Psychic baggage.

The first argument against this theory came from Melanesia. Bronislaw Malinowski, the Polish anthropologist who spent the years of World War I in the Trobriand Islands, concluded that for the communities he studied, myths were essential tools for expressing values and safeguarding morality. They may not have contained historical truths, but they were nonetheless vital ingredients of civilization.

This might explain why there is a common underlying structure to myths from various corners of the world. Creation stories are a good example. In Genesis, Yahweh shaped man from dust. In Banks Island *kastom* stories, the ancestor Qat carved man from a hunk of wood. A serpent in the Garden of Eden convinced Adam and Eve to taste the forbidden fruit. A snake did the same thing to the first man and woman in the legends of the Bassari in West Africa. The great flood is the most universal myth of them all: the Greeks and Romans told of a cataclysmic flood that transformed the world, but so did indigenous people on Canada's west coast. Qat made a deluge, too. It spilled out from the volcano on Santa Maria and carried him away forever.

Carl Jung carried these stories into the realm of social psychology. He argued that myths represented the wisdom the human species had gathered over the millennia. They contained essential truths that the "collective unconscious" had carried for generations and that science should never be allowed to displace. Some of these truths were straightforward: Thou shalt not kill. Honor thy father and thy mother. Marry someone other than your sister. Some were more abstract, and concerned the nature of the soul and its relationship with the universe. The Garden of Eden, according to Jungian sympathizer Joseph Campbell, was not a lush corner of Mesopotamia so much as it was a description of the geography of the human heart. It is the place of innocence that lies within all of us, the place we cannot return to because we have tasted the knowledge of good and evil.

If you subscribe to these theories, then you cannot say the Christian faith in an intervening god is any more or less valid than Melanesians' traditional belief in spirits, stones, and sorcery. If the god-ancestor Qat is a mythical character, then so is Jesus, and so are Bernard the Dane, John Frum, and John Coleridge Patteson, because regardless of their histories, they have been kept alive in stories in order to perform certain mythic functions. They represent ideals. They inspire. They offer their believers clues about the nature of the universe.

But these theories mortally wound myths, because even as they value them, they defang them with deconstruction. A myth without believers is a fairy tale. It is fantasy, fiction, stripped of sacredness. It is mere entertainment. It is a loss, perhaps, of something unfathomable.

Consider this: After decades studying the tribes of southern Sudan, the pioneering social anthropologist Edward Evan Evans-Pritchard returned to Oxford in the 1960s and announced that nonbelievers would never come close to understanding religion and myth as well as believers. Nonbelievers tended to try to explain religion away as illusion, using sociological, psychological, existential, or biological theories. (It's exactly what most anthropologists had been doing for decades, despite the fact that, in the absence of historical evidence, they had absolutely no way of knowing whether the spiritual beings of primitive religions existed or not.) Believers, on the other hand, explained religion in terms of how people conceived and related to reality. Since believers have an inward experience of religion, they understand it better than nonbelievers. According to Evans-Pritchard, even a missionary would make a better anthropologist among pagans than an atheist; while the atheist might find Jungian allegories or codes for living, the believer experiences epiphanies, tendrils of some divine thread.

I was discovering this in Melanesia. As soon as you stand apart from myths, divorce them from faith, pick apart their function and their origins, you become like an anthropologist, like Frazer peering through his ancient texts. You may be fascinated and amused, but you will never see a ghost, or magic, or the hand of God, because you have stepped outside the realm of faith. People say that religious fanatics are blinded by their faith. Evans-Pritchard asserted that there is something just as blinding in rationalism. You must make room for mystery before you can reach for it.

My journey in the Hotel Santo should have ended with that vision of my great-grandfather collapsed beneath the blinding cloud of his god; hearing, knowing, certain. It did not. I had my own memory of that place, and it was too strong to erase. I had flown to Ireland long before I hit the South Pacific. I had driven up the In-ishowen Peninsula, along the darkened Lough Foyle past the villages of Muff, Carrowkeel, Drung, and Moville. I had found what remained of Henry Montgomery's garden on a knoll above the lough.

The family manor was boarded up and surrounded on all sides by "heritage-style" vacation homes. The garden was a shambles. The roses were gone. I tromped through the ivy where our ancestors appeared to Henry as ghosts. I forced open the door of the moldering stone church where the god cloud had shone and had asked Henry, "Lovest thou me?" It was cold in there, and empty. I spent an afternoon lingering beneath the granite cross that marked my great-grandfather's grave, challenging the old man to appear, to speak, to offer a sign, anything. I did pray. I did promise to be open to the divine. I waited hours, willing him into being. If there was ever a time for a ghost to make himself known, this was it. All that came was a bitter wind that shook the oaks and ripped the slate tiles from the roof of the church. A storm rolled over the moors. A single patch of sunlight raced across the lough and was gone.

It's reasonable to demand proof if you are going to let miracles flood your dreams and guide your life. Isn't it? Proof. That's what should guide you. But now the certainty, the solidity, of memories were mingling with the fantastical inside the blurred walls of my fever. I rolled and sweated, clear and then unclear, fighting and then not fighting the incandescent visions, the tingle of closeness to something else, the immeasurable longing for the glowing cloud that would descend on me when I reached my myth island, Nukapu, to ask the question and then answer it.

On the fifth morning I awoke to dry sheets, my fever gone.

8

The Island of Magic and Fear

And, behold, the Lord passed by,
and a great and strong wind rent
the mountains, and brake in pieces
the rocks before the Lord;
but the Lord was not in the wind:
and after the wind an earthquake;
but the Lord was not in the earthquake:
and after the earthquake a fire; but the
Lord was not in the fire: and after
the fire a still small voice.

—I Kings 19:11–12

I found Mary Jane taking coffee on the veranda with her rumpled Australians. She wore a full-length silk gown.

"I need a ship," I said.

I had awoken clear-headed, and feeling a new vigor for my path, which led north to the Banks and Torres islands—the stronghold

of Anglicanism during my great-grandfather's time—and then beyond to the Solomons. According to my maps, it would only be a few
days' sail from the last of the Torres to Nukapu. I wanted to get
closer to the old stories. It was time to see the proof behind all the
magic talk.

"No ships, my dear," said Mary Jane.

"No ships," agreed the ranchers.

What captain would bother sailing to the northern islands?
There was no cargo to carry, other than the odd bag of low-grade
copra, the kiln-dried coconut flesh that once fueled the South Pacific economy. There was, however, a weekly mail plane that left
Santo and zigzagged its way north between a network of grass
airstrips.

At Pekoa, the last of Santo's World War II airfields, I climbed
inside a scuffed de Havilland Twin Otter along with a dozen other
passengers, a clutch of grass mats, and twenty sacks of rice. We
bounced off the tarmac, and the plane's shadow danced away between the tidy rows of coconut palms, through a herd of cattle,
over a dusty road, and into a powder blue bay. We glided over a
coral reef that stretched like a pink stain along the coast, over the
rust-red skeletons of wrecked ships and over the open sea, which
was rippling and empty and expectant.

My first stop would be Maewo, a thirty-mile-long spine of uplifted coral rock just south of the Banks Islands. I had been assured
that Maewo magic was even stronger than Ambrym magic. Maewo
didn't have Ambrym's volcanoes, but its mountains squeezed torrential rains from every storm that came Vanuatu's way. Hundreds
of fast-running streams tumbled down its flanks, and those streams
gave Maewo magicians their power. This was water magic, not fire
magic. Everyone knew that water magic could extinguish fire
magic. Back in Port Vila I had been assured that if I was ever the
victim of an Ambrymese curse, I should go straight to Maewo and
seek a cure from a *kleva*, a *kastom* medicine man.

Another thing. My great-grandfather had felt Maewo's *mana*. The mission had established seven schools on the north coast by the time he arrived in 1892. The *Southern Cross* stopped in to fill its water tanks at a cascade on the coast. Henry Montgomery observed that the people, once "wild and cannibal," had largely been pacified, but supernatural power was being manifested in a new and wondrous manner. "Two women had gone into the church after dark for prayer. There was no lamp there, but over the Lord's Table they saw a bright shining light, which remained there while they prayed and knelt. That same appearance was mentioned as having occurred at another school. There can be no doubt at all events of the simple and real faith of these people." The light was similar to the one Henry would see in his garden decades later. It was clearly proof of the catalyzing power of faith. I figured there was no better place than Maewo to launch my challenge to those who claimed to control or witness supernatural power.

After half an hour, Maewo appeared below us like the serrated back of a surfacing crocodile. My seatmate, a gaunt, sincere man, peered over my shoulder. He introduced himself as Alfred, adding that his brother was the Right Reverend Hugh Blessing Boe, the Anglican bishop of Vanuatu. Alfred said he was proud of his famous brother, but he was even prouder of his other brother, whose name was Dudley. Not only did Dudley own a truck—one of four on Maewo—but he was a *kleva*. When the previous prime minister of the Solomon Islands had heart trouble, it was Dudley who healed him. Dudley could make the ocean spill over the land, said Alfred. He could dump sea snakes into the coconut groves.

"Do they get along, Dudley and the bishop?"

"Yes, they do. Why do you ask?"

"Because of the magic, of course."

I had met Bishop Boe in Santo. He was a kind fellow, and smart, too. I had asked him about the persistence of traditional magic in Vanuatu. The bishop told me (and I was sure he meant it as a criticism) that many Melanesians still used religion as a kind of technology. For example, if a man was sick, he would see a medical doctor, but he would also ask a priest to pray for him. If that didn't work, the man would turn to traditional magic or make a sacrifice to some kind of spirit. Sometimes he would pursue all three methods at the same time. Sometimes, said the bishop with a sigh, Melanesians had trouble separating what was God from what was not God.

Now, yelling above the drone of the propellers, Alfred told me what Bishop Boe had neglected to mention. It was the bishop himself who had advised the prime minister of the Solomon Islands to see his brother the *kleva* about his heart trouble.

"Dudley's magic is not against the church," explained Alfred. "It is a gift from God. It's his work. It's how he paid for his truck."

The pilot banked the Twin Otter into a steep, descending arc. We landed on an airstrip whose grass was as tall and robust as prairie wheat.

Dudley was waiting for us. He was no withered mystic. In fact, he seemed altogether plain for a witch doctor. He had the capable appearance of a roofing contractor or a mailman. He must have been about forty. He chain-smoked Peter Jacksons under a drooping mustache.

Alfred and I climbed into the box of Dudley's Mitsubishi. Dudley drove. We followed a cart track south along Maewo's leeward coast. The landscape reminded me of the greenhouse at the Royal Botanical Gardens at Kew, only more lush, more surreal: patches of big-leaf taro, flowers, and manioc exploded between great battlements of uplifted coral stone. Green parrots flecked with crimson flapped back and forth between palms and glistening breadfruit trees. White orchids sprang from tree branches. Piglets rooted in pens fenced with heaps of moss-covered rock. Smoke curled from makeshift sheds where men stoked fires in rusty steel drums and tossed bags full of coconut shells on the

racks above. It was copra-harvesting time. The air was sweet with
the scent of drying coconut.

Clear water flowed everywhere: it rushed down fissures in
the gray rock, bubbled along irrigation channels, cascaded from
stalactite-laden cliffs, over the road, down, down to the sea. We
forded thirty streams in an hour.

"Water, water," said Alfred. "All the people are scared of man-
Maewo because of our water magic. This island is full-up poison.
But no magic can hurt me, because I bathe in *tabu* water every day.
If you were a jealous man and you tried to kill me with a spell, it
would fail. Your poison will bounce back and kill you instead.
Would you like protection from evil? A charm? Dudley can make
you one."

Yes, of course I wanted a charm. I wanted love magic. I wanted
to see rain pour from a cloudless sky. I wanted to see Dudley turn
himself into an owl. Anything.

With all this supernatural wherewithal, Maewo should have been
the most blessed and peaceful island in the archipelago. It appeared to be idyllic at first, and wealthy, especially compared to
Tanna. There were cement-block houses with tin roofs. At first I
didn't notice the fences, the wire mesh that wrapped the yards of
Maewo's most prosperous families. I didn't make much of the
sullen faces or the suspicious glares directed at Dudley's truck.

We stopped beside a huge open-air church. Dudley didn't cut
the engine. He barely stopped long enough to say good-bye. This
was Betarara, site of the island's only rest house.

"The chief," said Alfred, as a filthy-looking man approached.
"*Yumi* can meet tomorrow after church."

I jumped out, and then they were gone. Strange.

The chief scratched his belly through a rip in his shirt and
smiled at me anxiously. I handed him a letter of introduction I had

obtained from the National Tourism Office. The letter advised readers that I had come to promote tourism and that they should help me. The chief peered at it, furrowed his thick brows, and studiously ignored the young man who panted and squirmed behind him. The boy rolled his eyes, giggled, leaped in the air with a yelp, then dashed away squealing.

"My son," said the chief shyly. I turned away so that someone could turn my letter right-side up without completely embarrassing him.

The rest house inhabited a corner of the village church hall. It had all the ambiance of a medium-security prison. It was protected by a tall wire-mesh fence, which baffled me, because people in Vanuatu did not steal.

I cooked myself a dinner of instant noodles and ketchup. I lay awake in the dark, listening to the groans and howls of the chief's son somewhere in the distance. And closer. The crunch of careful footsteps on gravel, then a sound that made me shiver: a barely perceptible rasping, like tiny fingernails or claws scratching against wire mesh. The sound was faint enough and brief enough to dismiss as an imagining.

Alfred did not come to meet me the next morning, so I walked south until I reached his village, which was really more of a family compound, several cement-block houses encircling a broad lawn.

Alfred and Dudley had a sister. Faith Mary was a broad woman with a stern brow and a voice like a diesel engine. She wore an Anglican Mothers' Union T-shirt and was constantly digging through the dusty leather purse she carried around her neck. When I arrived, she spread banana leaves on the lawn and served baked taro root and coconut crab on it. Alfred, Dudley, and a dozen others gathered around to eat. Faith Mary told me that Maewo was a very modern place. Look at Alfred and Dudley, she said. They cooked and washed the dishes if she told them to. Alfred laughed. Dudley exhaled a plume of cigarette smoke and gazed at the sky. Faith Mary smiled and pushed more food toward me. Then she narrowed her eyes.

"Now," she said, "tell me what you want from us."

"Well, I know that people everywhere are afraid of Maewo because of the magic here," I said as soberly as possible. "I want to see that magic. Not crazy stories. Not conjuring tricks. Proof."

"You know why the people are afraid of Maewo? For the same reason we are all afraid: death! You make a Maewo man angry, and he will kill you with poison, right now!" she said, slapping the earth. "And Dudley is the strongest magic man of all. Tell him what you can do, Dudley."

Dudley was not so enthusiastic. "*Mi mekem kastom meresin.*"

"Tell him what kind of medicine, Dudley!"

"*Wanfala drink blong curem cancer.*"

"And . . ."

"*Wanfala drink blong bringim daon blad presa.*"

"Tell him, Dudley, tell him more." Faith Mary clearly wore the pants in this family.

Dudley sighed and made an attempt at English. "Okay, suppose *yu garem wan nogud* devil living inside you. I take a white cloth *blong yu* and I sleep on it. Now I travel inside your body to look at that *nogud* devil, then figure out how to make it leave you. Okay? Now suppose *yu ded* from a mystery something. I put a stone on the grave *blong yu* to make you rise up and tell me what *killim yu i ded*. Okay? Now suppose you knew you were going to die and you wanted to make sure your wife didn't go marry *narafalla*, I give you a special drink that would *killim hem i ded* five days after you."

"But Dudley doesn't do the bad magic, only the good magic," interrupted Faith Mary.

"So what is your most popular, um, medicine?" I asked.

"Well, suppose you want some girl to love you, I could make a leaf for you to eat at night. Then you would get up early *tumas long morning*, and say the name of the girl just as the sun hits you. By and by you will *stap* inside her dreams. She will come find you."

"Ah, sweet mouth," I said. This was the same medicine Graeme had bragged about on the *Brisk*. "Why don't you show me one of these tricks?"

Dudley looked away. Alfred fidgeted. Faith Mary cleared her throat. It was against the rules for the men to share their *kastom* with me, she told me. The provincial council had decided that white men couldn't be trusted.

"When a white man sees magic, he learns it and he kills it. We know you white people have got *savve*. For example, a few years ago an Australian came here. He threw a piece of tin can on the ground and it turned into a snake. Then he told us that white man's magic was stronger than ours."

Faith Mary said she liked me. She said I should not be staying in Betarara, because the people there would certainly poison me— that's just the kind of people they were. I should come and stay in Navenevene, where Dudley could protect me. Dudley showed no particular enthusiasm for the idea, and I had already paid for a week's stay at the rest house, so I thanked her and left.

Dudley caught up to me a short way down the road. He rolled down the window of the Mitsubishi and sheepishly offered me a ride.

"I've got legs, I can walk," I said.

"*Hem i tru*. But you might step over *wanfala* black magic on the road, *wanfala* leaf that would do terrible things *long penis blong yu*."

The gravel felt suddenly hot beneath my sandals. "My penis?"

"Now and again people here get cross with each other. They leave poison lying *albaot*. The worst is the poison that makes your penis shrivel," he said, holding his thumb and forefinger together, "and swim up inside your body. I cure people of *disfala* curse all the time."

No wonder people on Maewo protected themselves with wire

fences. I got in the truck. Church was out, and everyone in every village along the way saw me riding with my good friend the witch doctor. At the time I didn't think that was such a bad thing. Dudley dropped me off at Betarara and promised to meet me the next day.

Most communities in Vanuatu have a *kastom* chief, a man who holds no political power but whose job it is to sustain and promote the old ways. Geoffrey Uli was Maewo's *kastom* chief. He lived in a shack near Betarara. I figured his mandate might logically encompass public relations, which meant he should help me.

Uli managed to evade me for four days. I finally caught him in his yard one afternoon just before kava time. He was an old man. With his shirt off, his skin looked as though it had been shrink-wrapped to his bony frame. His eyes were birdlike, sharp and cunning. They darted back and forth across his garden as though looking for an escape. Eventually they settled on me.

Uli told me that people on Maewo already had God before the missionaries came. Their *kastom* stories were the same as the ones in the Bible. Only a few names had been changed. Maewo's own version of Eve was created not from Adam's rib, but from his collarbone. There was a great flood, and Tagaro had weathered it in a big canoe, like Noah. As Uli told me these things, his wife, who was sitting in the dirt, howled with laughter.

"That rubbish woman had me baptized when we got married," he said. "Now I must pray twice a day. First I do *kastom* prayers, then I pray to the church God."

Uli wouldn't say exactly to whom his *kastom* prayers were directed. Not to Tagaro, anyway. But he did make this point: The old gods never had a problem with magic, so why should the new one?

"But isn't the Christian God opposed to *kastom* magic?" I asked.

"The Anglican missionaries never told us our *kastom* was rubbish. It was their students, boys from Maewo, who smashed the *tabu* stones. They went into the *nakamal* and spoiled the kava grinders and the drinking shells, too. They thought that this would get them into heaven. Now we know better. We have our kava back. And there is plenty of *kastom* magic left on Maewo."

"I don't believe it. I don't believe you people still have the power," I said, hoping to shame him into a demonstration.

"Sir, you are wrong," said Uli. " We have rocks that can make rain, wind, and sun."

I looked at the sky. There was rain, wind, and sun every day on Maewo. "How about thunder?"

"The thunder man lives far, far away in the bush. You'll never find him."

"There must be something, some way to prove . . ."

Uli's wife spoke up from the shadows. "*Sipos hem wantem looklook long kastom magic, hemi mas findem tufala ston blong etk-wek*," she suggested.

Uli shot her an irritated look. She ignored Uli's glare and turned to me. She lifted both hands as if shaking an imaginary rock. Then she trembled and fell over on her side. I got it.

"Yes, yes, earthquake stones. Wonderful," I said. "When can we go see them?"

"I cannot help you," said Uli.

"Why not?"

"Because I have no time. Sir, I have been keeping an eye on you. I know you have been on this island for four days already. If you had come to see me first, I could have helped you. But I know what you have been doing. You went off with Dudley, didn't you? You have not paid me respect. You have spoiled your luck."

I tried to explain that he was wrong, that Dudley had been avoiding me for days. But there was no point in arguing. Uli had told me just enough to make it clear to me that he was the real *kastom* expert on Maewo. He hustled his wife back toward their shack, clucking and poking at her, shaking his head like a bird. How was I to know that Uli and Dudley were bitter rivals? I was left to gaze east toward the serrated crest of the island and ponder the location of the stones that made the ground shake. I wanted to find those stones.

I met Faith Mary on the coast road.

"Dudley is avoiding me," I said.

"You have chosen the Betarara people and Geoffrey Uli."

"No, I haven't—"

"You have chosen," she said again. "We won't interfere, but we can't protect you anymore."

My fever returned. I spent most of my days in bed. Once they realized that Dudley had spurned me, the citizens of Betarara took me on as their cause. They brought me crackers. They boiled water for tea and instant noodles. They sat and watched me for hours. First, there were the chief and his wife, who mumbled to me soothingly. One night, a handsome young catechist dropped by to read me excerpts from the New Testament. Then came the lady with magic hands. She leaned over me, her immense breasts inflating the expanse of her island dress. She prodded my belly, grunted knowingly, then kneaded my internal organs for an hour, whispering, "God, *plis mekem alraet disfala* boy."

The people at Betarara told me stories, and all their stories were infused with magic and fear. Like the one about the pelicans that had recently appeared on a beach near the airport. Pelicans were not native to the island. Everyone was terrified of them. "They haven't attacked us yet, but they are huge. We are quite sure that white men brought them," said one kava-drunk visitor. But there was hope. A boy had brought one of the pelicans down with his slingshot. His family cooked and ate the bird. Now there were only four.

The villagers were suspicious of foreigners. Once, a white yachtsman came ashore near the village and dug for an hour in the sand. When he sailed away, the village children discovered that he had buried the eggs of man-eating crocodiles. Once, a Russian ship had anchored just off the coast. Villagers insisted that a crew member came ashore and let loose a copra snake. The snake slithered up a tree, and now everyone was afraid to go into the palm groves. Perhaps, the villagers whispered, the sailor had also let a tiger loose on the island. There was so much to fear on Maewo.

Curses were a constant danger. The strongest kinds of poison on Maewo were not sprinkled on your food or left on the road for you to step on. They were administered to you after the fact. In other words, a sorcerer could use your footprint or a banana peel you might have discarded to make you sick. The best way to stay healthy on Maewo was to bury your dinner scraps and sweep away your footprints. It was especially important not to make enemies, since many sorcerers kept their talents secret. Never forget to lock your door at night, they said.

The people of Betarara were scared of things they could see and things they could not see. Some things they did not wish to discuss at all. Like the earthquake stones about which Geoffrey Uli's wife had pantomimed, and which I very much wanted to see. Very bad, they said. Very dangerous. End of the world.

Each night, after the villagers went home and I had extinguished my oil lamp, the noises would start again outside my window. Scratching on wire. Rustling. Clucking. Whooshing. I locked my door and did my best to contemplate the rationalist tradition.

Then a white man arrived at my doorstep. Wes was Texan, barely out of high school. The Peace Corps had sent him to Maewo to teach English. He had the trusting face of a puppy and the glassy eyes of a kava enthusiast. Wes explained to me why the chief of Betarara's son spent his time howling and barking like a dog. The boy had once been considered quite clever, and had been sent to the Anglican high school over on Santo. That's when he had fallen in love. The boy's passion went unrequited, so he turned to *kastom* for help. He tried using some version of sweet mouth love magic on his beloved, but the prayers and leaves failed to make her crazy with love. The magic boomeranged. The boy had been crazy ever since. No exorcism could save him.

It was Wes who helped me find the earthquake stones. It was no secret, he said, that the stones resided in Kwatcawol village, which clung to the crest of the forested ridge that ran the length of Maewo. I was still too weak to make the trek on foot, but a track had recently been bulldozed up the mountain from Betarara. Wes's adopted brother had a truck.

We left at sunset, following the red scar of the new road up through the jungle. The evening's first fireflies twittered like green sparks. Flying foxes dropped out of the banyan trees to chase them up and down the road.

We pulled into a field in the middle of the village. A crowd formed around the truck. I stood up in the box and explained my mission. There was a whispered debate. Wes interpreted. He told me my timing was perfect. The custodian of the earthquake stones had never permitted outsiders to see them. But the old man had died a year before my arrival, and his seven sons, all Christians, were not quite sure how they should handle their pagan legacy. Voices were raised. Heads were shaken. Finally, one man's eyes lit up: perhaps the visitor could offer a gift. Ah yes, a gift. It was not so much a bribe or an admission fee as a tribute to Melanesian *kastom*. Traditional relationships in Melanesia were always based on symbolic exchange. A murderer could be let off the hook with the right exchange of pigs.

I handed over a bag of rice and a can of corned beef, and we all filed somberly toward the sturdiest hut in the village. It had been built in the traditional style: one great room under beams of black tree fern trunks, with palm leaves hanging so low to the ground they were spattered with mud. The roof beams were reinforced every few inches with smaller poles. This was the Melanesian version of the earthquake-proof bunker.

Inside, it was dark, crowded, and confused. Then someone lit an oil lamp, revealing what looked like two bundles of garbage hanging on the wall at the back of the hut. The earthquake stones. I moved closer. Hands reached out from the shadows toward me, not touching me, but straining and ready.

The stones may have been the size of potatoes, or they may have been bigger. I couldn't actually see them. They had each been wrapped in strips of dirty canvas, then bound in chicken wire and suspended from a crossbeam by lengths of hemp rope. It hardly seemed dignified.

The new guardians of the stones appeared to be a husband-and-wife team: he was bare-chested, tattooed, and scowling suspiciously; she was plump and beaming warmly in the glow of her oil lamp. At first nobody said anything. Then an old man stepped out of the shadows. He wore a towel wrapped around his head like a turban. His pupils were opaque. He pushed his face into mine. I will translate his monologue into English:

"Ages ago, in the time of the ancestors, the people found three stones in the forest," he said—or rather, shouted through the silence. He cupped his leathery hands together as though he were holding a great weight. "The stones were all hanging in midair, and they were shaking. One man touched them, and they stopped moving. He played with those stones. He put one of them on the ground—that caused the ground to shake in another village. Oh, yes, that man saw how powerful the stones were. He played so much and caused so many tremors that one of the stones rolled into the ocean and was lost forever. Since then we have been very careful with the other stones."

"Can I touch them?"

The old man made a gurgling sound, as though he were choking. The guardian exhaled through his nostrils like a bull, but his wife steadied him with a glance, then nodded her head at me encouragingly. I reached for the bigger of the two bundles, lifted it, turned it in my hand, peered through the chicken wire. It was an industrial-strength cocoon.

I felt a hand on my elbow. Foreigners could not be trusted. It was true. I was desperate to test the stones' magic.

"Can I untie it? Just touch it to the ground to see if the stone still works?"

"No! Of course not," croaked the old man, now breathing hoarsely. "If you did that, you would cause a terrible earthquake."

"But if we did it quickly, you know, a quick touch to the floor, perhaps we could make the ground shake for only a few seconds. Wouldn't that be fun to see?"

It was rude to push, I knew it. But the stones did not radiate power or history or the slightest whiff of danger. They looked like cobblestones. I wanted to give them a chance to be something more or nothing at all.

"*Yu no savve!* The last person to try anything like that was this boy's grandfather," said the old man, pointing at the bare-chested guardian. "He made Maewo shake for eight days. Eight days! It was one awful something. But at least the *olfala* knew how to make the tremors stop, he had a special leaf. But he never passed on his secrets. The knowledge is dead in the ground. That's why we have to take such great care of these stones. They are very sensitive. When a big wind comes, someone has to stay here to hold the stones tight, even if the house collapses around him. And if a rat or a pig was to find its way inside this house, watch out! The ground would shake, because the stones don't like those animals. We have to be careful!"

The story wasn't good enough. Proof. Part of me yearned to pull out my knife, cut the hemp, pound that rock on the bare earth even as the people screamed and leapt on me and beat me senseless, because in those moments we would all know. I could feel my muscles twitching. The bare-chested guardian took a deep breath and said in a commanding baritone, "*Yumi go long drink kava nao.*"

"Um," I said.

"*Nao ia,*" he said, and he stepped toward me like a bull. "*Yumi go raet nao.*"

I looked to Wes for support. But he had already turned for the door.

"Kava," Wes was murmuring to the men who clung to him like a teddy bear. "*Mi likem kava.*"

Late that night, after three shells of muddy kava and a dizzy ride home, I lay awake in bed listening, for the last time, to the distant cries of the chief's son and the rain on my tin roof, drumming and dripping me toward sleep. And then I heard the rasping, the same staccato click and metallic hum I had heard every night on Maewo, and I knew that something was tapping at the wire-mesh fence outside my room. I rolled quietly out of bed and crept to the window, holding my breath. The rain had stopped. The yard was empty. The sky was starless and muddy. A shadow teetered on the curled edge of the mesh fence. Before I could focus, there was a sudden, explosive beating of wings, and the creature flapped through space and landed on my porch. I could just make out a great plume of tail feathers and the glint of tiny eyes. A rooster. I exhaled. I suppose I should have felt relief. I didn't.

"Out!" I shrieked.

The rooster didn't take flight. It simply cocked its head and glared at me with cunning, familiar eyes. I hung a towel over my window and locked my door. When I did fall asleep, I dreamed of the *kastom* chief, Geoffrey Uli. I saw him in a clearing in the forest, standing with a knife in one hand and a stone cup in the other. There were black feathers tied to his arms. At his feet lay a pig with its legs bound together. I saw Uli bend down. I saw his knife slice through the beast's throat, saw the blood run in bright red streams into the stone cup, overflow, and trickle over Uli's talonlike hands. I saw his eyes narrow with pleasure and secret knowledge, and I recalled what he had told me: I have been watching you.

It may be true that people all over Vanuatu were scared of men from Maewo. But here on the island of water magic, people were fearful of absolutely everything. They trembled at the thought of unseen curses and charms, at the terrible power of two small cobblestones. They suspected treachery from visitors, from their neighbors, and from the natural world. All that magic made them vulnerable. It always had. My great-grandfather described an encounter between a white missionary and a murderer on nearby Ambae. The missionary only had to fix a disapproving gaze sternly on the man to send him scurrying for safety. The murderer returned to his home village, declared, "The man looked at me!" and promptly collapsed. He died, I suppose, of shock, or fear, or some life-sucking disorder he felt the white man had directed at him. My great-grandfather was intrigued, not so much by Melanesian magic as by Melanesian fragility. "Like peaches ripened in the hot sun, the slightest shock seems to upset their balance and cause death," he wrote.

Bad intent, hostility alone, could be lethal. I felt the truth of this on Maewo. I couldn't shake the idea that the rooster that had been prowling my yard each night for a week had something to do with my recurring fever, and with Geoffrey Uli. Yes, this would be a silly hypothesis if proposed from an easy chair in an apartment in London or Toronto or Los Angeles. But when you are breathing the air of sorcery and fear, it is difficult not to absorb the local wisdom about these things. If myth is the form we give to our idea of the universe, of God, then it must also occasionally be the vessel into which we pour our fears. I flew away empty-handed, without proof of anything, and yet carrying an acute sense that the farther I got from Maewo, the safer I would be.

9

The Curse of Gaua

One day, long ago, a man was fishing on a reef, and he saw something out in the sea. It appeared to be an island, but it moved. He ran to the beach shouting, "An island is coming here," and quickly the people gathered on the beach to watch a sailing ship approach and anchor on the reef. The inhabitants of the island came ashore, and our island world ceased to be.

—CASPAR LUANA, *Buka! A Retrospective*

When the *Southern Cross* first appeared in the Banks Islands, islanders assumed the ship could not be of the world, because nobody in the world could make such a big canoe. They assumed the creatures aboard the vessel were not human: after all, humans were black, not white. So there was much debate wherever Bishop Patteson stepped ashore. Some elders thought he might be the ghost of a dead man. But it was the general consensus that Patteson was not a ghost at all but Qat, the mythical hero of all the Banks Islands, returning after thousands of years away.

Qat was born on Vanua Lava. His mother was not a woman

but a stone that had cracked apart to bring him into the world. Like Jesus, he had no earthly father, but Qat was not a god, or even the son of a god. He was a *vui*, a spirit. He was not the world's creator. But he did make men, pigs, rocks, and trees to amuse himself. He did not make day, but he did paddle to the edge of the world and return with a piece of darkness so that his brothers could have night to sleep in.

I wanted to know more about Qat. I imagined sitting by a cooking fire and listening to some *olfala* ramble on through the night about the wonders of the cunning ancestor. There should have been no better place to do so than Santa Maria, southernmost of the Banks Group. Qat's story was written into the remarkable geography of the island. I could see it all through the porthole of the mail plane. Santa Maria looked like a green doughnut floating in the bubbling fat of the sea. The island had clearly once been a volcanic cone even grander than Lopevi, but at some point that cone must have exploded or imploded, leaving a four-mile-wide hole in its center. The doughnut hole was occupied by a lake. Steam billowed from a small cone of ash and orange muck at the lake's edge.

The island looked strange and mysterious and just as it should have, and it was all explained by the Qat stories that Codrington had recorded in *The Melanesians*.

In ancient times the caldera had been quite dry. It was Qat's playground. He spent his last earthly years frolicking there with his companion, Marawa the Spider. This is how the lake came to be: When Qat grew tired of the world, he carved himself a huge canoe from a tree he found in the caldera. He loaded his wife, his eleven brothers, and every living thing, even the smallest ants, into the canoe, and built a roof over them. Then came a rainstorm of biblical proportions. Water filled the caldera and flowed over its rim. Qat steered his canoe over the edge, ripping a channel through the crest and tearing a ditch all the way to the sea. Then he floated away beyond the horizon, never to return.

Flying above Santa Maria was like drifting above Oz. There was the mythical lake. There was the gaping wound in the side of the caldera, and a cascade, and a river marking the path of Qat's escape. I saw all these things as the Twin Otter drifted out of the clouds toward a patch of grass at Gaua, the name given to Santa Maria's east coast.

Once the plane had bounced away and its drone had subsided, I went looking for signs of Qat. A family had built a bungalow for tourists by the airstrip. They fed me. I was their second guest in five months. I asked the man of the house for the old stories. He didn't want to talk about Qat. I wandered the cart track that served as the island's only road. I sat with people in the dirt. Nobody cared much about Qat.

You would think islanders would never forget Qat. You would think that with his stories imprinted on the landscape, thoughts of the *vui* would occupy their days. But this is not the history about which Santa Marians now concern themselves. Finally, Paul Wudgor, the paramount chief of Gaua, a thoughtful, shoeless man of about thirty, took me for a walk through the forest beyond the coast road, and showed me why.

The coastal lowlands were covered with ruins: hundreds and hundreds of stone platforms, broken walls, chest-high foundations, all built from stones fitted tightly without mortar in a style reminiscent of Peru's Inca palaces, though more modest in proportion. The ruins appeared in gardens, under mounds of grass among the coconut groves, and in the darkest glades, bound by knots of banyan root. They collected moss in the shadows on the mountainsides, and they whispered that once, long ago, there had been something of a metropolis on the Gaua coast.

That was certainly the impression gained by the island's first European visitor. The Portuguese navigator Pedro Fernandez de Quirós—who journeyed on behalf of the king of Spain, and who gave Santa Maria its name—noted in 1606 that the island was populated by "innumerable natives" of three different colors: yellow, black, and off-white. Other early visitors estimated the island's population at twenty or thirty thousand.

But now there were few people on the Gaua coast. They lived in a scattering of small hamlets, their houses rustic pole-and-thatch affairs with no tin roofs or stonework or milled timber to speak of. I never saw a car or truck on the coast road, and I rarely saw people. What had become of the metropolis and all its citizens?

Codrington blamed a turn-of-the-century population decline on the labor trade. Tens of thousands of Melanesians had been taken to work on the sugar plantations of Queensland and Fiji in the nineteenth century. But most of the laborers completed their "contracts" and returned home after a few years. That explanation wouldn't do.

Henry Montgomery, who was carried to shore by a young man in 1892, blamed the islanders' own bloodlust. War, he wrote, was as regular and systematic on Santa Maria as cricket tournaments, with marked battlegrounds and strict start times: "Still more curious, is that when such a battle is announced the young men of a neighbouring village, who have nothing to do with the quarrel, will take their bows and arrows and start off to take part in the conflict. Strangest of all, is the fact that such a party, who go from sheer love of fighting, usually divide into two parties and choose to oppose each other."

The sport resulted in a cycle of murder and vengeance that my great-grandfather insisted only got worse when laborers returned from Queensland with rifles.

But this explanation won't do, either. Such blood sport rarely ended with more than a single death and could not account for the almost complete decimation of Santa Maria and almost every other island in Melanesia. Each year, fewer and fewer canoes came out to meet traders and missionaries. A resident missionary at Wango in the Solomon Islands was shown the sites of forty-six once-prosperous villages, of which only three remained. In the nineteenth century, the population of Erromango, north of Tanna, fell from more than three thousand to less than four hundred. Some historians estimated that the population of the New Hebrides was reduced by 90 percent in the late nineteenth century. What was killing people?

My new friend Chief Paul had a theory about that. I should have seen it coming. He said it was *kastom* magic that had decimated the island, and it was God who eventually came to the rescue. Santa Maria was once like Maewo: a place held hostage by sorcerers so treacherous and lethal that those who weren't poisoned or murdered finally just got in their canoes and fled.

"Once we had twenty thousand people on this island," the paramount chief told me as we gnawed boiled fish in his hut. "But then came a time of terrible magic. Sorcerers cursed people using their garbage, their poo-poo, whatever they could find. People had to throw their dinner scraps into the sea to make sure sorcerers didn't use them to cast evil spells on them. Bad men used secret leaves to kill our *pikinini* even before they were born. They used smoke from fires to curse people. Hundreds and hundreds of people died this way."

By the 1960s, said the chief, there were only seven women left on the Gaua side of the island. Finally the church took action. Esuva Din, an Anglican district priest from Vanua Lava, sailed south to confront the evil with an act of boldness and Old Testament audacity. He harnessed the Holy Spirit to create a boomerang curse: all black magic would now bounce back and kill anyone who tried to use it. Within days, dozens of known sorcerers had dropped dead. One sorcerer confronted the district priest and said, "I don't believe it's true; I don't believe you really have the power to curse anyone who uses black magic." Esuva Din did not like to be challenged. He said, "Rubbish man, just you wait and see." The sorcerer keeled over and died the next day.

The chief's version of the crisis and its resolution seemed good enough for almost everyone I met on Santa Maria. I suppose you remember things in the manner that most suits you. But the truth is, the church was the cause, not the solution, of the death plague that landed on the islands. You can see the signs in the early mission writings. You can see the truth dawning, too late, on the Anglican brotherhood.

After a visit to a village on Vanua Lava in 1861, Bishop Patteson complained that local men were avoiding him and that some had remarked quite rudely about the "unusual sickness" connected with his new teaching. Patteson found Mota in good health in August 1863; two weeks later, he returned to find the island in the grip of a terrible scourge of dysentery and influenza. Fifty people had already died from it. Four of every ten baptized Melanesians died in the decade straddling the turn of the century. It would take the missionaries decades to realize—or admit—the part they played in the Melanesian apocalypse. The Reverend W. J. Durrad was horrified to realize it was his own arrival on isolated Tikopia that sparked an epidemic of pneumonia that killed dozens. The incident convinced Durrad, finally, that the *Southern Cross,* oozing with New Zealand–bred germs, was the chief agent of disease. The ship's legacy of death lasted well into the twentieth century. "A fortnight after its visit everyone is ill," he wrote in 1917. As late as 1931, a stopover on Malaita unleashed an epidemic that killed eleven hundred islanders.

Even when Europeans acknowledged the role they played in spreading disease, they put the catastrophe down to a lack of stamina among Melanesians. As Durrad put it, "There is a fatalism in their outlook which reacts upon their physical organism." When they fell sick, Melanesians tended to give up and wait to die rather than fight their illness. It was the same with sorcery: anyone who so much as believed he was the victim of black magic died within hours or days. If only they were made of stronger stuff! The third bishop of Melanesia, Cecil Wilson, responded to all this by suggesting that all that could be done for this "dying race" was to try to ensure its members went to their graves as Christians.

I didn't have my history books with me on Gaua. But I wanted to let the chief know I was ashamed and sorry for my ancestor's ignorance, sorry for the slow dirge of pneumonia, dysentery, and influenza that had decimated the island. He just laughed.

"You just don't understand," he said. "We have been saved. Esuva Din saved us."

Once the coast had been purged of evil, hundreds of families arrived from nearby islands to till new life into Santa Maria's ancient gardens. That was during the 1970s and '80s. Now the population had rebounded to almost forty-two hundred people.

Still, the Gaua coast felt eerily empty, like so many of those places—the highlands of Peru, the Thai plains of Ayuttaya, the Turkish Aegean—whose time has passed and where foreigners pay to see the rubble of once great cities. Only there weren't any tourists here. Nor were there ghosts or *vui*.

Who would the ancient souls of Gaua have haunted? Most of their own descendants were dead, and the rubble of their ancient city was suffocating under a thickening blanket of vines. I walked the ruins and the empty forests, bought the last can of tuna from a village canteen, sat out a rainstorm, and then lay down in the tall grass and waited for the mail plane. A crowd of giggling children gathered around me. Since nobody on the island could remember the stories of Qat, I told them one I had learned from Codrington.

Before there was a lake in the caldera, Qat played games there with his companion Marawa the Spider. Once Qat spent six days carving bits of wood into the shapes of men and women. He danced for those dolls, and they stirred. He beat his drum, and they moved some more. He kept on dancing and drumming until he had coaxed them all to life. Qat was pleased, because he had made the first humans. He had made life. Marawa tried to imitate Qat, but the spider was so startled when he saw his own dolls stir that he buried them in the dirt. After six days Marawa scraped the earth away to find his dolls rotten and stinking. He was horrified. Marawa had made death.

10

The Parishioners' Paradise

*Warning: It is not wise to be dismissive of religion,
particularly Christianity, if you are a nonbeliever.
Islanders are likely to dislike you strongly if you are
hostile to Christianity.*

—*Lonely Planet: Solomon Islands*

When I was young, I learned that paradise was an island. There
were mountains on it, and they were shaped like sand castles
melted by the rain. There were pink marshmallow clouds around
those peaks, but not over the beaches or the kaleidoscope of reefs
that sheltered the lagoons from the surf. You approached paradise
by plane and drifted between those peaks and circled over its estu-
aries, and you saw the palm shadows cast over sand. When you
landed, you were greeted by a white-suited Mephistopheles who
said, "Welcome to Fantasy Island," and you knew that paradise
would be whatever you willed it to be.

Vanua Lava was twenty minutes by Twin Otter north from

Gaua. The volcanoes, the beaches, the shining estuary, I did glide above them all, and I was carried into the lushness of a vivid green airfield, and then I was welcomed not into an exotic fantasy but into the arms of the church. The secretary to the bishop of Banks and Torres was a large, backslapping fellow, and like almost all Anglican clergy in the islands, Melanesian. He was waiting at the airstrip with the only truck in the village of Sola.

I jumped in the back and was deposited shortly at a seaside rest house owned by an Anglican priest. We prayed before lunch, then again before dinner, and then again at breakfast.

"I want to go to Mota," I told the priest's wife.

"Tomorrow is Sunday," she told me. "You'll go to church."

"Oh, yes," I said. "Of course I will," knowing there was no way out of that one.

Vanua Lava's tiny neighbor, Mota, was the epicenter of the explosion of Anglicanism that reverberated across Melanesia in the nineteenth century. The church now defined life on both islands. When I asked people in Sola to tell me a *kastom* story, something from the past, they did not tell me about Qat. Instead, and without fail, they related the tale of their favorite hero, a lad who had been born in Darkness Time. His name was Sarawia, and his curiosity would lead him on an adventure stranger than anything he could imagine, an adventure that would forever link the names of Vanua Lava and Mota in the new Christian mythology. When he was an old man, Sarawia wrote down his story so it would not be forgotten. The bishop's secretary gave me a copy. It went like this:

In the days when people still relied on ancestors and spirits for help, Sarawia lived in the forest above the wide bay that now cradled Sola. He was paddling his dugout canoe in the sheltered waters one evening when he saw what looked like a floating village on the horizon. As if by magic, the village drifted into the bay and ceased moving, despite the strong tide. There were creatures with shocking white faces on board. Everyone who saw them was certain they had come from the rim of the sky, because they were clothed in the colors of the setting sun.

Sarawia paddled out for a closer inspection. Two of the creatures were dressed in black robes. They beckoned him to come closer, but he stayed in his canoe, remembering his father's warning that the spirits would kill and eat him if he was not careful. But Sarawia was even more curious than fearful, and he wanted the fishhooks and biscuits that they held out to him. One man called so gently that Sarawia could not resist taking his hand and climbing on board. He saw the leather-shod feet of his hosts and was horrified: "I said to myself that these men were made partly of clamshell, and my bones quaked." But Bishop George Selwyn and his young protégé, John Coleridge Patteson, did not hurt Sarawia. They sat him down and asked the names of people and things on Vanua Lava, and when Sarawia told them, Selwyn scratched symbols into what Sarawia later discovered was called a book.

The *Southern Cross* returned to Nawono the following year. Sarawia was still unsure if his hosts were men or spirits, and he was unsure about the dangers that lay ahead, but like Ulysses, Sinbad, and Skywalker, his mind was set on fortune and adventure. "I wanted to go myself to the real source of things, and get for myself an ax and a knife, and fishhooks and calico, and plenty of other such things. I thought they were just there to be picked up, and I wanted to get plenty for myself," he recalled.

Sarawia got on board and sailed away. Selwyn took him far beyond the edge of the world, and after more than a hundred nights, Selwyn brought him home again to Vanua Lava and presented him with a very large ax, and his family was immensely proud. After the *Southern Cross* sailed away, Sarawia joined in a few battles against other villages.

The next year, Sarawia and twenty other boys traveled with Selwyn to his school near Auckland, where he was taught by both Codrington and Patteson. One day Patteson asked Sarawia which spirit had made the sky, the sun, the moon, the stars, the world, and its people. Sarawia answered that of course it was Qat. No, said Patteson. It was God alone who had made everything. Sarawia did not think much of the bishop's idea: "I said to myself that this was just another spirit whom the white people think about, whereas we think about Qat."

After Patteson was consecrated bishop of Melanesia, Sarawia sailed with him to Espiritu Santo, Gaua, Ambae, and Ambrym. He sat in the rowboat and watched fearfully each time Patteson swam to shore to sit among bands of strangers armed with bows, arrows, spears, and clubs. The strangers wouldn't shoot, not until Patteson had finished handing out his presents and was swimming back to his boat. Sarawia was not on board the day Patteson was chased from the beach by a bloodthirsty crowd at Santa Cruz. But he knew the two half-caste boys who were pierced with bone-tipped arrows as they rowed Patteson to safety. One of them, Fisher Young, was buried near the beach at Port Patteson.

Patteson taught Sarawia to read the Bible. Sarawia was duly impressed. The stories were like nothing he had ever imagined, and if they were true, Patteson's God was certainly more awesome than Qat or any other *vui*. Patteson baptized him and gave him the Christian name George, after Bishop Selwyn.

After four years of training, Sarawia concluded that his kin and his race were prisoners of Satan. He returned to Vanua Lava to deliver the unsettling news. He told his people that Qat was not a true spirit but a lying spirit, that there was only one God, and it was Patteson's god. "He alone created all things, in heaven and on earth, and it is he who looks after them, loves them, pities them, people and animals, birds and fish and plants, and every kind of thing in the world, he alone looks after them because he loves them."

Sarawia was ordained Melanesia's first native deacon in 1868 and, with Patteson, set up a model Christian village on Mota, transforming the tiny island into an Anglican stronghold. Motese men were sent to evangelize throughout the archipelago. Sarawia stood fast even after Patteson's murder at Nukapu three years later. He was a living legend by the time Henry Montgomery landed to conduct a mass confirmation service on Mota twenty years on. My great-grandfather declared that "Dear George" had shepherded the entire island to its Christian destiny. Men were no longer afraid to walk from village to village for fear of attack by humans or spirits, as they had once been. My great-grandfather waxed poetic about the new age Christianity had brought to Mota: the hymns, the merry children's dances, the prayer gatherings (twice daily!), and the congregations whose members were more gracious and humble than in any English country parish. "No spot in the whole extent of the Mission has so settled a Christian life," he enthused. The bishop had indeed found his Fantasy Island.

Before my own journey, several South Pacific scholars had advised me that if I wanted to get anything done in Melanesia, if I wanted doors opened, if I wanted to achieve any kind of intimacy with the place, I would have to strike up a friendship with the church. The church had trucks, boats, influence, and many friends. I suppose that's why I joined the people for Sunday Eucharist in Sola.

The service was conducted in a tin-roofed shelter by the gentle but long-winded local rector. We sprawled on grass mats while Father Saul rambled on for close to three hours, giving an extended remix of Jesus' walk on water. The rector stroked his woolly chin, ruminating on the Word, offering the incantations that would be repeated before thousands of altars across the former empire during the course of the day. I prayed along with the people—"For Thine is the kingdom, the power and the glory, for ever and ever"—and before I knew it I was dutifully accepting the blood and body of Christ from the rector's hand. I glanced up to see a look of intense concern on his little face. He knew I was not a believer.

After the service I escaped before the rector could interrogate me. I headed down the beach, away from the village, restless, irritable. Clouds boiled around the peaks. Boys marched past me in their Sunday whites, Bibles in hand. There was no escape from Henry Montgomery's settled Christian life. Take the hill above the village, which had the twisting shape of a snake. Back in Darkness Time, that hill had been inhabited by the spirit of an evil serpent. Not anymore. The Anglicans had claimed it, exorcised the spirit, and built a residence for their bishop on its crest. The snake's head had been pierced with a tall white cross and the mystery banished forever.

The bishop's secretary spotted me at the edge of the village.

"*Yu go wea?*" he shouted from his truck.

"Away," I barked.

He insisted that the cook from the rest house guide me. She was a good Christian girl, he assured me. Great. I followed the wide sweep of the bay, chasing the coconuts that rolled in with the breaking waves, the girl steps behind. I had a sickening feeling she would want to talk about the rector's service. I tried to ignore her. I gazed out beyond the surf, beyond the whitecaps that danced in the riptide on the shallow bay to where Mota floated like a Chinese straw hat on the horizon.

I was beginning to resent my great-grandfather. It was the sort of resentment shared by many Western travelers when we discover that missionaries got to paradise and transformed it long before we packed our bags. It is similar to the anxiety we feel when we discover a McDonald's among the palms. Melanesia was supposed to be exotic and primitive, not familiar. It was supposed to be *otherly*.

I couldn't help feeling this way, even though I knew that the very idea of the tropical paradise was an invention. I carried a copy of Edward Said's *Orientalism* with me as a reminder of the dangers of romantic thinking. Said argued that the Orient never existed in the real world. It was a fantasy, a collection of exotic places filled with quaint but inferior races, constructed in order to justify England's colonial aspirations in the East. His theory could well apply to the Melanesian Mission: Henry Montgomery made no secret of his fatherly affection for his hotheaded and childlike "little Melanesians." So many dark-skinned people in need of improvement. We modern travelers claim to be different. We insist we don't want to change paradise. But we are frequently bothered by the version of it we encounter.

The American writer Paul Theroux, for example, expressed constant disappointment in his South Pacific travelogue *The Happy Isles of Oceania*. Theroux was irritated to find churches on every populated island and maddened by the ringing bells that reminded him that Sundays were more sacred in the Pacific than at home in New England. He fled to increasingly remoter shores, but the only islands uninfected by Western influence were, in fact, uninhabited.

I knew how Theroux felt. I had read my *Treasure Island*. I had studied the accounts of swashbucklers like Peter Dillon, the Irishman who claimed to have repelled a cannibal army from a mountaintop in Fiji while the torsos and limbs of his companions were cooking in the valley below. I had seen Mel Gibson bewitched by an Oceanic love spell in *The Bounty*. I had gaped at Bronislaw Malinowski's snapshots of Trobriand Island primitives, unaware that missionaries had arrived in the Trobriands decades before him. Despite everything that my great-grandfather had written about his mission's triumphs, I suppose I still wanted it to be more authentic, more savage, more like the South Pacific other travelers had invented. But the romantic primitivist is bound for disappointment in Oceania. The spear-shaking headhunters, the Man Fridays, the Bali Hai girls—if they ever existed—were long gone even before Robert Louis Stevenson and company began to package them for northern audiences. Now, not even a photo opportunity at Port Vila's Cannibal House can fill that void. No island has escaped the whorl of cultural convergence that began nearly two centuries ago.

But this does not mean that history ended with the baptism of Melanesia. I had realized on Tanna that the strangest bits of culture were those that had been infected by Christianity. *Otherness* lay not in some romantic stereotype but in the hybridization of myths, magic, and spirit, in the eight-legged, DayGlo love child produced by the union of church and *kastom*.

I shuddered at the thought of sitting through more prayers, and yet I knew the church was my conduit to the mutating soul of the Banks Islands. On Mota, where the well of faith had overflowed to spread across the archipelago, there was yet an unexplained chink in the mortar that held the church to its island foundations.

What my great-grandfather did not write, and what islanders won't admit about Vanua Lava's first native priest, was this: George Sarawia's great evangelizing influence came not from his office as a priest but from his stature in a secret society whose members' use of black magic and poison once led to a near-apocalypse on Mota.

The first missionaries didn't condemn the strange *suqe* and *tamate* societies to which the men all seemed to belong on Vanua Lava and Mota. On the surface, the *suqe* appeared to be nothing more than a social club. Each village had a men's clubhouse lined with cooking ovens, all arranged according to rank. Men gained status by sacrificing pigs, giving feasts, and paying long strands of shell money to high-ranking members. At first the Anglicans saw nothing overtly sacrilegious about the arrangement.

Tamate was harder to accept. It was a network of secret societies whose members met deep in the forest to communicate with *tamate*—the ghosts of dead men. The meeting place, or *salagoro*, was *tabu*, and strictly off-limits to women and uninitiated men. The missionaries stationed on Mota heard terrible noises coming from the *salagoro* at night. Sometimes "ghosts" clad in leaf overcoats and masks would emerge to rampage through nearby villages, beating anyone they could catch. Sometimes *tamate* members would march out of the forest in the full light of day, wearing bark hats bristling with red and white quills, and they would dance. This beguiled and softened the Anglicans, who had a weakness for pageantry that extended beyond the bells and incense of their High Church liturgies (some taught converts Gilbert and Sullivan show tunes in their spare time). Codrington was delighted by the *tamate*'s finery, the outrageous frilled masks, the dancers who posed with their leaf fronds much like the paintings he had seen of Christ the Martyr holding his palm.

On one occasion, Codrington heard the bloodcurdling cry of Mota's great *tamate* ring out across the island. All business ground to a halt: the island was now in occupation by the *tamate* and its members. The great *tamate* was angry, apparently, because a man had disobeyed Bishop Patteson's teaching by pointing his bow and arrow at another man. The "occupation" continued until the offender paid a pig to the society. This could hardly be a bad thing, noted Codrington, who concluded that the *tamate* and *suqe* societies were a means of regulating political authority. He was sure that, after much encouragement, the natives had divorced their societies from any association with ghosts and spirits. Patteson found both societies "distasteful," but still he advised Christian converts to make up their own minds about whether or not the rituals broke God's rules. They did make up their own minds: for decades, *suqe* and *tamate* rituals were simply delayed until the missionaries had sailed back to Norfolk Island after their annual visits.

Not until 1900, when a white missionary was stationed permanently on Mota, was the truth about the societies revealed. H. V. Adams reported that George Sarawia's church school was sparsely attended, while the *tamate* and the *suqe* were as strong as ever—and shockingly religious in their rituals. Sarawia had ascended to the grade of *suqe* headman. It was clear that people listened to Sarawia because he had followed more rituals, knew more secrets, and obviously held more *mana* than most anyone on the island. One native deacon lamented on his deathbed that the *suqe* had become the church's biggest enemy. In order to gain rank in the *suqe*, he noted, a man needed wealth. And in order to be wealthy, he had to resort to sacrifices to the old pagan spirits. "Rain, wind, sunshine, health and sickness were all bought from those who had power over these things," the Reverend Robert Pantutun confessed tearfully, then died.

In 1910, the third bishop of Melanesia, Cecil Wilson, pronounced that the *suqe* was *nalinan Satan*—an utterly vile thing— and its members would be excommunicated if they persisted. George Sarawia was safe by then: he had been dead for nine years. The age of *suqe* and *tamate* was declared over.

But every generation interprets the will of its gods differently, and I had heard talk of a new dance across the water on Mota about which everyone was proud, even the clergy. Had the church taken the pagan sting out of *kastom* or not? We hiked back to Sola as clouds boiled up over the peaks. A light rain swept along the beach. The sky turned shades of pink and gold, and so did the hibiscus flowers that littered the brick-red sand. I ditched my guide and found the bishop's secretary in a commercial kava shack beneath the snake hill. The shack was unlit save for a dim lantern hung on the stoop. The secretary was well into the grog. He smiled, but his words came slowly.

"The diocese has a ship," he whispered. "You will get on that ship. Tomorrow you are going to Mota. Big party."

Father Saul, the rector who had served me communion, was there, too. His gray beard glowed like an accusing puff of smoke in the semidarkness. He padded forward, kicked at the dirt floor. "We must talk," he mumbled softly, but couldn't bring himself to say more. We all drifted into kava's peculiar silence.

11

Death and Marriage on Mota

Partly because of empire, all cultures are involved in one another; none is single and pure, all are hybrid, heterogeneous, extraordinarily differentiated and unmonolithic.

—Edward Said, *Culture and Imperialism*

The flagship of the Diocese of Banks and Torres, it turned out, was a wooden skiff the size of a station wagon. The craft felt vaguely seaworthy until it was loaded with ten passengers and the fixings for a week of feasts on Mota. We chugged out from Sola on a slack tide, following a series of ragged bluffs along the southern edge of the bay. It was calm there. I was glad the disapproving rector from Sola was not on board. Sunlight reflected off the water, illuminating the weathered face of our skipper, Alfred, and his teenage son, who stood proudly with him at the tiller. Alfred's wife, Jocelyn, crouched glumly in the boat's tiny cabin with an armful of squirming children. I was not exactly sure why these people were heading for Mota. I had heard something about a wedding, but nobody on the boat seemed particularly festive, except for one man, whose face was stretched into a permanent grin. He was not part of the family.

Alfred had an unruly beard and aged, mournful eyes. He steered toward Kwakea, a palm-covered swath of sand just off the coast of Vanua Lava, and ran the skiff right up onto the beach. A bullock—or rather, the carcass of a bullock—was waiting for us onshore. The animal had been skinned and cut in half. Its shoulder muscles shone in the sun. Blood dripped from its buttocks as we wrestled the hind section into the boat. We took the beast's head, too. There was still a half-chewed wad of grass between its teeth, and its eyes were fixed in a terrified stare.

The journey to Mota was far from bucolic. When you are in a small boat, you do not cut through the ocean swell. You ride each wave as you would a great wrinkled beast. The wave rises above you, threatens to break over you, lifts you onto its broad back so you can see down into the blackness of the approaching trough, even as the next swell is bulging, shape-shifting, lumbering toward you. And then you fall.

I was coming to dislike the sea immensely. I held fast to the gunwale as we left the shelter of Kwakea. The bullock glared at me. The grinning man cupped his hand around my ear and told me why Alfred had such sad eyes. It was on a crossing just like this that the last diocesan skiff had taken a rogue wave over the bow. The boat was claimed by the sea. So was Alfred's six-year-old daughter. I watched Alfred wrestle with our boat's forty-horse outboard motor, which groaned with every ascent, then screamed with every descent. Alfred pulled that tiller and watched the sea silently, his face pulled into a smile or a grimace. The closer we drew to Mota, the more doleful Alfred seemed to appear. I had thought we were coming for a party.

From a distance, Mota resembled a great nipple poking from

the ocean. Closer, the island looked more like a shark's fin served on a thick platter. The fin was a dormant volcano, the platter a two-mile-wide plateau of uplifted coral rock, cut short on all sides by black cliffs, down which spilled vines with purple flowers, trailing all the way into the surging ocean. There were no beaches, only shelves of wave-beaten coral hanging over the edge of the electric blue abyss.

Alfred drew up against a submerged shelf on Mota's leeward side. We waded ashore, carrying the bleeding bullock on our shoulders, and then ascended the side of a deep, mosquito-filled ravine. The cracked rock was imprinted with the shapes of seashells. Alfred's village, Mariu, sat in a grassy clearing on the edge of the plateau. There were dozens of the usual thatch huts. Next to them was a church with cement foundations and the only tin roof for miles around. I pitched my tent under a grapefruit tree behind the church.

That evening the men lit a great bonfire in a pit outside Alfred's house. An ancient woman heaped rocks on the fire and tended it into the night. Through the mesh wall of my tent, I could see her bent frame as she stirred the embers and poked at the glowing stones long after the flames had ceased licking them, long after the rest of the village had gone to sleep. She ignored the hoots and the choruses of grunts and squawks that echoed through the forest. I did not, mainly because, apart from the odd gecko or bat, I had seen next to no wildlife in the islands, and assumed they had all been hunted to extinction. The forest should have been silent.

I was awoken early the next morning by the sound of the church bell, which was not a bell at all but an old propane tank against which someone banged a steel bar, over and over. Then the wailing began. It came from the direction of the firepit. It was the voice of a woman. It began like a song, rising softly in the cool morning air, but it grew more insistent and less melodic. The crying broadened until finally it was one long, repeated chorus of anguish. I slipped on my sandals and crept around the edge of the church. There was the firepit steaming in the cool morning air. There was the old woman furiously sweeping around the pit with a straw broom. There was Alfred gazing silently into the embers. And there was his wife, Jocelyn, who had not said a word since we left Sola. She was on her knees, rocking back and forth, clenching her fists so tightly I could see the whites of her knuckles. Tears were streaming down her face, and she was howling her agony to the dirt, the fire, and the empty sky.

Later, I asked Alfred to take me to George Sarawia's grave. As we wandered through the jungle, I asked him if the story about his daughter's drowning was true. He wore the same strange, meek smile he had worn on our crossing to Mota, and he recounted the story as though it were a fairy tale.

It had happened eight years ago. They were more than halfway to Mota when the wave hit. The boat sank within seconds. Alfred was left in the swell with his little girl clinging to his neck. He tried to swim for Mota, but the island just kept getting smaller and smaller. He tried to swim west toward Sola, but the current was too strong. Alfred and his daughter drifted north through the morning and the afternoon. The sun sank toward the mountains of Vanua Lava. The girl grew weak. She had swallowed too much salt water. Alfred lost strength, too, as he treaded water and surveyed the explosions of surf along the reef that separated him from the beach at Port Patteson. He felt his daughter's body go limp. He felt her fingers slipping from his neck. He held her as long as he could. A few hundred yards from shore, he felt her slip off his back, saw her slide into the blue shadows.

"I gave my daughter to God. I let her go. I buried her inside the sea. Then I said to God: 'You have taken the daughter of me. Now will you please let me live?' "

In a clearing just outside the village, Alfred showed me his daughter's grave. I was confused.

"I thought your little girl drowned. I thought the sea took her body," I said.

It had, he said. This was another daughter, a teenager, who had died exactly a year ago. Cancer got this one. Tomorrow, Alfred would give a feast marking the anniversary of her death. Alfred and Jocelyn would share out their bullock, let the second girl go as they had the first. Alfred would shave for the first time in a year, and Jocelyn would stop crying until God or luck pulled them down into the deep blue of another tragedy.

The old woman who had been tending the fire was waiting with her broom at my tent. I had been told she was a *romoterr*, the last of the Mota big women. She was also Alfred's mother. Her name was Lengas. Her face was as furrowed as a walnut. She had black flowers, or perhaps they were stars, tattooed on each of her cheeks. The tattoos were proof that she had been a high-ranking woman in the time of the *suqe*, she told me. Her father had killed many pigs and paid many lengths of shell money in order to give Lengas her high status.

"So the *suqe* honored women as well as men," I said.

"Yes, but it doesn't matter anymore, because the *suqe* is dead," she said in Bislama.

"Right, because the church killed it a century ago," I said.

Lengas chuckled. The church certainly did not kill the *suqe*, she said. In fact, the *suqe* had grown stronger after the death of George Sarawia, through the patronage of another powerful Anglican priest—who just happened to be Lengas's late husband, Mama Lindsay Wotlimaru (*mama* is Motese for "father"). But there were problems. In the 1940s, *suqe* members had grown increasingly competitive. Their jealousy led to fighting and a renaissance of black magic. Sorcerers used all the usual tricks: poisonings, curses, leaves to induce miscarriages. By 1949, Mota's population had fallen to a hundred. The island was as devastated as Santa Maria had been, and everyone knew that sorcery, not disease, was to blame. That's when Mama Lindsay summoned every man, woman, and child on the island to his village and ordered them, one by one, to put their hand on the cross and swear that they would abandon the use of poison and magic. Those who lied or resisted would face the immediate wrath of God. It worked, said Lengas. A handful of sorcerers died. Everyone else was so scared of the *mama*'s curse that they forsook all *kastom* magic. Even the good spells were abandoned. Now the population of Mota had climbed back up to nearly eight hundred, but nobody had any idea how to induce the spirits to bring sun, rain, or bigger yams.

"But why did the *suqe* have to die, too?"

"Because these days our men work for paper money, white man's money. To go up-up in the *suqe* you must have shell money." Lengas pulled a plastic bag from her skirt and drew out a long string of red-brown discs from it. They were dirty and chipped. It looked like the kind of necklace you would buy from a beach vendor in Cancún.

"Shell money. It takes days and days to make these beads, put holes in them, make them smooth. Mmmm," Lengas said, cooing and stroking her beads. Then her eyes narrowed. She scowled and waved her arm toward the village, where the men were preparing the day's first round of kava. "Look at these men. They got no *savve*. They would like to have rank, to go up-up in the *suqe*, but they can't without shell money, and they don't know how to make it anymore. This is the last of ours," she said, shaking her string of beads. A few tiny discs broke free and fell into the dirt.

"Why don't you teach them how to make it?"

"*Mi no savve!*" she howled. "This is men's business. Only a man can make shell money. And the shell carvers are altogether dead now. When I die, the *suqe* will die with me."

The village women fussed at the firepit all afternoon. They wrapped taro, cassava, and root puddings in banana leaves, then buried them beneath the hot rocks, which they covered in more damp leaves. The men sat around in the grass and prepared kava. They didn't get their sons to chew the root as was the *kastom* on Tanna. Instead, they stuck pieces of it inside a short length of plastic drainpipe, plugged one end, then pounded the kava to pulp using a wooden rod as a piston. Next, in plastic buckets filled with water, they massaged the pulp through cloth towels until the drug seeped into the water.

"You'll be drinking a bit of kava today," I said to Alfred.

"A lot of kava," he murmured.

"And tomorrow," said another man.

"And the next day, too, for the wedding," said another, whom I recognized as Father Saul, the rector who had served me communion in Sola. He was as soft and furry as a koala, and he grinned like a teenager who had just raided his parents' liquor cabinet—until his gaze turned to me.

"We must talk," he said for the second time in a week. Despite his shyness, it sounded like an order.

"Yes," I said. But we didn't talk. He lay down on the lawn and closed his eyes.

The death feast proceeded like a Sunday barbecue back home. The women did the work. The men got drunk and melted into the grass. We ate root vegetables and bullock stew. Alfred's brother showed me a copy of the Motese dictionary that Codrington had written. He said that two things made islanders proud. One was Mota's history as an Anglican stronghold. The other was dancing: the Motese still had the best *tamate* dancers in all of the Banks Islands. The *tamate* had never died, Alfred's brother said. In fact, half the village men were deep in the forest as we spoke, practicing their dances at their *salagoro*. I asked if I could I go watch. Of course not, he said. The ghosts would not permit it. The *salagoro* was sacred.

"But you wait," he said. "You'll hear the *tamate* coming." He rubbed his eyes and lay back on his mat. The kava had done its work.

There was a woman on the far side of Mota whose job it was to remember the old stories. I went to see her, following the red dirt track that circled the island and the instructions of the chief of Mariu, who advised me to seek permission from each village chief before moving through his territory. This made for an arduous journey. Each chief had me served a plate of *laplap*, and crowds gathered to watch me lick the pudding and coconut milk from my fingers. At each village, after each meal, after I shook hundreds of hands, a hush would descend, and the question would come. Always the same question.

"Is he dead?" the chiefs asked.

"Is who dead?"

"Bin Laden. Is he dead?"

People on Mota had radios. They felt close to the great dramas of the world. They had heard about aircraft crashing into very tall buildings.

"I'm sure he's dead," I tried to reassure one chief.

"Well, that is not what they say on the radio," he replied. "They say that the Bible predicted the rise of bin Laden. And they say that when bin Laden dies, the world will end. The Apocalypse will be upon us. So please do not tell me he is dead."

I found the storyteller. She was a vast, fleshy queen ant who seemed to be sinking into the earth by her little cooking fire. Her name was Hansen Ronung. Her cheeks were tattooed with a grid of black spots. In a low drone, she sang me a story of Qat, who had apparently spent his happiest days on Mota. This story was like one Codrington had recorded in *The Melanesians*, except for one detail: once, when Qat's brothers had stolen his wife and his canoe, Qat made himself very small so that he could ride the ocean inside a hollow bamboo stick. In this way he caught up to his brothers. One of them, the cunning one, said, "Qat is near, I can smell him," but the rest did not believe him. Finally, another brother saw Qat's bamboo boat in the water and picked it up. Qat used a secret weapon to repel the brother, said Hansen. Oh, yes, she said, Qat had let out *wan bigfala* fart. The smell was so bad that Qat's brother dropped the bamboo stick before he could peer inside it, and Qat escaped. This detail may have offended Codrington's Victorian aesthetic; there was no mention of flatulence in his version.

I asked Hansen where she had learned the old stories. Some, she said, came from her father. But others, she had learned from a Norwegian anthropologist who had visited Mota six years previously. Since none of his stories contained naughty bits, I suspected that the Norwegian had brought a copy of Codrington's *Melanesians* and that he had used the book to reunite the old myths with their onetime home.

The Norwegian anthropologist's name was Thorgeir Storesund Kolshus. Mota's *kastom* chief lent me a scuffed copy of the thesis Kolshus had written for the University of Oslo. I took it back to my tent. In it, the anthropologist, who lived on Mota in 1996 and 1997, argued that Christianity had not sterilized traditional religion on the island: it had remystified it. The *suqe* had crumbled, but the *tamate* and the ghosts they celebrated were stronger, more respected, and more feared than when the missionaries first arrived. After a year on the island, Kolshus had been partially initiated into a *tamate* society and taught the steps of a simple dance. He was shocked to learn that the dance hats the Motese constructed in their secret glades were treated with more reverence even than the goblet used to serve the blood of Christ on Sundays. The hats were more than decoration: they were the abodes of powerful, living *tamate* spirits. To disrespect or mishandle a *tamate* hat would be to anger the spirit and thus to invite sickness or death. When Kolshus was finally permitted to dance in public, he caused a panic by nearly allowing a *tamate* hat to slip from his head. If that hat had touched the ground, the entire village would have had to be evacuated until the *tamate* energy had been contained and removed.

While *tamate* hats shared the sacredness afforded Christian objects, Kolshus noted that the church on Mota had taken on the Melanesian concept of *mana*. Priests had the power to work miracles, bring rain, even inflict sickness as punishment for wickedness (though, when pressed, they always named God as the source of the power). That's why Mama Lindsay's antimagic curse had worked so well.

How did the islanders reconcile these two conflicting worldviews? Kolshus insisted that the Motese had split their souls in two: there was the one they were born with, and there was the one they received when baptized. When a Motese died, his first soul, the soul of the world, became a spirit and roamed the island as a *tamate*, while the second soul, the soul of heaven, rose out of the grave after three days and flew up to meet God. I liked that idea.

I dozed off, not sure if the faint howls and echoes I heard were coming from the forest beyond the church or the ether of my dreams, which carried me away from the tin-roofed church, through the forest, to the place where mysteries were revealed. Two souls.

In the morning, we gathered in the church for the Christian half of the marriage ceremony. First came another excruciatingly long sermon in which the priest rambled on in English for a good two hours. There was chanting and much waving of incense. It was as formal and anesthetizing as Eucharist at Westminster Abbey. I found myself sitting down-bench from the rector from Sola, who gazed dreamily into the rafters and yawned periodically. He still had kava in his veins. I realized with some irritation that we were among the few who actually had arrived early enough to catch the entire service. Most dribbled in just in time to kneel down and accept the body and blood of Christ. I didn't join them. The rector, shuffling back from the altar, noticed this. He sat close, leaned in, and issued his usual disquieting greeting.

"We must talk," he said.

There were two brides and two grooms. One bride was bare-foot; the other wore a new pair of sneakers. They both wore white dresses. Their hair was combed out Afro-style, and powdered white. The grooms wore hibiscus flowers behind their ears.

Later, both couples sat outside the church in a row of plastic chairs. One by one, we came forward to shake their hands and place gifts of rice and sugar at their feet. Then the brides began to wail. They pulled down their veils to cover the tears that streamed down their faces. The two grooms stared at their knees dejectedly. A string band struck up behind the wedding party: three guitars and a washtub bass. The musicians thunk-thunked and jangled away maniacally, and they sang:

Kava! Kava! Mi likem kava,
Kava, oh kava hem i numbawan.

Now the grooms began to cry, too.

Just as the scene began to feel unbearable, the brides and grooms stood up and went their separate ways, as though the marriage had never taken place. The crowd dispersed, and the village grew quiet. Mota's Christian soul had had its moment.

The rector shuffled up to me and, for the first time since he had served me communion in Sola, looked me in the eye.

"Hum. Yes. We need to talk," he said, jerking his head toward the edge of the forest. I followed him there reluctantly. He held out a palm full of *gnali*—almondlike nuts—and I accepted them.

"You took communion in my church," he said.

"Yes," I said, remembering how our eyes had locked just for a moment as I licked the wine from my lips.

"Your granddaddy was Anglican," he said.

"Yes."

"Good. Yes, good," he said, clearly uncomfortable. "And you are Anglican."

The rector was anxious for me to say yes, to know he had not shared the blood and the body of Christ under a false pretense. I did not want to tell my story, to rupture my friendship with the church. I felt my face flushing.

"You are Anglican," he said again, hopefully. "You are Christian."

"I was confirmed into the church when I was twelve," I said. True enough.

"Of course! Good! Yes! Good!"

The rector was immensely relieved, and he was also transformed. He offered me more nuts and led me through the forest to the neighboring village, where members of one groom's family were gathering. There was a strange, apprehensive energy about the crowd: they reminded me of troops preparing for war. Old men argued. Young men paced back and forth, fidgeted, yelped. Girls tied red flowers in their hair. And then they all began to march, solemnly at first. There were more than a hundred people, all led by a dignified old man wearing a *lavalava* and a starched white shirt. He carried an unopened yam shoot—a sign of peace, according to the rector. The others carried bags of rice, sugar, and root vegetables. One yam was so big it had been strung from a pole so two men could carry it. Men hauled buckets full of kava. As the marchers made their way through the forest toward Mariu, they began to whoop and howl. The string band appeared out of nowhere to lead the procession, which now bounced and shook with the joy of a giant conga line. As we entered Mariu, the guitarists strummed faster and the crowd broke into a sprint. They ran to the lawn at the center of the village. They kept running as they were joined by Alfred and his neighbors, now all dashing together around and around in a wide circle, skipping, jumping, leaping, shouting, laughing ecstatically, heaving their yams and their sloshing buckets of kava high in the air until they had run themselves breathless and the circle closed in on itself.

Then the *kastom* wedding ceremony began. Banana leaves

were spread on the grass. The father of one groom made a great show of arranging the bride price. First, he produced a thin string of shell money that had seen better days. Then there was a pile of cash: a stunning 42,000 vatu—about $340. The bride's father made his own pile of gifts, without money. There was a moment of uncomfortable silence, then whispers. A man in a Brazil soccer jersey stepped forward, shook his fist in the air, and started yelling at the father of the groom. Something was very wrong. It wasn't about the money, explained the rector. Someone hadn't done their homework, someone had botched part of the ritual. The whole thing hadn't gone according to *kastom*.

"Shhh!" someone hissed at the critic. Three or four more men joined in.

"Shhh! Shhh!"

The groom's father pointed his finger at the critic and yelled at him. The bride and groom stared at the dirt while the old men angrily debated the fine points of bride price etiquette. Lengas had told me this was just the kind of confusion that happened all the time now that the *suqe* societies weren't around to reinforce *kastom*. Men didn't know their traditions. They didn't follow the rules.

"Shhh!" hissed the crowd. The string band started up again, young men joined in the kava song, and the critic was eventually drowned out. Meat was shared. Kava flowed. I sat with the rector, who was in his cups again and content. We were friends. I tried to tease him with a story from the Norwegian anthropologist's thesis. Kolshus had written that ghosts were so strong, so present, on Mota that they could be cajoled into playing games with humans. The most popular spirit game was called *ravve-tamate*, or pull-the-ghost. The object was to go out into the forest and engage in a tug-of-war with the spirit of a dead man. What could be more heretical?

"Oh, I know about *ravve-tamate*," said the rector, pausing to wipe the kava scum from his beard. "When I first came to Mota from the Solomon Islands, they told me about it. I just laughed at them. I said, 'I am a leader of the church, so of course I do not believe in your ghosts.' Well, one night they showed me their game. They filled a basket with the favorite food of some dead fellow. Taro, I think it was. They tied the basket to the end of a long pole, and we went out into the forest. There were a dozen of us, men and boys. Everyone started to shout at that devil. They were cheeky with him. They teased him and they called him weak. And I tell you, I heard him answer back."

The rector paused, peered into the forest, cocked his head as though listening for something, and continued: "We followed the voice while one man shouted out: 'Hey devil, if you think you are so strong, why don't you prove it? Why don't you try to pull this food from us?' We were all holding on to the pole when something grabbed the basket and tugged it. It was strong, I tell you. It dragged us through the forest."

"Weren't you afraid?"

"Oh, yes! The devil was very rough. It dragged us through the rocks and the bushes. I was bruised! I was bleeding! But the strange thing was, I never felt the pain of my wounds."

I didn't know what to say. The rector was not at all troubled by his demonic flirtation. He was enthralled by it. I sat and thought about the two souls of Mota, the church and the *salagoro*. I remembered that morning's church service and the crowd that had trickled in just in time to take Holy Communion. Kolshus had written that the Motese took communion as often as they could. They were swallowing the body and the blood of Christ not only as a way of remembering their Messiah's sacrifice but as an act of pragmatism. He was sure the Motese believed that the bread and wine of Holy Communion made them strong, not just spiritually but physically. It was a way of soaking up the *mana* of Jesus. No wonder the rector had been so concerned about wasting it on me.

A storm was building in the late-afternoon sky. The wind was up. I glanced around the crowd, looking for Alfred, who should have been readying the skiff for our trip back to Sola. His face, when I found it, always seemed to be obscured by the base of an upturned kava cup.

The rector peered into the forest again, grasped my shoulder. "They are coming," he said. "Stand back!"

Then I heard a familiar sound, a faint owl-like hooting. It echoed through the forest. It was the sound I had heard every night on Mota, the sound I was certain was a product of imagination or dreams, only now it was louder and undoubtedly real. *Whoop. Whoosh. Coo.* Then silence. Children ran squealing from the garden at the edge of the village. Shadows ducked among the glistening leaves. The brush stirred, gained legs and arms. The devils leapt out into the open. There were half a dozen of them. Their heads were crowned with brambles, bamboo branches, and feathers, like oversize birds' nests, from which sprouted the tentacle-like bodies of snakes: Medusa meets *Apocalypse Now*. Their eyes were completely obscured by leaves. They wore leather thongs around their genitals. Their legs and arms and gaunt buttocks were smeared with charcoal mud and bands of chalk paste. They crouched and shuffled with bowed knees. They leapt through the air. They peered into the doorways of houses and shook long white sticks at the villagers.

Alfred's brothers grabbed wooden poles and began to pound on a plywood drum in front of the church. Everyone else drew back and watched from the fringes of the clearing. Parents held children close. The dancers drew around the drummers, lurching, ducking, craning their necks like snakes. This was the dance of the *mai*, the poisonous black-and-white-banded sea snake, the rector said. He grunted and cackled with pleasure. The dancers had been practicing in the *salagoro* all week—hadn't I heard their shouts at night?—and this was their gift to me. I was too busy fumbling with my camera to answer, or to say, "What the hell kind of priest are you? Shouldn't you be outraged?" I got on my hands and knees and began to crawl toward the melee. I wanted to fill the frame of my memory. The crowd stirred behind me. I looked back to see the rector gesturing at me frantically to stop.

"You must not approach the dancers," he said when I had retreated to his side. "The ground is hot. If you stop too close, you will break it, and it will take days, weeks, to fix the ground. We will all have to leave the village."

It was clear that violating the dancer's space was more than a breach of etiquette. This dance was more than a dance. But nobody could explain the source of its power, or its apparently volatile nature, or if it had anything to do with the *tamate* at all. The ground had been wound up like a spring by the energy of the dancers, and it needed to be unwound carefully. That was all the explanation I could get.

I was struck by the geography of the spectacle. The snakes strutted and ducked below the eaves of the church, ignoring the house of God completely. The church and the *salagoro* shared congregations, they knocked against each other, and now the serpent was dancing in God's garden, and there was no competition, no conflict at all, because neither acknowledged the other. Strangest of all, the man who had served me the blood of Christ had also served as my interpreter to the world of pagan spirits. The island really did have two souls.

The snake dancers retreated into the woods. The wind picked up. The sky darkened. The storm was upon us. Alfred threw back one last cup of kava and shuffled liquidly down the ravine toward the ocean. I followed. The swell had risen even here on the leeward side of the island. The sea shivered and heaved, then surged across the rock shelf that served as our dock. Two of Alfred's surviving children refused to climb aboard the skiff, which bounced dangerously off the rocks. Alfred did not force them. He just smiled dejectedly and left the boys with their uncles and the beaming rector, standing knee-deep in the storm surge. He bade them a soft good-bye, gunned the outboard motor, and steered us into the endless gray cordillera of swell. Alfred had plenty of fuel for our journey back to Vanua Lava: at his feet was a half-gallon jug of kava.

12

The Secret of West Vanua Lava

How colonial of me, I later thought: I want into their lives, but only as a voyeur.

—DEBORAH ELLISTON, *The Dynamics of Difficult Conversations: Talking Sex in Tahiti*

Melanesian history has long belonged to foreigners, because the written word always trumps oral history. It was white men who first wrote down the islanders' stories even as they sought to erase their *kastom*. Through sermons and schoolbooks, the words of those early missionaries, traders, and colonial administrators lived on to shape collective memory. Now, Melanesians casually refer to the time before contact as *taem blong darkness*, reducing thousands of years of trading, agriculture, fishing, and storytelling to a shadow world of fear, violence, and suffering. Whether this memory is accurate or not, its foundations lie in the scribblings of foreigners.

On Mota I realized that European accounts of the island's *kas-*

tom always seemed to carry the most weight. Thus Hansen Ronung, whose job it was to sing her way through Motese history,
could be corrected and humbled with a few anecdotes from Codrington's *Melanesians*, and when Motese argued about modern
culture and rituals, their disputes were now arbitrated by whoever
was holding the tattered copy of Thorgeir Kolshus's University of
Oslo thesis. Was Kolshus an expert on Motese culture? The islanders evidently thought so. Before Alfred and his brothers
drank kava, one of them always said a little prayer and spilled a
drop of it on the ground. But the men admitted it wasn't their fa-
thers who had taught them that prayer. It was Kolshus. And he, it
turns out, picked up that gem from anthropologist W. H. R.
Rivers's 1914 book *The History of Melanesian Society*. Alfred's
brother had told me that he thought Kolshus's big idea, the one
about the Motese having two souls, was just plain wrong. His
words faded amid a haze of kava, conversation, and guitar strum-
ming; and they will be transmuted with every year, as conversations do. But Kolshus's versions of *kastom* will live on, unchanged.

When Codrington published *The Melanesians* in 1891, it was
hailed as the first thorough study of "primitive" culture. Ever
since, anthropologists have flocked to the South Pacific looking
for remnants of a primitive Other that they might romance, penetrate, and ride toward scholarly recognition. These foreigners
and their books have frequently been lauded as preservers of
truth and traditional culture in modern Melanesia. Some communities are thrilled to be the subject of research. It brings them
status and attention. But anthropologists, like the missionaries
and traders before them—not to mention travel writers—don't
necessarily get their stories right. The godmother of modern anthropology, Margaret Mead, proved that much. In *Coming of Age
in Samoa: A Psychological Study of Primitive Youth for Western Civilization*, Mead presented "evidence" that cultural—rather than
biological—factors were the most important determiners of human

behavior: testimony from a trio of Polynesian girls who claimed that they were not subject to any of the sexual taboos and shame faced by American teens. The girls led Mead to believe that they were both carefree and promiscuous. Mead, eager to prove her nature vs. nurture theories, ate the stories up. The book propelled her to fame when it was released in 1928, but half a century later, one informant confessed that she and her friends had been so embarrassed by Mead's interrogation that they had simply fibbed to her.

After nearly two months in the islands I had yet to pierce the thick skin of the Melanesian Other. I thought an anthropologist might provide me with the tools. Before leaving Canada, I had learned about a German scholar who had been living at Vureas Bay, on the west side of Vanua Lava, researching a doctoral thesis. She received my e-mail message at the post office in Port Vila during one of her quarterly visits to the capital. Just drop by, she had responded. Easy.

I had a map that showed a perfect red line wandering all the way west across Vanua Lava to Vureas Bay. Everyone in Sola insisted the red line was a road. But when Melanesians say "road," they aren't thinking about a highway or even a cart track. They mean there is a way. They mean that yes, once upon a time, perhaps someone walked in that direction.

I filled my pack with bags of rice, corned beef, and Webster's Cream Cookies, then followed a gravel road over the snake ridge and down onto a plain bristling with rows of coconut palms. The road became two furrows in the tall grass. The wind hissed through the tops of the palms but did not stir the soupy air beneath them. My shadow shrank beneath me. Flies landed to sip from beads of sweat on my neck. At midday, the copra plantations gave way to jungle and merciful shade, but then the road disappeared, swallowed by a mound of boulders and an extravagance of shining leaves and knotted vines. Bewildered, I marched back along the track, looking for the turn I had missed. I poked around the roots of a giant banyan. Nothing. I drank the last of my water. The road had obviously intended to go west, so I went west. I clambered through the boulders and realized that the moss and lichen had been worn from some of them. I followed the route of bare rock until it became a trail. It led over a mountain, through a mosquito bog and down along a great bay, where the sea rose into house-high curls that slammed onto the crags below me. I saw no one.

The trail faded, reappeared, then was joined by others in the afternoon. Like a river, it strengthened and gained certainty with each new tributary. I stopped by a creek and opened my bag of cookies. I listened to my breathing and the roar of the distant surf. The solitude was a gift, but it did not last. Melanesians do not believe in solitude. They will rescue you from it when they can.

It was midafternoon when the red-eyed man emerged from the forest. He carried a broad machete and used it to cut open a coconut for me to drink. He told me that yes, he knew my German scholar, Miss Sabina. She was a good woman, he said, but her story was a sad one: "*Hem i no gat famili. Ino gat husban. No gat brotha. No gat pikinini. I sad tumas.*"

The man insisted that I needed his help to reach Vureas Bay. The problem, he said, was the big water. He took my pack and marched off, pleased with himself. I followed, irritated. Cattle stood beneath the palms. The heat had made them so lethargic we had to push them from our path. We descended into a black rock canyon and forded a river, hopping across a series of submerged boulders. The clear water tugged at my shins. "Men have been swept away here," said the man. "Yesterday the big water was so high you could not cross it. You should pray for God to keep the sun shining, or you will not be able to leave Vureas Bay for a long, long time."

As if on cue, the sun disappeared behind a mound of billowing cumulonimbus.

We splashed through water gardens bursting with big-leaf taro, all irrigated by dozens of narrow earthen canals. We hit the suburbs of Vetuboso just before dark. This was supposed to be the biggest town in all the Banks Islands, but there were no roads and there was no power, just hundreds of huts scattered through the forest, all strung together by a network of trails slicked by centuries of bare footsteps. In the middle of the town, beneath the eaves of her own thatch bungalow, was my anthropologist.

Sabina was a sparrow compared to her meaty neighbors. She was pretty but also somehow harrowed, thirsty. When she saw me, she ran a hand through her blond hair, which she had trimmed into a precise bob, and sighed deeply. She seemed relieved to see me, embracing me like an old friend. The neighbors were scandalized, but I understood. I carried the aura of chocolate, books, rock videos, conversations in cafés, bad language: things that were as familiar in Heidelberg as they were in Houston or my own hometown, yet absolutely foreign to Vanua Lava.

Sabina introduced me to the village's *kastom* chief, Eli Field. He wore no shirt or shoes, but he did have a silver watch on his wrist. He had the chest of a bull and the sparkling eyes of a storyteller.

"*Bi yumi dringim wanfala kava tonaet!*" Eli said, crushing my hand inside a callused paw.

"*Kava, hem i numbawan,*" I replied.

Sabina rolled her eyes and led me inside to her kitchen. A thin dog rubbed his haunch across the dirt floor.

"One more month," she sighed. "Just one more month, then I will escape."

Sabina set a kettle on her fire and made me a cup of tea. She said she had come to Vureas Bay because the locals had put in a request for an anthropologist to the national cultural center. Nobody had completed an ethnography here since Codrington.

"All their old knowledge is scattered, it's disappearing. The chiefs thought that if I wrote it down, at least they would have a picture of the *kastom* they still possess. But . . ." She waved a thin arm dejectedly toward her door.

"Yes?" I said.

"But it has been difficult. Officially, these people want their knowledge preserved, but in reality they are incredibly possessive of it. These are jealous people."

A crowd gathered around Sabina's hut. Heads poked through the window, which was not a window but a rough gap in a wall of woven pandanus leaves. Men and boys strained to hear us. Sabina smiled weakly. "And there are other problems. It's hard to be a single woman living alone here. To the men, I'm a temptation. To the women, I'm a threat. I have informants, but as soon as I establish a rapport with them, their wives get jealous. They gossip. Some men aren't even permitted to come drink tea with me. And then there are the creepers . . ."

I laughed. I had heard about creepers. As in pagan times, men and women on most islands were forbidden almost any physical contact until they got married. But boys will be boys. Men who couldn't control their libidos would literally creep through their villages at night, tapping softly at the windows of prospective lovers. It was regarded as a sport by some, but I imagined a creeper's approach would be terrifying for a woman sleeping alone. Unless she was unusually bold.

There were a generator and a television in Vetuboso. Someone had returned from Port Vila with porn videos. From them, the men had learned that white women were insatiable and eager to break all kinds of sexual *tabus*, especially the one forbidding oral sex. As a result, there was constant knocking at Sabina's window. The creepers didn't scare her, she said, but what a bloody bother they could be. The trick was to yell as loudly as possible, yell until the creepers were shamed into flight.

You would do that if you wanted them to go away, I thought.

But what if you didn't? What if you were lonely? What if you were curious? What then?

"I might leave my door open now and then," I said.

"That makes you a man," she replied.

And naive, I thought. Since Victorian times, anthropologists have claimed to follow a simple rule, which, though unwritten, is as powerful as any Melanesian *tabu*. Edward Evan Evans-Pritchard was said to put it simply for his students at Oxford: Don't fuck with the natives. Study the Other. Insinuate yourself into its life. Befriend it. Do its dances. Eat its food. Learn its secrets. Become intimate with it. Love it, even. But never cross the line. Anthropologists are less articulate when they try to explain why they should keep their distance, but the sex taboo is about more than scholarly high-mindedness.

Bronislaw Malinowski won fame in 1929 by revealing the amorous secrets of Melanesians in *The Sexual Life of Savages*. However, it wasn't until the posthumous publication of his field diaries that Malinowski's own erotic fantasies about his Trobriand Island hosts were revealed. After observing one local woman, Malinowski panted: "I watched the muscles of her back, her figure, her legs, and the beauty of the body so hidden to us whites, fascinated me. . . . I was sorry I was not a savage and could not possess this pretty girl." Why could Malinowski not claim his exotic prize? Postcolonial critics say it was because sexual intimacy would have broken down the last barrier between the anthropologist and his Other. The sex taboo reinforced Malinowski's superior status; as long as he remained pure, he was not part of the Melanesian system but above it. Malinowski was the one with the right to ask questions, and unlike his "savages," he would not be expected to give up his own secrets.

Plenty of Malinowski's intellectual descendants have broken the sex taboo, but few are keen to publicize their adventures. That kind of story could have you lumped in with three hundred years of sexual exploiters, or it could reveal you as weak, soft, vulnerable. Either way, it could ruin your reputation. The community of anthropologists is hierarchical, one field-worker explained to me in Port Vila. To rise to the top, you must guard your power and your secrets as fiercely as a *suqe* society member.

After dark, Sabina led me to the compound Eli had built for his family in the forest far from the village. Eli had decided that I should stay in a hut he had built behind his own. It was cluttered with dusty audiotapes and stacks of *National Geographic* magazines, the effects of a linguist who came to make a dictionary of the local dialect, then took one of the local lads home to Australia with her.

We arrived just in time for kava. Eli's eldest son pushed chunks of the root into a cast-iron meat grinder on the porch. His bright eyes and bare torso shone in the silver light of Sabina's headlamp. Cali was eighteen. He had a wife and a baby. He wore an ear stud with a tiny pink star.

Eli held up an oil lantern and began his lament.

His great-grandfather had been the most powerful *kastom* chief in Vureas Bay. Then the *Southern Cross* arrived. The missionaries converted Eli's grandfather and his father, too. The missionaries built a school and started a coconut plantation. The children learned English and, along with it, the new religion. Esuva Din—the district priest who had cursed the sorcerers of Gaua—arrived in Vureas Bay to stamp out *kastom*. Ten sorcerers died within a week. Magic stones were smashed. The *suqe* and its secrets were lost.

Eli grew up hearing the old folks whisper about *kastom* and about the power and secrets the church had banned. As a young man he was struck by the idea that his family was following someone else's religion. He had had enough of it. "I had looked at the world, and I knew there wasn't only one true religion. I knew about the Buddhists, the Muslims, the Hindus. The world had always been full-up with religion. I decided that my *kastom* was the religion of my country, and I wanted to start living by it again. Don't tell me my *kastom* is darkness!"

The more excited Eli grew, the more he fell into speaking Bislama. It was hard to keep up, especially after my second shell of kava. I caught this much: Eli had planted *kastom* herbs and built himself a house amid the ruins of the old mission schoolyard. He had started a culture club and invited the elders to come and share their knowledge. He had stopped attending Sunday services. The church elders declared him a heathen and a backslider.

The kava was strong. The night was dark. I was sitting on a high wooden bench when Eli lifted a plastic cup of kava in the air. Cali gestured for me to get down, squat on the floor. "*Taem kastom chief i drink, yu mas stap daon nomo,*" he whispered. Eli gulped his drink, stepped outside, spat into the wind, and barked an elaborate incantation. It was an exaggeration of the *tamavha* rituals I had seen on Tanna. It felt like an imitation, an approximation of what had once been sacred.

"What about magic?" I asked Eli. "I suppose that has been lost for years."

Sabina let out an annoyed sigh. I had forgotten she was with us. This definitely wasn't Tanna, or no woman of any color would have been permitted near a kava session.

"It has not been lost," said Eli. "Some old fellows hid their magic stones from Esuva Din, and now we are learning how to use them again."

"What about you? Can you do it, Eli?"

"Sabina knows I can. I have proved it. One time, Catriona, the last researcher, made me *cross tumas*. She spent two weeks interviewing me, making demands, asking me to *walkabaot* with her here and there. Then, to show me her appreciation, she gave me a box of matches. A box of matches! I said no worries. I did not complain. But when she went to the airport at Sola, I sent my boy

to give her a message. I told him to tell Catriona that she had better find somewhere to stay in Sola because she would be stuck
there for two weeks. Then I made it rain. *Hem nao!* I made it rain
so hard that the airstrip flooded and the big water swelled. Didn't
I, Sabina?"

"Well, it did happen to rain, and Catriona happened to be
stuck, but . . ."

"Look," I interrupted. "On every island, people tell me they
can use *kastom* magic, but nobody ever proves it. I'm tired of
magic *toktok*. I want magic action."

"*Disfala* rain magic takes time. The rainmaker has to make
sacrifices. No sex. No talking. He has to fast for three, four days."

"Fine. I'll stay five days, until Wednesday."

"Is that a challenge?" said Sabina.

"You bet it is."

"You careful," Eli said with a mischievous smile. "If we bring
rain, you won't be able to cross the big water."

"Well then, hold off on the rain until Wednesday afternoon."

There was more said that evening, but I had taken a third cup.
Shortly after my last spit, I lost Eli's voice in a congealed soup of
mumbled thoughts, shards of flickering lamplight, and distant
dog howls. I remember the silver-blue glare of Sabina's headlamp,
shooting across the yard. Swirling nausea. A fight with a mosquito
net. A damp mattress. Rain seeping through the rafters.

The next morning, I was back in the village, sitting in Sabina's
kitchen, when a few members of Eli's culture club arrived. Sabina
stepped back and tended to her cooking fire. One man had the
hungry eyes of a creeper. He sat down and told me that the club
was working to start up the *suqe* again. It would be difficult, he
said, giving up all those pigs, spending all those months in medita-
tive seclusion.

"If the *suqe* is so hard, why bother reviving it?" I asked.

"For power!" he said. "Our grandfathers, they went to the

salagoro and prayed, and they would *walkabaot* down into the ground, deep, deep, until they reached a place under the bottom of the ocean. There they met the sea snake, and he gave them secret knowledge so they could become wealthy." There was more. Something about eating a *tabu* fire in order to kill some distant and unsuspecting person. His ideas were a muddled fusion of *suqe*, *tamate*, and *The Lord of the Rings*.

"So when will you start killing pigs again?"

"This will take a few years. We have to convince enough men to join us. Right now, most Christian men are afraid of this kind of *kastom*. They call it devil worship. So we have secret meetings each week to gather the old knowledge and rebuild *kastom*."

"How many have joined you?"

"Um, hum, six, I think." His voice trailed off. He scratched his beard and stared over my shoulder. I followed his gaze across the room. Sabina was bending over her fire, revealing the peach-smooth skin at the small of her back.

Vetuboso sat on a forested plateau above Vureas Bay. That afternoon, Sabina led me down a footpath to the sea. The mountains were girdled with low cloud. The breeze was warm and sticky. Waves curled along a black sand beach. Sabina swam fully clothed—it was *tabu* for a woman's thighs to be seen in public.

My conversation with Eli's culture gang had made Sabina grumpy. "You know, I have never heard those stories," she said. "The *salagoro*, the *suqe*, the snake spirits—the men won't tell me about any of that stuff."

Once, said Sabina, an informant had told her a *tabu* story, a particularly erotic one involving the god of taro and his tree-sized penis. When Eli got wind of the informant's indiscretion, he was furious. He said it was not a story to be shared with women or outsiders. He became even more angry after Sabina defended the old man and told her he would have nothing more to do with her. It took weeks for Eli to warm up.

"But why would Eli block you? You are here to help him save the *kastom*."

Sabina wiped the seawater from her eyes and swam closer. "You have to understand that women here are seen as a threat to male power. I don't mean politically; men honestly believe that women can drain their energy. That's why, when men practice their dances, they steer clear of women. When the men go fishing, women are banned from walking on the beach. Some fish will simply refuse to be caught when women are around. Men even abstain from having sex with their wives for fear of losing this kind of energy."

Sabina had come to Vetuboso to write about people's sense of self. Who do you think you are? she asked them. Why are you that way? All she had gotten were superficial answers. "*Mi no savve,*" people would tell her. *I can't say. I don't know. It's just our way.* The more time she spent in the village, the more an invisible grid of *kastom* rules and relationships closed in around her. The moment Sabina arrived in Vetuboso, she had become Eli's adoptive daughter and a member of Eli's wife's tribe. Her maternal cousins—of which, according to the mathematics of extrapolated kinship, she now had dozens and dozens—became like brothers and sisters. Half the village's unmarried men had suddenly become potential marriage partners.

The system landed her in a minefield of manners in a landscape filled with uncles, aunts, brothers, sisters, friends, and enemies by default, all people who were bound by *kastom* to speak to her in specific ways or not to speak to her at all. Sabina was forbidden to utter the name of her "sister-in-law," Cali's wife. She couldn't even use words that sounded like that name. Sabina couldn't tease or joke with Eli or any of her maternal uncles. She had scribbled diagrams to remind herself whom she could talk to.

This, she said, was the real story of Vetuboso. The rules were everything. If a man took the wrong person—for example, an unmarried woman—to his garden, the gossip would start immediately. Then the elders would levy a fine. Or worse: they would send a party to trample all the man's garden, and perhaps those of his family as well. But it was the gossip that hurt the most. Trust me, Sabina said with the gravity of one who knew from experience: you do not want to break the rules in Vureas Bay. She had given up trying to extract *kastom* secrets—the *suqe* and *salagoro* mysteries would have to survive without her help—and she had focused her research on the intricate web of rules she had to follow. The rules, she told me, were everything here. You write what you know.

I learned this in Vureas Bay: the rules were catching up to Sabina, tightening around her, suffocating her. I liked Sabina. We agreed on things, on the subjectivity of morality, for example, a concept that was a world away from the kinship codes of Vetuboso. Sabina had a secret of her own, I knew that much. She had made one mistake, she had broken one rule. The backsliders let it slip between belts of kava. The creepers whispered it at night, when they circled like sharks in the shadows of her garden. We know who you are, they hissed. We know you are not as strong as you pretend. You have opened your door once. Now open it again.

Sabina would not reveal her secret in her doctoral thesis on kinship rules, and I have promised not to reveal it here. I suppose we are attempting to make the story of Vureas Bay our own by erasing the details that do not suit us, just as the missionaries did with the myth of Patteson's death and the conversion of Nukapu. Now I know that Sabina's secret has been passed from fire to fire and village to village across Vanua Lava. It has climbed on the mail plane and bounced down to Vila. It has flown around the world. It has entered e-mails. It has arrived like a scandalous guest at university cocktail parties where cold-handed academics snigger and debate the rules of engagement but cannot begin to imagine the lonely nights, the knocked-on doors, the jealousies, the dimmed lanterns, of Vanua Lava.

The secret's mobility and tenacity have proved to me that writers are not the only arbiters of history. And Vureas Bay proved that *kastom* secrets are much heavier, much harder to unearth than gossip. It's the things that matter most that people are slowest to reveal. Eli Field taught me that lesson, in a roundabout way.

Eli was hard to catch, which seemed to be a trend among people I had challenged to prove their magic. He spent his days away from the compound. Cali explained that he was doing Very Important Things Related to Culture. I caught him after dark on my fourth night. He wouldn't talk until I had downed a cup of kava with him.

"Sabina came here to help you, but you and your friends won't share *kastom* stories with her," I said.

Eli scratched his belly and smirked. "She can always ask the women for their stories."

"But women don't know about men's *kastom*, do they? They don't know about the *suqe* or the *salagoro*. How is Sabina supposed to make a full report?"

Eli threw back another cup of kava, went to the door, and spat into the night. He lowered his voice and spoke solemnly in English. "Let me tell you what makes a Ni-Vanuatu different than a white man. You people share out all of your knowledge, but you don't like to share your money. Your thinking is backward. Here in Vanuatu, we are not too rich, but if you want our food, we will cook for you. If you want our money, we will give it to you. We are generous with these things. But knowledge, that is our power, and there are some things only men should know. If you take the secrets that belong to us men, if you write them down or show them to women, you take our power away. And then we would have nothing. Sabina was cross first time I explained this to her. She cried for weeks. But this is our *kastom,* and she must accept it."

"But the men have told me all kinds of secrets, and I am writing them down," I said.

"Mmm, but we will never tell you the most important things."

"But you said you'd prove to me that your *kastom*, your magic, still has power. Didn't you promise to bring a big rainstorm on Wednesday?"

"Hmm, well, *yumi garem wanfala* problem. It has rained so much this year, our mangoes are rotting on the trees. It would be irresponsible for me to make rain right now."

The truth was that it had been drizzling constantly since I arrived in Vetuboso. A rainstorm wouldn't have been much of a miracle anyway.

"Okay then, how about sun?" I suggested. "Let's have some sun for Wednesday."

Eli shifted uncomfortably on his bench. His voice lost its authoritative tone. "*I gat wan narafala* problem."

"What? What now?"

"I have been trying to help you. I have. But the men who keep the *kastom* stones are scared. Today, I went to see the man *blong* shark stone, to see if he could bring you a shark in the bay. He refused. I told him that you would write a *bigfala* story about him . . ."

"To prove that your *kastom* lives," I said.

"But he was afraid *tumas*. He said if he played with the stone, the *tasiu* would kill him."

Eli lowered his voice. The *tasiu*, he said, was a powerful man of God. He lived with his apprentices on a hill near Vureas Bay. He had a magic walking stick. Wherever Eli had tried to promote *kastom*, the *tasiu* had smashed it. Even as we spoke, the *tasiu* was hunting down *kastom* stones, exorcising their spirits, wiping away their power. The *tasiu* confronted the owners of those stones: he told them they must wrap their hands around his magic walking stick and confess their crimes or face a terrible punishment from God.

"I tell you," said Eli, "it is not easy being a *kastom* chief these days."

In fact, it was much harder than he admitted. It was common

knowledge that black magic was being practiced in Vetuboso. In the most recent case, a boy had been struck with a mysterious illness that caused his leg to swell up like a giant sea slug. Before the boy died, a *kastom* doctor had told his parents that he was the victim of a curse. "Look in the dirt under your house," the doctor had told them. They did, and found several sinister-looking parcels—lumps of ash wrapped in coconut bark—under the boy's sleeping platform. The *tasiu* had come down from his hill to investigate. He declared that the parcels were evil charms. He dabbed holy oil on the suspected sorcerers to lubricate their confessions. One of them insisted that it was Eli Field who had paid for the curse. Rumors were as effective a weapon in Vanuatu as black magic, and these rumors were enough for village leaders to take away Eli's title of *kastom* chief for several months.

I knew the word *tasiu*. It is Motese for "brother," and it is reserved for members of an indigenous Anglican order called the Melanesian Brotherhood. I had been hearing stories about the brotherhood for weeks. Some said the brothers were a kind of spiritual SWAT team, dispatched by the church to douse the fires of backsliderism and paganism. "You behave," I heard a mother tell her squealing child at the market in Sola, "or the *tasiu* will come and take you away!"

I sent a message up the mountain and waited to hear from the *tasiu*.

Meanwhile, the drizzle continued, and my clothes began to rot. One afternoon an acquaintance of Eli's named Ben produced a magician. We all met outside Sabina's kitchen. The magician had the long, stubborn face of a mule. He handed Ben his wooden staff. Ben and I kneeled in the dirt and grasped the narrow end of the staff, hand over hand. The goal was to keep the heavy end of the staff pointed upright. It would be difficult, said the magician, because soon a spirit would come to tug at it. It would be like a miniature version of Mota's *ravve-tamate* game.

"Why can't Chuck and I play the game together?" asked Sabina.

"Because you don't know the special prayer," barked Ben dismissively, then under his breath added, "girl."

"*Yufala mas sarem eye blong yu,*" said the magician, closing his own eyes to demonstrate his request. "*Sipos yu openem eye blong yu, devil hem i runaway nao.*"

By now a dozen people, including Eli, had gathered to watch. I closed my eyes, and Ben made a short incantation to harass the soul of some dead man. The stick swayed slightly. I strained to hold it still. Ben's fists flexed against mine. He was clearly trying to push the staff from side to side. I felt tempted to do the same, to make the staff bob and bounce and swing—what a show we could have produced—but I didn't. I held firm, and the staff did little more than tremble. Ben gave up after a few minutes. "Open your eyes," he said.

"I don't know what went wrong," said Eli. Sabina just stood at her door with her arms folded and a half-smile on her face, like a mother whose teenager had once again come home drunk.

The magician was not deterred. He led us into the forest for Round Two. We pushed through groves of sharp-leaved shrubs and bamboo thickets where spiderwebs hung like wet laundry. The ground had been ravaged by rooting pigs. Birds screamed. Mosquitoes rose up from the muck. The magician hacked a clearing with his machete. He built a fence of pandanus leaves and gestured for Sabina, Eli, and I to stay behind it.

The magician picked a coconut off the ground, cut a hole in it, and turned it over so that we could see the milk pour out. Then he cut open a second coconut and turned it over. No milk this time. But Ben, who was kneeling a couple of yards away, had turned his face up and was gulping enthusiastically at the air. His mouth swelled like a fish, and his Adam's apple bobbed up and down. The idea here was that Ben was drinking the invisible stream of coconut milk that the magician had mysteriously transported across the clearing into his mouth.

"*Bigfala sapraes, no?*" asked the magician after repeating the trick a few times.

I could feel Sabina's eyes burning into me disdainfully.

"*Yu lookim power blong devil. Yu bilif, no?*" he said hopefully.

"Well," I said, glancing back and forth between Sabina and the magician, "it would have been easy for you to have come out here and empty three of those coconuts early this morning, wouldn't it?" I felt a sudden pang of guilt, or maybe something closer to pity, for the magician. "Oh, hell, sure I believe. *Hem tru-yu garem bigfala savve.*"

Sabina was not impressed with the magic show, or, for that matter, with me. Back in her kitchen, she spooned the last of her peanut butter onto a crust of bread and handed it to me. "What a performance! What a miracle! Now you have seen your *kastom* magic. Have you had enough yet?"

I gnawed on my bread glumly. "You've spent a year with these people," I said. "You have heard them talk about magic and spirits. Instead of acknowledging these things, you ignore them. Aren't you at least curious about what drives these beliefs?"

"What drives them? Fear. Jealousy. Superstition. We have all those things at home in Germany. I am not interested in fantasy. I am writing about what I see. You, on the other hand, are romanticizing these people. Look around. Look at this remarkable community, the complex society they have built. I don't understand why this isn't enough for you. Why the world isn't enough for you. Why you are so obsessed with magic when you have all the wonder of humanity around you."

What could I say? I hadn't left home with the intention of seeing magic. I thought I could remain aloof in my travels, record the stories I heard, chart the legacy of the missionaries while pretending indifference, like a journalist or an ethnographer. But the approach was coming to feel entirely dishonest. Modern anthropologists parachute into communities, dig around for people's secrets and myths, listen wide-eyed and stone-faced, as though they believe, pretending all the while to be neutral in matters of spirituality—or worse, converts to the local way of thinking—when in reality they hold very strong convictions about the nature of the universe. They may analyze the origins and usefulness of their study communities' beliefs, but they don't hold them to the same standard of critique to which they subject those of their own society.

Field anthropology is a business of deception generally performed by unbelievers. Thorgeir Kolshus was so convincing that the men of Mota welcomed him into the *salagoro*. They taught him how to dance. They even let him leap around with that sacred and dangerous *tamate* hat on his head. But when Kolshus defended his thesis at the University of Oslo, did he insist that his dance hat actually contained a ghost? Not likely, unless he wanted to end his academic career.

At least the Victorian missionaries had been honest about their bias. They never stopped telling islanders just how false their spirits were. (To her credit, Sabina was equally honest about her skepticism about magic and the boasts of Vanua Lava's rainmakers.) Yet despite this cultural scorn, my great-grandfather wrote enthusiastically about the spiritual gift that Melanesians offered their English counterparts. Just as Melanesians needed governance and moral instruction, he felt that Englishmen needed help in the essential act of seeing the unseen.

"I have heard of no race indeed that lives in the tropics, whether civilized or uncivilized, that does not look upon the continued presence of an unseen world as a fact beyond argument. The feeling engendered may be one of fear, but the belief is there," he wrote in an essay on faith. "It is all very wonderful, and the conclusion of the matter is just this: that all the races of the world need each other to make up one another's deficiencies. The tropical man says to us, 'I can easily believe in God, come and help me to make my religion and my conduct one complete thing.' The temperate clime man says, 'I should find no difficulty about obeying God's commands if only I could first see God and believe that He is. Come and help me to see God, I ask no more.'"

This is an entirely racist idea, and its foundations should not be sheltered from the blows of the postcolonial wrecking ball. And yet now I sensed a truth within it. Were Melanesians hardwired to believe more fervently? Was it in their genes? I don't believe so, any more than they were hardwired to be ruled by Englishmen. But there was something about the closeness of the air, the seething forests and reefs, the precipitous shadows, that demanded a new way of seeing, as though the physical world was a jigsaw puzzle whose cracks offered glimpses of an entirely different picture. How could one not be captivated by it? How could you resist trying to reach through the cracks to the shadow world? Henry Montgomery credited Melanesia with confirming his mystic beliefs. Melanesians shared these certainties with him: The world is more than an accident. The cosmos is not empty. Humans are not alone.

The islanders I met may have had differences about which gods deserved their allegiance, but they did not doubt the existence of any of them. I was disoriented and enthralled by the natural extension to this incongruity: If one cosmology was a conduit to the mysteries of the world, then couldn't they all be? And if the islands could produce magic, if some shred of Oceanic faith would just reveal itself as grounded in something I could touch and feel, then it followed that the Christian myth that had sustained my family for generations might also contain more than a metaphor.

Here is the thought I was too shy to admit to Sabina. Despite everything I was sure I knew about superstition, fiction, and science, I was allowing a small part of myself to imagine the impossible: that *mana* did flow through the air, that ancestors and gods could make rain, that men could transform themselves into owls, sharks, and *tamate*. It was a good thing to imagine. I envied the believers, including my great-grandfather. I was drawn by the notion that perhaps they were on the right track when they knew that the world was more than a collection of serendipitously bonded atoms and spinning electrons; more than a series of accidents, collisions, explosions, and diffusions bubbling endlessly in an insignificant corner of an otherwise empty cosmos.

13

My First *Tasiu*

*The day of the Lord cometh as a thief in the night
and when men shall say, Peace, and all things are
safe, then shall sudden destruction come upon them,
as sorrow cometh upon a woman travailing with
child, and they shall not escape.*

—"A Penitential Service to Be Used on
the First Day of Lent," in *The Book of
Common Prayer of the Church of Ireland*

Sabina would not be the one to take me closer to magic. She had given up on secrets. As for Eli Field, his heathen revival had only served to weaken him, making him enemies in the church and putting him in the crosshairs of the mysterious *tasiu*. If supernatural power was being exerted in Vureas Bay, Eli and his friends were not the ones directing it. The coconut trick was proof enough of that. Everyone knew the real power was coming from the hill above the village, where the *tasiu* lived with his apprentices. The latest news of the *tasiu*? He had issued a curse that resulted in the death of a theological rival. Spectacular!

The morning after my argument with Sabina, a long-legged runner arrived bearing word from the hilltop: the *tasiu* was expecting me. The rain had been dumping for two days—incidentally, ever since Eli had rescinded his promise to open the skies. The big water was rising. At the risk of being stranded in Vureas Bay, I went to meet the *tasiu*. Ben, the magic coconut milk drinker, insisted on guiding me. Hymns were echoing from Vetuboso's church when we set off. It was the one hundred and first anniversary of George Sarawia's death. The service went on most of the morning. Ben was terrified the priest might spot him from the open-air chapel, so we slunk around the edge of the village, dashing from hut to hut like commandos.

"*Yu wanfala backslider!*" I hissed at Ben conspiratorially.

He nodded in agreement, then lowered his voice: "You must never talk this way around the *tasiu*."

We followed a mud track into the forest, up along a low ridge, through a dozen small clearings planted with young banana trees and trailing vines. The earth was the color of boiled yam. Ben whispered to me as we walked. He said I should not run away even if I became frightened. Higher, the wind pulled at the forest. The trees creaked and shuddered.

A terrible scream rose from the forest. Two boys leapt out of the bush onto the trail in front of me. They wore loincloths and had smeared mud over their faces and thighs. They carried spears, which they pointed at me. Two more approached from behind. The boys grunted and yelled until their adolescent voices broke. The ambush was baffling but not scary in the least. It was a performance. Ben winked at me. The lads jumped up and down threateningly, and slapped me gently with lengths of vine rope, which they then wrapped around my wrists. I put on a grimace and allowed them to poke me, prod me, and pull me through the forest.

We headed for the top of the ridge, a bare bluff that appeared to have been entirely seared by fire. We trudged through a patch-work of broken tree limbs and charcoal until we reached a white cross and a chapel overlooking the desolation. The *tasiu* met us at the chapel door. He was a magnificent-looking man with the physique and rough face of a rugby forward and the deep-set eyes of a mystic. He wore a black T-shirt and black shorts secured by a black-and-white-striped sash. A copper medallion hung from a coral necklace. He said nothing but waved me into the chapel.

My faux-savages led me to a bench. The *tasiu* stood with his novices in a line near the altar, and he led them in song, much as a schoolteacher might lead children in a variety show number.

"You have traveled far from home across the sea. Welcome, welcome, we welcome you," the boys sang in English while flakes of crusted mud fell from their cheeks. It was sweet and heart-breakingly sincere.

Over coconut milk and cream cookies, the *tasiu* explained to me that the ambush was a traditional welcome for European visi-tors, so that we would know what captured laborers felt during the days of the blackbirders.

"Thank you, I think," I said. I was their first foreign visitor in months.

The *tasiu* told me his name was Ken Brown. He was twenty-nine years old. When he was half that age, emissaries of the Melanesian Brotherhood had come to his village near Vureas Bay. Ken was captivated by the stories the brothers told him about their adventures in heathen places. He followed them back to their base on the island of Ambae, where he trained, prayed, and emerged after three years as a full-fledged member of the Melanesian Brotherhood.

"But what do you do here in Vureas Bay?" I asked. His English was sparse, so we spoke in Bislama. Ben helped with translation.

"Many things. We negotiate to stop land disputes. We help

married couples work out their problems. We make rebaptisms for backsliders . . ."

"Magic?"

"Oh, yes, we take care of that. We also organize a youth choir . . ."

And I felt the sense of urgency returning, and though I had intended to play ethnographer, I knew I did not care about youth choirs or rebaptisms, and I could not stop myself from interrupting him: "But the magic," I said. "What do you do about it?"

"Well, if there is a rubbish spirit hurting people, we stop it. For example, did you see the black stone down on the beach at Vureas Bay? That devil stone was making people sick, so we took some holy oil and made a small service, and we banged that stone with our sticks to drive the devil out of it, in the name of the Big Man."

"I'm sorry, who?"

"The Big Man, our Lord in Heaven."

Ben interrupted. *Tasiu* Ken was like the policeman of Vureas Bay, he said. If you stole something and hid it, he could find it just by praying. And if you were a bad man, if you worked black magic on someone, he could curse you.

"*Yu mas look-look woking stik blong mi*," said Ken. He left for a moment and returned with his walking stick. It was black. A carved snake wound its way up the shaft, the snake's eyes shining with inlaid abalone. Exodus: God turned Moses' staff into a serpent to prove his power to the Egyptians. Ken had carved this stick himself. It had been blessed by the bishop of Banks and Torres. It was the first of dozens of snake staffs I would see before my journey was done.

"I heard that people are scared of your walking stick," I said.

"He is one powerful something," said Ken, running a muscular hand over the carved wood. "For example, suppose I go to a heathen village and want to show people the power of God. I always bring my staff. I throw it up high and it hangs in the air. After the people see that, they know they must follow the Big Man."

"I can't even imagine it."

"*Hem ia nao!* It does take a big, long prayer to make the stick fly. We pray and fast for two weeks before visiting the heathens. That helps us work closely with the Big Man."

I wanted to ask him about the man he had cursed, but it seemed a rude question after all his hospitality, all those cream cookies. I didn't quite know how to bring it up. In the end, I didn't need to.

"You killed a man who defied you, didn't you, *tasiu?*" said Ben. "Tell him about Jim Bribol."

Ken lowered his head and spoke quietly. The trouble had started back in 1997, during a time of denominational turmoil. While he was away visiting the island of Ambae, the Seventh-day Adventists had gained a foothold down in Vetuboso. Even Eli Field's brother had joined the new church. But the Adventists weren't content with stealing Anglican sheep; they accused the *tasiu* of being a false prophet.

The *tasiu* challenged the entire Adventist congregation to meet him in their church. The Adventist pastor was the only one brave enough to show up. Ken put his staff down and challenged the pastor to an unusual duel. He suggested they point their Bibles at each other and see which one of them was still standing after three days. The pastor refused to face him.

Ken had been due to return to Ambae after winning the standoff, but things got ugly before he left. His own cousin, Jim Bribol, switched churches. One day, Jim decided that his wife's King James Bible was a symbol of Anglican hegemony, so he burned it. That was his first mistake. He would have survived if that was all he had done. But then Jim Bribol announced to the village that he was going to march up the mountain and break the *tasiu's* walking stick in half. Ken's response was swift and unequivocal. He sent his cousin a message: I will leave Vanua Lava, and then you will die.

A few days after the *tasiu*'s departure for Ambae, Jim Bribol went wading in the sea. A strange fish—a swordfish, perhaps— swam up through the shallows and cut his shin. The wound became infected. Bribol fell desperately ill. His family rushed him to the hospital in Santo. The doctors couldn't temper his fever, nor could they stop his flesh from rotting. They called in a *kleva*, a *kastom* medicine man, who told the family that no medicine could save Bribol because he had been cursed. Bribol's family sent a message to Ambae by teleradio, begging for *Tasiu* Ken's forgiveness.

"And you didn't help him?" I said.

"No," said Ken, solemnly.

"You just let him die. How could you?"

"Listen: we have our *kastom*, and we must stick to it. We have one Church and one God. We were all born Anglican, and we must stay that way. If Jim Bribol lived, people would forget the power of the true God."

Either the *tasiu* had capitalized on a coincidental death to reinforce his own mythical status, or he was guilty of some admittedly awesome, but extremely un-Christlike, behavior. It didn't seem polite to point this out at the time. Ben and I retreated from the mountain in silence. The oaks had ceased their creaking. Mist drifted up from the sea. Drizzle fell like sadness.

The southeastern trade winds had eased for the first time in weeks, but the rain continued to fall through the night. The trails around Vetuboso were as gummy as *laplap*. My sandals were useless. I left for Sola in bare feet, letting the puree of mud, cow shit, and rotten mango squeeze through my toes. In lieu of a sun-producing miracle, Eli sent his son, Cali, to help me across the big water. The river had swollen. The water was waist-deep and flowing swiftly. Cali held my hand tightly as we crossed. I felt like a grandmother.

I carried on alone through the warm drizzle. I was surprised at midday by Ken Brown himself, who emerged from a trailside shack halfway to Sola, rubbing his eyes. He was now more Ken than *tasiu*. He wore his civvies: baggy surf shorts and a tank top that gave him the aura of a Santa Monica surf bum. He had crossed the river the night before, hoping to intercept me. He wanted to carry my pack to Sola. There was no dissuading him.

We walked through the afternoon. The rain ceased, steam rose from the grass, and the overcast sky radiated white heat. Ken was silent.

The path became a road again. We crossed the plain of palms and climbed the hill above Sola. Ken stopped on the crest of it and set my pack on the ground. This was as far as he would go. He said he couldn't walk into Sola without his uniform; the bishop might see him. I wasn't ready to part. I hadn't been able to shake the image of Jim Bribol, rotting to death in some dreary hut.

"Are you still glad you cursed that man?" I asked. "Did you do the right thing?"

A thousand tiny beads of sweat had broken out on Ken's forehead. He looked to the sky, kicked the gravel on the road. Here, without his local audience, he was less keen to take credit for Bribol's misfortune. "Maybe I made the curse," he said slowly, "but I didn't kill Jim Bribol. No, I asked the Big Man to decide on his fate. I made prayer for hours. I said, 'God, it is for you to choose. You make Jim live or you *killim hem i ded.*' So it was truly the Big Man who ended the life of Jim Bribol."

"So your God is an angry God."

"He is a god *blong* love. But yes, He is also a god *blong* vengeance. The unrepentant will be punished."

Of course. This was the same conflicted god my great-grandfather had worshipped, a spirit vacillating between love and anger, war and power. It was a god who behaved very much like the ancestor spirits of old Melanesia. Later I would learn that the bishop of Banks and Torres had given Ken a firm talking-to about the whole Jim Bribol episode. Apparently the punitive direction of divine power wasn't the kind of work a member of the Melanesian Brotherhood should be doing. I did not approve of cursing. But I was enthralled to have brushed against the bounds of a mystery so foreign and yet so familiar. I resolved to seek out more members of this strange order as I moved north.

14

Guadalcanal, the Unhappy Isle

In the last days perilous times shall come. For men shall be lovers of their own selves, covetous, boasters, proud, blasphemers, disobedient to parents, unthankful, unholy, Without natural affection, truce-breakers, false accusers, incontinent, fierce, despisers of those that are good.

—2 Timothy 3:1–3

I met the deputy mayor of Honiara, the capital of the Solomon Islands, somewhere in the stratosphere between Fiji and Guadalcanal. I had the window seat. He leaned into my shoulder, peered out into the blue, and exhaled into my face. Rotting carrots. Grass mulch. Compost. The deputy mayor did not wish me a pleasant stay in the Solomon Islands, nor did he recommend a favorite restaurant. But he did roll up his pant leg to show me the bullet wound in his calf. The scar was the size of his thumb and the texture of tire rubber. "I am going to kill the man who did this," he said. "Fucking kill him." I didn't reply. I just stared into the deputy mayor's mouth, which was like nothing I had ever seen. His teeth were the color of rotten cedar, and his tongue lolled beneath a worrying gob of pinkish fiber. A drop of red juice had dried at the corner of his mouth, like something from a Transylvanian nightmare. It was the mouth of a betel nut addict.

I did not want to be breathing recycled air with the deputy mayor. I wanted to be crashing north toward Nukapu aboard a cargo vessel, a mission ship, a yacht, a canoe, crossing the ocean that Henry Montgomery had once crossed, whipped by salt spray and nautical hardship. It should have been easy to arrange a passage to the Solomons from Vanua Lava: Sola is the last jumping-off point for boats traveling north from Vanuatu. In theory, the two nations are just a day's sail apart. Barely ninety-three miles separate Hiu, the most northerly of Vanuatu's Banks and Torres islands, from Vanikoro, the most southerly of the Santa Cruz Group, of which Nukapu is an outlier.

But each time I shook awake the customs officer in Sola— which I did every afternoon for nearly two weeks—he assured me there were no cargo ships bound for the Solomons. Finally, he lost his patience. Why would there be a northbound cargo ship? What in God's name would it carry? Didn't I understand that Solomon Islanders had no money left to buy cargo?

There were yachts, though: a sail grew out of the horizon every day or so. Vanua Lava sits smack in the middle of the trade-wind route that carries yachties from New Zealand and Polynesia to their storm-season havens in the Gulf of Thailand. The Solomon Islands offer the next batch of good harbors on the route. With each new arrival, I would wait for the sails to come down, the anchors to fall, and the dinghies to bob toward shore. I would shave and put on a clean shirt, and then I would catch the sun-ravaged yachties on the beach and tell them my story about Bishop Patteson and my mystery island, Nukapu. We could be there in four days, I would tell them. They could drop me off on the reef and carry on toward Torres Strait or Papua New Guinea. The yachties were universally horrified by my proposal. Hadn't I heard about the guns? The blood feuding? The pirates? The awful Chinese food? "We're not bloody idiots, mate. The Solomons are no place for children," one yacht dad told me sternly.

It was September. I was two months into my journey, halfway through my savings, and facing the advent of the storm season. One by one, the yachties all turned west for Cairns. As I watched the last sail disappear, I realized that Sola was a dead end. My only hope of getting to the Solomons was to backtrack: hop the mail flight south through Santa Maria, Espiritu Santo, and Malekula to Port Vila, catch the weekly shuttle east to Fiji, then loop northwest again, three hours by 737 from Fiji to Honiara, on Guadalcanal. After that 2,200-mile detour, after trading the rolling uncertainty of the open ocean for the crystalline detachment of the stratosphere, I would try to reach Nukapu from the north.

Which is how I met the deputy mayor of Honiara, whose first act upon reaching his homeland was to spit a stream of crimson mucus onto the tarmac of Henderson Field, the Solomon Islands' international airport. Betel nut juice is apparently tremendous fun to spit, which is why the most striking thing about the airport was that everything was spattered blood red. The arrivals hall looked like the scene of a mass murder. The rest of the city was the same.

I was met at the airport by Morris Namoga, the manager of the national tourism bureau. Morris was a jovial man with a Rhett Butler mustache and a rugby player's physique. I had faxed him from Port Vila, promising to write happy stories about the Solomons if he helped me. I felt a pang of guilt as soon as I saw his generous grin.

Morris drummed the steering wheel and hummed the Canadian national anthem as we drove into town, trying to distract me from the storm of dust and refuse, the plastic bags that rolled like tumbleweeds across the road, the heaps of garbage that smoldered like castles after a siege. And this, spray-painted across an abandoned building: Welcome to Hell.

"Haw! haw! Sorry about the mess," Morris said in English. "The municipality doesn't quite have the means, haw haw, to clean up anymore."

Honiara was perfectly safe, said Morris, before I had a chance to ask.

"And in case you are wondering, it's not true what they are saying about the deputy high commissioner of New Zealand. She was not stabbed to death. She fell on her kitchen knife."

The heat was unbearable. Morris didn't seem to be in a hurry, so I suggested we drive out of town and go for a swim.

"Haw haw! I don't think so. No, I don't think so. Well, of course you can go, but it would not be a good idea for me to come with you. Oh, no. Guadalcanal people are still being, shall I say, assertive."

Morris was from the island of Malaita. Malaitans controlled Honiara, he said, but they tended to get shot at if they left the city.

We passed an open-air cathedral. I could see hundreds of people inside.

"Funeral!" said Morris. "For the national minister of sport. Tsk, tsk. Very sad. Murdered two weeks ago. Father Geve—yes, he was also a Catholic priest—he went back to his constituency to talk to Harold. Not a good idea. You know about Harold Keke, of course."

I had been hearing Harold Keke's name for weeks. Harold the militant leader. Harold the Guadalcanal nationalist, Harold the warlord, Harold the madman. Keke was all these things. He had been hiding out on Guadalcanal's storm-battered southerly Weather Coast ever since refusing to sign a peace agreement in 2000. Someone had recently convinced a gang of eleven lads from Malaita to go looking for Keke. The boys were given guns and a boat, and they buzzed around the Weather Coast until they found Keke. Or rather, until Keke found them. He killed them all. That was three months before my arrival. People were starting to think Harold had cooled off, but then he went and put a bullet in Father Geve's head.

"Harold thinks the war is still on, which it certainly is not," said Morris, wiping the perspiration from his neck. "None of this is good for tourism. Haw! Sorry about the mess."

Morris left me at the Quality Motel, a fortress of steel mesh and barbed wire overlooking the port. That night I sat with the motel's guards—there were five of them, earnest young men with broad chests and billy clubs. We watched a gang fight in the orange glow of the streetlights below us, and we listened to the radio. The news was read both in English, the official national language, and Solomon Islands pidgin, which floated in a linguistic swamp between Bislama and English. On the news: Harold Keke had sent a communiqué from the Weather Coast, saying Father Geve had died from "lead poisoning." Lead poisoning! Everyone got a chuckle out of that. Other news: four people were dead and six wounded in a shootout on an oil palm plantation east of the airport. Police suspected the combatants were neighbors. (But how would they know? The Royal Solomon Islands Police had been too scared to drive beyond the city limits for months.) Last item: the police had made a formal request for citizens to please stop stealing government trucks and vans.

The brawl on the street below us ended abruptly when the power failed. Honiara was left in darkness punctuated only by garbage fires and the sparks that rose out of them like fireflies. I heard one disembodied voice howling and bawling late into the night. "Go home," it cried. "Go home, oh please go home."

People in Honiara did not like to call the darkness a civil war. They did not like to call it chaos, or even conflict. The preferred phrase was "ethnic tension," as though the past four years had come like a migraine, a condition of suffering over which no one had any power or responsibility. But it looked like war to me.

The trouble had begun with hatred, guns, and money. Sometime during the 1990s, men on Guadalcanal became irritated with the settlers from other islands who populated Honiara and the rich plains around the capital. The Guadalcanalese were particularly bothered with the thousands of Malaitans who had arrived and prospered in the years following the nation's 1978 independence from England. Malaitans treated Honiara as if they owned it. They ran the businesses, took the government jobs, built proper houses with tin roofs and TV antennas, and they let their young men run wild at night. The locals blamed Malaitans for a string of murders, including one machete massacre on the outskirts of the capital. Malaitans were greedy, crude, and aggressive, they insisted. Malaitan *kastom* was not good *kastom*.

The Guadalcanalese armed themselves. Some borrowed hunting shotguns. Some found leftover World War II rifles, which they oiled, polished, and loaded with salvaged ammunition. Some made their own guns from drainpipes and auto parts. The gun collectors had a vague but passionate notion of "getting their island back"—even though most of them, including Harold Keke, hailed from the Weather Coast, which was nowhere near Honiara. The militants were more interested in money than justice. They demanded $20,000 for every murder allegedly committed by a Malaitan since independence. The prime minister cut a check for the compensation claimants, but it bounced. Chaos mounted. With their homemade guns, their axes and spears, and their anger, Keke and his *wantoks* crossed the island and rampaged along the north coast, chasing Malaitan settlers from their gardens and setting fire to their homes. Thirty thousand refugees—a third of the population of Guadalcanal—fled, seeking shelter in the heart of the capital or crowding onto rusty passenger ships and retreating to the provinces. Most were Malaitan. By June 1999, almost every settlement on the outskirts of Honiara had been trashed and burned.

It was not hard for Malaitans to take their revenge. During the previous decade, the country's leaders had grown increasingly nervous about a war that was already taking place on the Papua New Guinean island of Bougainville, just an hour's paddle from the Solomons' most westerly islets. The fighting had occasionally spilled across the border, so the Solomons government bought $10 million in automatic weapons from the United States, ostensibly to protect the country from invasion. The guns were held in the Royal Solomon Islands Police armories. Since most of the police happened to be Malaitan, it was a cinch for the newly formed Malaita Eagle Force to make off with two thousand machine guns. The Eagles forced the prime minister to resign and transformed Honiara into a Malaitan fortress. They ripped off a wide-gauge machine gun from the bow of a police patrol boat, mounted it on a bulldozer, and voilà, they had built the islands' first tank.

Not to be outdone, their Guadalcanalese enemies raided a gold mine and made off with a dump truck that, with a little creative welding, became the country's second tank. The two sides blew up bridges and gas stations. They burned down hotels, churches, and villages. They strafed mission stations, and they invaded hospitals and clinics in order to finish off the wounded. Heads were mounted on sticks along the highway. Decapitated bodies began turning up amid the pineapples at the central market. Neither side would admit casualties, but at least two hundred people were killed in the first half of 2000.

Finally the militants squared off at Alligator Creek, just east of the international airport. The creek's coffee-colored waters were streaked with whorls of blood. The tension was revealed as the war it really was. The fighting let up only when a group of men wearing black shirts, black shorts, white sashes around their waists, and copper medallions strung from their necks marched to the middle of the bridge. The Melanesian Brotherhood had had enough of the killing. They held their walking sticks in the air: sunlight reflected off shards of inlaid abalone, white snake eyes glowed. The *tasiu* prayed for peace. Some fools actually shot at them, but witnesses all agree the bullets were deflected by those magic walking sticks.

After a cease-fire was declared in 2000, Solomon Islanders managed to elect a government. International aid was flowing in. Life in Honiara should have been getting better. It was not. Every month of peace brought more dysfunction, more anarchy, more bloodshed. The economy was in the toilet. Foreign businesses had packed up and left. The government was beyond broke. The villagers who controlled the capital's water source turned off the tap each afternoon to punish the government. Machine guns were still floating around the countryside. Neighbors were settling scores in hillbilly-style shootouts. Schools had been closed. Hospitals were running out of medicine. Malaria was making a comeback. Money did not flow. Phones did not ring. Boats did not sail. Planes did not fly.

With its potholes, ruptured drains, dust, wire mesh, tree stumps, and open sores, Honiara looked like the worst of suburban Mexico City. It had the crude aesthetic of an industrial park and the haggard air of a refugee camp. The sidewalks were crowded with hundreds of makeshift stands selling cigarettes and betel nut, the city's two favorite addictions. The ground was stained indelibly red, like the hands of Lady Macbeth.

I headed down Mendana, the capital's one avenue, past the Anglican Cathedral with its memorial to Bishop Patteson, past the yachtless yacht club, past the diesel generators that kept the air conditioners flowing in Honiara's three office buildings, past the video club where Chuck Norris beat the shit out of the Vietcong again and again on a wide-screen TV, past the spit-smeared walls and unkempt grounds of the National Museum, past the Ministry of Finance, which cowered behind a giant Slinky of razor wire. I stopped by the office of Solomon Airlines, where a relief map on the wall showed an airport at Nendo Island in the Santa Cruz Group. Nendo was three days' sail east of Honiara, but less than forty miles from Nukapu, my grail, the center of the Patteson myth. Sign me up, I said. Not so fast, said the agent. Santa Cruz was the Hotel California of flight destinations: a plane could get to the group, but it could not return. Nendo had run out of fuel months ago. The only way to get there now was by ship.

So I headed for the port. Two ships made the run to Santa Cruz. They were tied up to the same crumbling cement pier. One, the *Eastern Trader*, looked like hell: she was a garbage heap of grease, great flakes of exfoliating rust, and flapping laundry, but her deck was stacked with fuel barrels.

"When can we go?" I asked her skipper.

"We wait," he said.

"For what?" I asked.

"Petrol," he said.

"But your ship is loaded with fuel," I said.

"That's the airplane fuel. We need diesel, and we don't have the money to pay for it just yet."

"So when will you have the money?"

"When our passengers pay us."

"And you've been waiting how long?"

"Not long. A month, maybe."

It was the same story across the dock, on the MV *Temotu*, which looked slightly more reliable, and whose Chinese signage revealed a long life on the Pearl River Delta trade.

At least ships had run during the civil war. There had been money then. Now everything was grinding to a halt, and I was stuck.

So I wandered around and met the unhappy people of Honiara, who were not like the fresh-scrubbed, just-blessed innocents of

Vanuatu. It was as though all ease and subtlety had been drained from them. Men told me things like, "Our country is fucked." Urgent women invited me to meet their daughters. Everyone was afraid: of ex-militants, thugs, and extortionists, but also of the police. No wonder: after the armistice, as many as two thousand ex-militants had been enlisted by the Royal Solomon Islands Police as "special constables." Putting them on the government payroll certainly hadn't convinced the militants to turn in their stolen guns, nor did it reform those who had been responsible for all the torture, rape, intimidation, and murder during the war. People were afraid of Harold Keke, afraid that in a moment of utter madness the last of the Weather Coast militants might march across the mountainous spine of Guadalcanal and storm the capital. But they were even more afraid of Keke's enemies, men like Jimmy Rasta, one of the supposedly reformed Malaita Eagle commanders.

War had been good for Jimmy Rasta. The man was a nobody before the tension, but now he commanded a private army of former militants. Everyone in Honiara had a Jimmy Rasta story. Some people were impressed by the way he passed out handfuls of dollar bills in the street. Most weren't. They talked about how Rasta's boys had extorted thousands from shopkeepers, bludgeoned protest leaders, and assassinated at least two police officers. Rasta's gang could be hired to rough up or kidnap anyone you didn't like.

I figured if I couldn't escape Honiara's darkness, I might as well confront it. Rasta ran a bottle shop on the highway near the airport. I went there and asked the dull-eyed lad behind the counter to pass a note on to Rasta for me. I was curious to know if Jimmy thought he was going to hell. That's not what I wrote in my note. I wrote that I was meeting with all the most important men in the Solomon Islands.

I returned to the bottle shop three times. Finally, Rasta rolled up in a battered Toyota SR-5, reggae pumping so loud the car's doors rattled. He must have been about thirty. He was Bob Marley gone gangsta: thick dreadlocks, baggy jeans, and a delicate gold wristwatch. He handed me a warm SolBrew and led me out back. We sat on a couple of beer crates by a pond of discarded oil.

Rasta, whose real surname was Lusibaea, told me that he had been a peaceful guy before the ethnic tension. But one night in 1999, some of Harold Keke's boys had burst into his village and shot up the place. Rasta's grandfather was so scared, his heart stopped beating. In the following months, the bodies of Rasta's *wantoks* started turning up in creeks and gardens. The police did nothing, so Rasta and his friends raided the police armories and took their revenge. But all that was in the past, he told me proudly. Now that the tension was over, he ran a private security business, providing employment to more than thirty boys. No, they didn't use guns. How could they use guns? The boys had given their guns back: all their SR-88s, their M-16s, and their LMGs, all long gone.

I wanted to say, "Jimmy, you're lying. Everyone in town says that your boys are always shooting at people," but I was too scared. I sat and drank my beer, listening to him rant about his enemies, which included the Melanesian Brotherhood.

"The *tasiu* are false prophets. They *garem* no magic powers. Look, they stopped at my headquarters one day, trying to cause trouble, and my boys went and broke two of their walking sticks. Has anything bad happened to us since then? No. Nothing. *Mi no fraet long olgeta tasiu.*"

This was not the story most people told. They said that the boy who broke the walking sticks was now crippled. His hands had shriveled up.

"Some people think you should be in jail," I said quietly.

"What?" Rasta grunted.

I chickened out. "When will your country have peace?" I asked instead.

"Peace? We *garem* peace. Look, my store is open. Business is good."

He winked at me, beamed, slapped me on the knee.

"Look, I'm a Christian boy. South Seas Evangelical Church. Are you a Christian boy?"

"Um . . ."

"Well, if you are, then you know that everything happens according to God's plan. From the day we are born, God knows what will happen to us. He has a plan for us. All will be well, my friend. All will be *gud tumas*."

But all was clearly not good in Honiara. Hundreds of people had returned from the provinces to demand payback for land, property, or relatives they had allegedly lost during the conflict. They called it "compensation." The price for killing a man? In Darkness Time, it had been a life for a life. Under the Western legal system, it had been a prison term. Now it was cash. If you had a gun, you didn't need any justification for your compensation claim. You just found the national finance minister and demanded he write you a check. That's why the Ministry of Finance had been wrapped in razor wire.

The tension ebbed and flowed like the tide. When it rose, you could feel it. It was thick and heavy, and it covered everything with a dark, sticky film, like betel spit. That's when you watched your step. That's when you looked into people's eyes, not too long but long enough to check their intentions. The streets were full of excitable young Rambos, bored mongrels with betel-stained lips, teeth razor-sharp with rot, wandering between the garbage fires in packs or squatting in the dirt, spitting red, smoking, waiting. Shortly after I returned from Rasta's place, a bright-eyed lad called to me across the street: "You watch out!" he shouted cheerily.

Then quickly:

Distant shouting.

Pop-pop, gunfire.

Suddenly we were all stampeding madly for cover. I hid behind a shipping container. There was the lad, giggling.

"What happened? What happened?" I asked breathlessly, peering out at the empty street.

"*Mi no savve*," he said, husking himself a betel nut. "But *long Honiara, taem olgeta pipol run, yu run olsem.*"

Christianity was supposed to have saved the Solomon Islands from this sort of chaos and violence. When I asked people in Honiara why their ancestors had converted, they usually answered with one word: peace. Christians did not raid neighboring villages at the behest of their ancestral ghosts. They did not hunt each other or eat each other. They did not live in fear. This was the gift of the imported god. It was, some of them said, as though Christianity had saved islanders from the savage part of themselves.

This idea was naturally supported by European versions of history. English chroniclers have long characterized Solomon Islanders as people in desperate need of spiritual and practical guidance. "The Melanesian Mission did not reach the Solomon Islands a day too soon," wrote Austin Coates in *Western Pacific Islands*, a 1970 Colonial Office–sponsored summary of British rule in the region. "This was a society in a state of rapid disintegration, due principally to an appalling, and evidently rather recent, spread of cannibalism, head-hunting and black magic," he wrote. "Brutality had reached such a pitch that it was brutality no more; it was normal."

This hysterical assessment was rooted in the writings of early chroniclers, who seemed to relish scenes of horror and brutality. There was the traveling mission historian A. R. Tippet, who noted that near a mission station on Choiseul, skulls were hung from the branches of a banyan tree somewhat in the manner of Christmas tree baubles. There was the resident trader, John C. MacDonald, who claimed to have witnessed a canoe-launching ceremony in 1883 at Nono Lagoon during which a slave boy was dunked underwater until exhausted, then decapitated. MacDonald reported with morbid fascination how the child's body was paraded around the village canoe house until the blood ceased to pulse from the neck, then cooked along with a pig. Travelers were hungry for stories of local depravity whether they witnessed them or not. In *The Light of Melanesia*, my great-grandfather offered these nuggets from Makira, just east of Guadalcanal:

"Often it has been a chief living only a few miles off who [starts] in the dead of night and, at early dawn, surprises the sleeping population, murders every one, takes their skulls for his new canoe or house, and paddles back with as much human flesh as his people can dispose of. Close to Wango, one of our school centres, I was shown a village which had been wiped out only a few years ago. The forty skulls then taken are probably still in existence, but the people near a school do not care to talk of such exploits, nor exhibit their spoils."

Here it is tempting to stop and wonder: If islanders weren't relating these stories to my great-grandfather, then who was, and what was the storyteller's agenda? Or, one could simply pass on more of his tidbits, like this one:

"Infanticide is terribly common, almost universal, and it is the old women who are in fault. They are eager to kill babies as soon as they are born, that the young mothers may not be kept from work in the fields, which then would fall heavily upon the old and childless. I asked, of course, in what way the population of a village was kept up. I was told that in all coast villages it is the custom to buy boys and girls of six or eight from the bush people, who apparently do not practice infanticide."

I am suspicious of this sort of history because it comes entirely from European writers who had much to gain in portraying Melanesians as degenerate savages. Whether all the details of these stories are true, they have helped shape modern Melanesians' own version of history. Darkness Time was a time of violence, slavery, gore, and depravity.

But a closer look reveals that Europeans delivered a cargo of shackles, swords, and gunpowder along with their Bibles.

Take the first encounter between Europeans and Solomon Islanders. In 1567, the Spanish viceroy of Peru sent his nephew, Alvaro de Mendaña, out into the Pacific Ocean. The Spanish believed that the Inca had once sailed a fleet of reed boats across the Pacific to islands inhabited by a fabulously wealthy black race. They fantasized that this was Ophir, the biblical source of the gold King Solomon used to build his temples in Jerusalem. The conquistadors wanted the gold, but Mendaña declared he would also bring the discovered race under the dominion of the Catholic Church.

It took Mendaña nearly a year to find an island big enough to resemble the imagined kingdom. He called the island Santa Ysabel and claimed all the surrounding shores for his king and his god, but the islanders refused to share their yams with his starving crew. Relations reached a low point when ten of Mendaña's men paddled to shore on Guadalcanal to obtain water. Only one survived. "The dead were cut into pieces," wrote chief purser Gomez Catoira. "Some without legs and without arms, others without heads, and the ends of all their tongues were cut off, and their eye-teeth drawn, and those whose heads were left had had the skulls cut open and the brains eaten." Mendaña certainly didn't turn the other cheek. His soldiers burned hundreds of houses and killed at least twenty men. The native dead were drawn, quartered, and left at the spot where his own men had been killed. Mendaña then headed home to report he had found the fabled islands of King Solomon, though he had found no gold, silver, or spices, nor had he converted any heathens.

Early British adventurers did not pretend their mission had anything at all to do with God. They were after hardwood, then laborers, and then the islands themselves. The traders were frequently sworn enemies of the church. They armed natives with shotguns and, according to Henry Montgomery, were indirectly responsible for murderous attacks on Anglican mission schools. "Mission work has no greater enemy than the ungodly white man, for the foes within the household deal the most deadly blows," he despaired, finding Guadalcanal still defiantly heathen.

Britain took the Solomon Islands on as a protectorate in 1893. Its first resident commissioner, Sir Charles Woodford, insisted the rambunctious natives needed a "firm and paternal" government. But one reason the islands were so unquiet was that Woodford was wresting land out of native hands so that it could be sold or leased to white planters. Why was Woodford so keen to sell land? He needed revenues to fund his firm and paternal government. It was a catch-22 with explosive consequences.

Some planters did buy land from hereditary owners: one district was bought for £20, two thousand porpoise teeth, two hundred dog teeth, a case of tobacco, a case of pipes, a case of matches, one piece of calico, two knives, and two axes. But elsewhere, Woodford simply annexed hundreds of thousands of acres of supposedly "unoccupied lands," most of which he had never seen, and licensed it out to planters. When islanders resisted the theft, Woodford or his allies responded with murderous force. For a time, Woodford's efforts to "purify" the Solomons looked a lot like traditional Melanesian blood feuding.

In 1909, for example, a government party shot and killed the wife and children of the warrior chief Sito on Vella Lavella. In retaliation, Sito sent his men to kill the wife and children of a white trader. Not to be outdone, Woodford sent a punitive expedition of government officers, "revenge-crazed traders," and a militia of Malaitans, who swept over Vella Lavella in a wave of random killing and destruction.

The missionaries frequently reaped the harvest of the government's brutality. A story pieced together by my great-grandfather illustrates the double-whammy effect that evangelical zeal and naval power had on the islanders.

By 1880, the mission had attracted a handful of followers in the Florida Islands, east of Guadalcanal, but most of the natives remained hostile. That year, the British naval sloop HMS *Sandfly* cruised into the Floridas. The ship's commanding officer, one Lieutenant Bower, took a boat and four oarsmen and landed on the islet of Mandoleana, which he assumed was uninhabited. He was right, but his landing was noted by Kalekona, a chief on nearby Nggela. Kalekona had some past grievance with white men, and he apparently required at least one white head in order to make things right again. Such was the *kastom*. He sent a party, led by his son, to ambush the sailors. They killed three men with their axes, then shot Bower down from his hiding spot in a banyan tree. Four heads. The Royal Navy returned, bombing a few villages to ashes but notably sparing a Christian hamlet. More importantly, HMS *Cormorant* arrived the following year with Bishop John Richardson Selwyn (son of the original missionary bishop, and Patteson's replacement) aboard. Selwyn cut a deal with Kalekona. A "ringleader" was hanged from the banyan tree where Bower had made his last stand. Others were tied to it and shot. Kalekona and his son were spared because of their new alliance with the church.

The incident did wonders for the mission. Floridans smashed their shrines and promised to give up their old gods. By the time my great-grandfather arrived, thousands had been baptized. Islanders, who were outgunned, learned that safety lay within the mission stations. Congregations grew. Churches and mission schools sprouted in the coastal forests from New Georgia to Santa Cruz. Head-hunting and the cycle of interisland war gradually petered out. Coconut plantations flourished. This peace, interrupted briefly by World War II, lasted for a century. So, while Christianity did accompany the arrival of peace on the islands, this peace was a product of superior firepower as much as prayer. Solomon Islanders' conversion to Christianity was about self-preservation, politics, and declaring allegiance, not to the Prince of Peace but to a god of war who was more powerful than their own.

I did not buy the argument, much circulated on the streets of Honiara, that the current crisis represented a falling-out with the Almighty and a return to the heathen savagery of Darkness Time. How could it when all the combatants were Christian? But the preference for framing the tension in mythical terms reached even the highest levels of government.

I was back at the Quality Motel, waiting for the pressing heat of midday to lift, when the national minister for peace and reconciliation arrived on my veranda. He lowered his fleshy frame into a deck chair and set down his grass handbag. Nathaniel Waena had come to explain the country's troubles to me. He spoke in Cambridge English. His voice boomed with authority. But he was at a loss to make sense of the tension or its lingering consequences. Perhaps it was all the Malaitans' fault. Or perhaps it was the fault of the British for sewing together a country out of such discordant fabric, for drawing people away from their home islands to the illusory riches of Honiara. Or maybe, said Waena, running his fingers across his spongy Afro, squinting as though trying to suppress a headache, the crisis was a riddle handed to the people by God Himself.

"We will never be one country, one people. We will always belong to our own islands, the places where the Creator meant for us to live and survive," he bellowed. He threw his arms in the air. "But I ask you, why did God create the Solomons the way they are? Why has He bound and separated us by the sea? Why has He made us so different from each other? What is it that the Lord is saying to us?"

Waena brought his fist down on the table, spilling his glass of bush lime juice. A drop of sweat dribbled down the left lens of his thick glasses. He lowered his voice. "We have been wrong in our ways. We have so many riches. Where did all those riches go? What is wrong with us? What does God want us to do? How can we know His mind?"

As the weeks passed, and as I came to know the islanders and their sadness, I began to see that there was, indeed, a spiritual element to the tension. The root of the crisis lay not in politics or logistics, but in *kastom*, which was the soul of the nation. *Kastom* had not fared well in the Solomons. For a century, missionaries had run a system of residential schools, which removed children from their home villages, much as they had done in Vanuatu. But unlike in Vanuatu, traditional chiefs in the Solomons were stripped of their power and prestige. These two changes combined to sever a link between young people and the stories and teachings of their forebears. People did not listen to the whispers of the ancestors—they had forgotten how. They remembered the martyrdom of Bishop Patteson on Nukapu, but they did not seem to remember his message of peace. The bond between islanders and all the stories that once guided their lives had been so frayed by rootlessness and change and greed that it had simply snapped.

Only one story gave islanders hope. It had many versions, many plots, but it always featured the same band of heroes, and it always ended in a miracle. I heard one chapter of it from my new pal Robert Iroga, a reporter for the *Solomon Star* newspaper.

I caught up with Iroga at the Mendaña Hotel, the once-posh resort where politicians and ex-militants now drank Johnny Walker together at the pool bar. The militants wore Hawaiian shirts. The politicians wore camouflage sun hats. There were fresh bullet holes in the ceiling of the hotel lobby. Nothing serious, said the waiter. A few of the special constables had had a party on the weekend and brought their machine guns.

I had hoped that, as the *Star*'s ethnic tension point man, Iroga would give me a sober analysis of the crisis and a list of its architects. But even the hard-news man seemed to prefer myth to political scoops. I bought a jug of beer to loosen his lips. Explain the tension to me, I asked him. Whose fault is it? Iroga was a strapping young man, but he was nervous. He glanced around the room, nodded here and there, and looked back at me gravely. He assured me it was not uneducated men like Jimmy Rasta and Harold Keke who had instigated the tension. No, no. The trouble didn't bubble up. It trickled down from the educated "elite," from lawyers, parliamentarians, and businessmen. But Iroga would not give me names. The one thing you didn't do in the Solomons was lay blame on people. Stories were more dangerous than guns.

"Look at our newspaper," he said. "Sometimes we are so careful, we don't even print the news. For example, the Malaitan boys who went to catch Harold Keke on the Weather Coast: I know those boys are dead, I know Harold killed them, and I know the *tasiu* buried them—the brotherhood even sent me a fax to confirm it! But we could never run that story. If we did, the Malaitan leaders would come and demand compensation from us for spoiling the reputation of their boys."

Everything in Honiara was broken, he said. Nobody could be trusted. Except for the church, of course. Except for the Melanesian Brotherhood. The country would have torn itself to bits if it weren't for the *tasiu*, who walked between the armies, who were now endeavoring to collect guns from the ex-militants, and who, with God's help, would lead islanders back to the light.

Iroga had agreed to meet me because he was interested in studying journalism in Canada. It would be natural for him to attempt to impress me with his objectivity and his journalistic detachment. Perhaps that is what he was trying to do, in a particularly Melanesian way, when he took a deep pull on his beer and launched into the story he really wanted to tell.

Once, while on assignment in south Malaita, Iroga was being guided through the bush by three members of the Melanesian Brotherhood. At some point, the travelers' path was blocked by a river too deep to ford and too swift to swim across. They looked for a canoe but couldn't find one. They considered building a raft but couldn't find suitable timbers. So the three *tasiu* came together and prayed for God's assistance. They had barely said their amens when a crocodile rose out of the murk. It was huge, as wide and long as a canoe, and one *tasiu* noted, it was the perfect size for riding. The crocodile was the answer to their prayers. One by one, the travelers climbed onto its back, and one by one, they enjoyed a gentle cruise across the river. When the crocodile had safely deposited all four men on the far bank, one of the brothers pulled a copper medallion from his bag. It was not the same medallion the *tasiu* wore. This one was reserved for the generous and pious individuals who pledged to support the brothers in their work. They hung the medallion around the crocodile's neck and told the beast it was now a Companion of the Brotherhood.

I laughed.

Iroga sipped his beer solemnly.

"I'm writing this down. You rode on the back of a magic crocodile," I said, waiting for him to chuckle, slap me on the back, wink, step back from the story.

"It takes great faith to perform miracles," he said, and I knew by his furrowed brow that he was utterly serious.

Now it's one thing to tell fanciful stories by a campfire on the edge of the jungle. It's one thing to believe a thousand-year-old parable or to accept that a miracle has happened to a stranger in some distant land. It's one thing to attribute fortune or misfortune to *mana* or some form of divine intervention, as *Tasiu* Ken had done back in Vureas Bay. But we weren't in the jungle here, and we weren't talking about the Old Testament, and we weren't stringing together coincidences or offering metaphors for life. Nor were we regular people. We were both trained journalists. Iroga was the closest thing I would find to a Melanesian version of myself, and here he was, swimming through myth, remembering things his five senses could not have shown him.

Part of me wanted to jump up, grab that big man by the lapels, shake him out of dream time, berate him: *These are not the sort of stories that journalists tell!* But a growing part of me wanted to be him, or at least to learn the method by which I might remember things the way Iroga remembered things. Like Iroga, everyone in Honiara wrapped their war, their suffering, their pain, and their idea of redemption in tendrils of magic. Everyone told, believed, and claimed to *experience* equally fantastical stories involving the *tasiu*. Everyone was sure that it would take a *tasiu* miracle to save the country. I knew that these stories were the key to understanding Solomon Islanders and their journey, and yet for me they remained distant and out of focus. I wanted to see with island eyes, but it seemed the only way to do so was to close my own, and I couldn't do it.

I had yet to understand that there was more than one way to see, to feel, to live a story. I had yet to be readied for my own journey with the Melanesian Brotherhood.

15

The Bishop of Malaita

Solitude lies at the lowest depth of the human condition.
Man is the only being who feels himself to be alone and
the only one who is searching for the Other.

—Octavio Paz, *The Labyrinth of Solitude*

I spent my days at the port in Honiara, looking for a passage to the Santa Cruz Group and thence to Nukapu. The *Eastern Trader* was always on the verge of sailing. So was the *Temotu*, its competitor. Neither ship budged.

I watched them from the veranda at the Quality Motel, I dozed, and I barely noticed when a sturdy-looking tub took on a load of passengers, pigs, and rice, then chugged away with a puff of black smoke. I was furious when I learned the *Endeavor* was bound for Santa Cruz. I was less furious when I learned the ship's fate. Someone had pinched all the *Endeavor*'s spare lubricant, so when she ran out of oil halfway to Nendo, the engineer poured coconut oil into the gearbox, fouling it completely. The *Endeavor* drifted west toward the Coral Sea, where the swell grew so big and so steep that the pigs began to slide across the deck. The rice was lashed down, the pigs were not. Each time a pig went overboard, sharks charged out from under the ship to rip it to shreds while the horrified passengers looked on. It took a week and a half for someone in Honiara to scrape together enough gas money to send the Royal Solomon Islands Police patrol boat out to rescue the survivors.

Nukapu would have to wait. Fine. I was after heathens and magic, and Malaita, the Solomons' second most populous island, promised both.

Malaitans are fierce. Malaitans are warlike. Malaitans are mysterious. These are points on which all people in the Solomons agreed, especially the Malaitans themselves. It was Malaitans who controlled the police, who had outwitted and humiliated the Guadalcanal militants, who had the government under their thumb. It was Malaitans who still offered blood sacrifice to the sharks and octopuses that prowled their lagoons. It was Malaitans, or at least a few thousand villagers in the island's Kwaio highlands, who still refused the church and the authority of the government.

It was the mountain Kwaio people I was keenest to meet. They were not like the heathens back on Tanna; they were not recycled heathens. They had never succumbed to the missionaries' charms. They had never abandoned their *kastom*. They did not put on dances for tourists. They were notoriously hostile toward outsiders. When coastal Malaitans joined the dance of blood and anarchy in Honiara, the mountain Kwaio went on tending their gardens and sacrificing to their ancestors as they had been doing for thousands of years. I wondered what stories the Solomons' last pagans told each other about the fractured world beyond their mountain home.

Malaita and Guadalcanal are less than fifty miles apart. On a map, they resemble two slugs crawling slowly northwest, parting just enough to make room for the amorphous Florida Group. Until recently, ships had departed Honiara for Malaita every day. This month there was a problem. A fiberglass canoe carrying eight men from the north end of Malaita had disappeared and then been discovered, half submerged, off the coast of the Florida Islands. Its bilge plug had been yanked out. The passengers were never found. The north Malaitans suspected their *wantoks* had been ambushed and killed by rivals from the Langa Langa Lagoon, farther south. Since it was Langa Langa men who built and sailed the ships on the run between Honiara and Auki, those vessels had become fair game in the feud. Being north Malaitan, Jimmy Rasta had taken it upon himself to pirate one of those ships, the *Sa'Alia*, and sail it back to his base east of Honiara. Now the rest of the fleet was afraid to make the journey.

So I lingered on the docks and was seduced by the port with its great silver oil tanks, its dust, its corrugated-iron warehouses, its crumbling cement piers, its milling crowds, its possibilities, its roughness. The waterfront was not delicate or charming. There were none of the gleaming sailboats that populated Port Vila's harbor, only working craft: coastal freighters, iron barges, weatherboard hulks, converted junks and secondhand ferries, all black smoke, rust stain, bullet holes, and dripping diesel.

The port was a crossroads for the western Pacific. Fair-skinned, straight-haired Polynesians moved among barrel-chested pygmies, dwarfs with spiral tattoos on their cheeks, fragile-looking Malays, and Indonesian fishermen, jet-black men with violently red hair or sun-bleached Afros, bony women with skin the color of licorice and eyes of mud. The Malaitan sailors were the most curious-looking and the most handsome. Their skin was like cinnamon and covered in blond down. Their cheeks bore scars from ritual cutting: spirals and stylized sun designs etched forever into soft flesh, so that Malaitan *wantoks* would always recognize home in each other's faces.

Some evenings, I wandered out past the candlelit betel nut

stands to look at the *Eastern Trader* straining at her lines and her crew lounging like cats on the rails or slumbering in hammocks, strong arms dangling, fingernails tapping the grimy deck. They were bored. They twisted their frizzy hair to resemble the dreadlocks they had seen on TV at the video cinema before their money had run out. Their bare feet were grotesquely callused. Their teeth were crimson with betel stains, but their smiles were pure and generous. I sat with them for hours. I asked about Nukapu. They all knew that the island was the beginning of the story that bound them to their church. They could all recount the familiar details of Bishop Patteson's martyrdom on that hallowed shore, how he had worn a smile on his face even after the islanders had smashed his skull. But none of them had actually been there. When we talked, the sailors would reach for my hand, grasp it, squeeze, and refuse to let go, even when our conversations ended. They craved beer. They told me their ancestors came from Africa, like Bob Marley. They weren't sure how old they were. They smoked sweet black tobacco rolled in notebook paper. I would listen to them and breathe in the scent of their hard work, and I would let my hand be squeezed, tentatively at first, but later I would squeeze back and gaze into their eyes like a lover imagining more, and I would allow something resembling loneliness to leave me, let it drift away across the sound, up into the sparkling fullness of the night sky.

Back at the height of the civil war, the only ships to ply the waters around Guadalcanal without fear were those run by the Church of Melanesia. The militants would never dare harass an Anglican ship. So it was now. And so it was that I was helped across the water by a band of church ladies. The Anglican Mothers' Union had planned a congress on Malaita long before Rasta's gang had paralyzed the seas, and they had no intention of being waylaid. After all, they had booked a mission ship.

The mothers, dozens of them, arrived at the port in T-shirts and skirts. They squawked and huffed and dropped their bags of sweet potatoes into the hold of the *Kopuria*, a cute wooden tub named for the founder of the Melanesian Brotherhood. The Kopuria was all of sixty feet long and painted honeybee yellow. We chugged off at a donkey's pace, plowing across the calm sound, rousing schools of flying fish, whose rainbow fins beat like the wings of hummingbirds and left trails of shivers across the water.

We reached Malaita at dusk. I hadn't given much thought to where I would sleep. Everyone else had. I would obviously be staying with the bishop of Malaita. Not only was the bishop born on the same island as me—Canada—but we spoke the same language. That made him my *wantok*, and therefore obliged by *kastom* to take care of me. In fact, they said, the bishop acted like everyone was a *wantok*. His house was overflowing with de facto *wantoks*.

That night we gathered in the bishop's yard. The mothers cooed and fussed over the bishop. They placed a flower garland around his neck. The bishop said grace in Solomons pidgin and reassured the mothers that, even though they were on Malaita, they need not be scared. Then he plunged into a plateful of pig fat and mashed yams, scooping the food into his mouth with his fingers while they watched approvingly.

"There is no helping it," the bishop told me, licking his fingertips. "The women refuse to serve themselves unless I have started eating."

I didn't trust the bishop at first. I suppose I had decided even before we met that he would be a strange exile living a colonialist fantasy. His very presence on Malaita made him suspect: after all, his mission included the quashing of Melanesia's most resilient pagan enclaves. Why had he come to Malaita, if not to bear the torch of cultural imperialism?

I studied him, looking for Victorian anachronisms, conspicuous paternalism, shades of my great-grandfather. But Terry Brown offered none of these things. He was a gentle, slightly awkward man who stumbled through small talk and lurched through his house in a threadbare T-shirt that read "No Fear." His trunklike legs shook the floor with every step. He seemed always to be rustling through papers, chasing some new administrative emergency, peering through his thick glasses at the ceiling, pondering, pondering. Sometimes his face bore a look of vague shock, as though seized by the first tremors of a heart-stopping epiphany.

The bishop kept a stained map of Malaita on the wall of his office. He had pressed colored pins into the map to show where the church had spread across the island. There were congregations all along the seashore, clustered in coves and strung out along the road that ran from Auki up the west coast. There were pins scattered through the northern mountain ranges. But in the dead center of the island, across a ragged mess of creeks and peaks and topographic contours, the map was pristine and unpierced: Kwaio country.

"That's where I need to go," I said.

The bishop hummed thoughtfully. "We can get you to the edge of the Kwaio bush, but our influence ends there," he said. "You just don't wander into Kwaio country without an invitation."

"But aren't you evangelizing up there?"

"Well, the Melanesian Brotherhood has certainly tried. But the Kwaio aren't interested in the gospel. They only come to the brothers asking for medicine or for help finding lost pigs. The brothers are getting a bit sick of it, actually."

"Why aren't you up there converting them?"

The bishop looked over the top of his glasses at me. He knew I was baiting him. "Because they do not wish to be converted. And, to be honest, I'm sure they could teach our Christians a few things. They are humble. They are generous. Their communities are strong. People support each other. Look, the Seventh-day Adventists have been trying to evangelize these people for a hundred years, but the bush Kwaio have been quite happy to go on killing pigs for their ancestors. If some of them decide to pack it in and get baptized, well that's fine, we'll take them, but I'm inclined to just, oh, live and let live."

"But if they die without being baptized, then aren't they bound for hell?"

"Ah! There's the question that we Christians have been asking ourselves for a century. Some Christians feel that traditional culture is demonic and must be overturned—you'll hear that from the Adventists. On the other end of the spectrum, especially in the West, people are saying that salvation is possible, um, yes, without any knowledge of Christ whatsoever. Universalism, they call it. The idea is that good Muslims and good Buddhists and, yes, even ancestor-worshippers, can go to heaven, too. So there is less of a drive to evangelize."

The pagans were the least of the bishop's concerns, anyway. He had his hands full with his own flock. It was Christians who were running around with guns, stealing boats and trucks, robbing their rivals' stores, burning down each others' houses. The bishop was going to have a serious talk with Jimmy Rasta for starters. But his biggest beef with his flock was theological. Malaitans were still guided by their belief in *mana*. They believed that *kastom* chiefs had it. Rich men had it, too. Most of all, they believed the clergy had *mana*. People asked the bishop to bless tree bark, oils, potions, and *kastom* medicine. They asked his priests for holy water to pour into the radiators of stalled cars. They pinched the bishop's dictionary of angels, believing that if they knew the "secret" names of those angels, they could control them, calling on their powers to bring them wealth or kill their enemies, just as the Kwaio called on the *mana* of their ancestral spirits. They were sure that God's power could be diverted, focused, distilled, and put to work for themselves.

And then there was the Melanesian Brotherhood, who had the most *mana* of all, said the bishop.

After performing an exorcism in a village near Auki, a group of *tasiu* had built a small stone cairn by the road to "protect" the village. Not long after, a drunk walking home from a party stopped to empty his bladder on the cairn. "According to the story people told later, that guy only got about a hundred yards before—pow!—he was struck by lightning, or an invisible bullet or, well, something. He died, or so the story went. I never saw any proof of any of this, of course, but the message is that one shouldn't mess with the brothers. All this is all rather problematic for Christian theologians. I'm very, very concerned."

"Don't you believe in miracles?"

"Of course I do. But our relationship is supposed to be directly with God. People here are trying to use angels like they once used their ancestral spirits. They are still trying to accumulate and direct *mana* like their ancestors did. There is almost no reference in this to Christ at all. Christianity is not about wielding power. It's not about personal charisma. It's not about *mana*. It is about meekness. Jesus gave up his power in order to die, weak and helpless, on the cross. This idea is repeated over and over again in Corinthians: Strength is made perfect in weakness!"

The bishop encouraged his priests to focus on the New Testament, on Jesus and resurrection through love, but Malaitans seemed to crave the battles and divine favoritism of the Old. In fact, they cherished the myth and miracles of the Old Testament so much they extrapolated them, drew them out through the centuries and across the oceans to include their island. Some Malaitans firmly believed they were descendants of one of the lost tribes of Israel, said the bishop. A few hundred generations ago, a descendant of the Hebrew tribe of Levi supposedly drifted across the globe, washed up on the shore south of Auki, and started again. The theory made a strange kind of sense: traditional Malaitan *kastom* paralleled the *kastom* of the Israelites, the ones given to Moses and written down in the Book of Leviticus. Rules around the impurity of menstruating women, the sacredness of worship sites, the details of blood sacrifice . . . Malaitans had followed them all, long before Europeans arrived. Somewhere along the way, the Malaitans had simply substituted their ancestors for Yahweh. The biggest sticking point in this theory concerned those blood sacrifices: the Israelites sacrificed lambs to their god, but there were no sheep in Melanesia, so the lost tribe had no choice but to switch to a less than kosher alternative. Pork.

The lost tribe theory had gained momentum during the civil war, particularly when Malaita Eagle commanders circulated a treatise whose author used quotes from Genesis and Deuteronomy to "prove" that Malaitans shared their pride and aggressiveness with the sons of Jacob. Malaitans, who had never gotten along particularly well with each other, suddenly had a myth to bind them: they were different from the primitives across the water. They were bound by history and collective superiority. They were the lost tribe! It worked until the armistice was signed in 2000. Then Malaitans turned their guns and machetes on each other again.

All this saddened the bishop. Christianity was supposed to free the Malaitans from their fears and their restrictive *kastom* rules, but a perverted version of *kastom* was enjoying a kind of resurgence. Various Christian sects were bringing the old *tabus* back, especially rules regarding women. They forbade women to wear shorts. They forced women to remain in isolation during menstruation. They jacked up the price of brides to include hard cash as well as the traditional exchange of shell money. One breakaway priest had a vision that told him that women should not be permitted to wear ribbons in their hair.

The greatest perversion of all had occurred with the age-old *kastom* of compensation, said the bishop. Islanders had once relied on grand feasts and the ritual exchange of pigs, shell money, and favors to create bonds between clans and to reconcile all kinds of disputes. But the cash economy had twisted compensation into a grotesque caricature of itself. Malaitans were now demanding mountains of cash for bride price, war damages, and affronts real and imagined. The compensation racket was making men like Jimmy Rasta rich. It pretended to be *kastom*, but it was extortion, pure and simple. Example: A boy in the bishop's youth choir had touched a girl on the shoulder. The girl's brothers had demanded $400 for the indiscretion.

The bishop put me up in the spare room of his tin-roofed bungalow. I studied him, his household, and what I had wrongly thought was his exile. In 1996, Terry Brown had been living in Toronto when the Church of Melanesia announced it needed a new bishop for Malaita. He had spent a few years teaching in the islands, so why not put his name forward? He was elected in a unanimous decision by a committee of Melanesian clergy. He came to Melanesia alone, but his aloneness was not tolerated. The bishop's Melanesian predecessors all had installed their extended families in the official residence, but Terry Brown did not have a family. It didn't matter. The residence was like a sponge. It gave him one.

There was George, a bright-eyed Polynesian teen who had adopted the bishop as his father. George's function in the house seemed to be to prance Pan-like about the house and hold guests' hands. He had discovered glitter paint at a church dance. It sparkled from his eyebrows the night I arrived.

There was Derrick of the deep facial scars and dark moods. One afternoon, Derrick asked to borrow the stick of underarm deodorant he had found while digging through my pack. I said fine. Then he rubbed it through his beard. Derrick had once been Auki's Casanova, but he had fallen in love with the wrong girl. Her family demanded fifteen lengths of common shell money, two yards of red shell money, two thousand dolphin's teeth, and a whopping $6,000 in bride price, all of which was taking Derrick years to raise. The bishop paid him to drive his truck.

There was jovial Thomas, who arrived for tea and toast on the bishop's veranda each morning, and whose wife would invariably come searching for him by midday. Thomas was very skilled at driving race cars on the bishop's new computer.

Then there was gentle Tony, who took care of the bishop and quietly nagged the others to do their dishes. They were an immensely likable bunch.

"Melanesian society is corporate," the bishop explained to me one night as he cooked sausage stew for the gang. "There are no individuals here. You are either part of the community or you are quite simply considered something less than human. I have never been alone here—I am not permitted to be alone."

The bishop's residence reminded me of a fraternity house. Dirty dishes were stacked high. Walls were flecked with dried tomato sauce. People came and went without knocking. Strangers lurked in the kitchen, poked their heads into the refrigerator, then froze when they spotted me watching through the screen door. There was a note tacked to the bishop's bedroom door: "Please don't search through drawers and take things that aren't yours." The boys in the house were not servants. The bishop did most of the cooking. The boys borrowed his slippers and sweaters. They went to the market with his money to buy yams and returned with pockets full of betel nut instead. They played games on his computer late into the evening. They teased him. They rarely called him bishop. They yelled at him from the veranda. "Big B!" they shouted. "Come out, Big B!" And the bishop would shake his head and chuckle to himself.

For a time, I thought the bishop was being taken advantage of. Perhaps he was, but no more than any other Solomon Islands big man. This is the essence of the Solomon Islands *wantok* system: if you are a big man, you are obliged to share your wealth. If you have food, your *wantoks* will come and eat it. If you have money, they will ask for it. If you start a canteen store, they will clear the shelves before you can sell anything. Clothes they will borrow, permanently. If you join the government and move to a house in Honiara, your *wantoks* will move in with you and pester you until you divert some of that government cargo their way.

The bishop confided to me that at first he had been shocked by the touching, the familiarity, the closeness, the relentless communalism of Melanesian life. Now it made him smile. He wanted to write a book to convince people in places like Toronto that this was a better way to live. It is hard to disagree. His peculiar home was the warmest and most loving I had entered in years.

I lingered for days while the boys planned my invasion of the Kwaio bush. One afternoon, as we shared tea and biscuits on the veranda, George grabbed my hand excitedly: we could climb over the spine of the island and surprise the Kwaio! Nope, said the bishop. Too dangerous. Better to start from the Seventh-day Adventist mission on the east coast. A dirt road crossed the island north of Auki; from there, I could catch a canoe down the coast to the mission. The road hadn't been maintained since the start of the war, but Derrick insisted that with him at the wheel, the bishop's truck could make the crossing. I told him I knew that "road" didn't really mean "road" in Melanesia.

On Sunday, I went with the boys to the tin-roofed cathedral, where I saw the bishop finally transformed into the Victorian version of himself. He towered above his congregation, a giant in cream vestments and shining tassels. He wore a honey-gold miter and clutched a great curled staff. He swung a silver censer full of incense, and the smoke drifted around him as he prayed. The bishop's magnificence carried me back to my childhood, to the morning of my father's death, to the bishop of Tasmania gazing down at me from his portrait, noble, good, at peace with God. Now the choir rose, and the cathedral echoed with the sound of pipe drums. Two dancers appeared, teenage boys with bare shoulders shining and stone discs clattering on their chests. The boys stamped their feet and shook their rattles. The cement floor vibrated as they punched the air and charged up the aisle toward the bishop. In their wake came two girls, breasts bound with strands of shell money, arms straining under the weight of a wooden tablet. The tablet was decorated with flowers. On it was an open Bible. The girls brought the Bible to the bishop. He lifted it and he kissed it.

This was not the moment that revealed the bishop to me. He had not imposed all this Anglo-Catholic ritual on the islanders. It was they who had preserved it since Victorian times and only recently layered it with *kastom*'s drumbeat. It was they who had provided the bishop with his finery and insisted that he read at least part of the liturgy in English, rather than Solomons pidgin. No, I saw the bishop most fully after the service.

Raindrops thundered down on the tin roof, but still the people poured out of the church onto the lawn. There, the drummers were joined by a pipe band. The pipers blew on hollowed sections of bamboo. The drummers smacked at the open ends of sections of PVC pipe with their flip-flops. The rhythm was playful. People formed a circle and began to dance under the flowering trees. They surrounded the bishop, who had changed back into shirtsleeves and shorts. They took him by both his hands and pulled him in among them, and they shrieked with joy as he lurched about, elbows high, eyes raised ecstatically to the sky. "Look at B! Look, he dances like a frog!" George shouted. And the rain fell on the bishop, and mud squeezed out from the lawn and splattered his great calves, and flower petals fell from the trees, and the big man closed his eyes and giggled like a tickled child.

I felt a surprising joy, and as the wind swept across the grass and the eastern sky, I allowed myself to be pulled into the dance. And I realized this:

The bishop had not come to Malaita to rule. He did not love Malaitans because they revered him, deferred to him, waited on him, or obeyed him—for they did none of these things. This bishop loved Malaitans because they bossed him around. They harangued and chided him. They yelled at him. They invaded his house, asked him for favors and money. They were not afraid to touch him, not afraid to pat him on the shoulder while he was cooking, not afraid to grasp his hand tightly, without reservation and for no particular reason at all. He loved them because they ate his stews, and when they were finished, they leaned back and belched in unself-conscious contentment; because he had spent years in a northern metropolis where good people lived half-lives, and he had known what it was like to rub shoulders with thousands of them and still feel an immense, crushing solitude. He loved Malaitans because they surrounded him like water, because they made him know beyond any doubt that he was not alone, and in this way they were proof that his god, the God of Love, was real.

16

A Short Walk
in East Kwaio

*Every considerable village or settlement is sure to have
some one who can control the weather and the waves,
some one who knows how to treat sickness, some one
who can work mischief with various charms.*

—R. H. CODRINGTON, *The Melanesians*

It was not easy to reach the heathens in East Kwaio. The road
across Malaita's mountainous spine was more like a mud luge
track than a road. Descents were easy. Ascents were a problem.
The bishop's truck sank like a hippo in the red clay at the bottom
of each hill, and I climbed out and pushed along with Tony and
Thomas and the dozen-odd hitchhikers we had collected en route.
Derrick would stomp on the gas, the tires would fling great gobs
of doughlike mud at our faces, and the truck would lurch from rut
to rut, groaning more emphatically with every new bluff. Finally,
it refused to advance any farther.

The boys were outraged and shamed at the thought of my carrying on alone, but they felt better after they had cajoled one of the hitchhikers into guiding me to the coast and carrying my gas jug. (I had brought along five gallons of fuel because there was none left on the east side of Malaita. Without fuel, it would be a long paddle down the coast to the Adventist mission at Atoifi.)

"Oh, no," I told the hitcher weakly. "*No, yu no kari petrol blong mi*," and then I handed the jug to him. He glared at me and strode off with it. I scurried behind. An hour later, he dumped the jug on the road, accepted a month's wages for his effort, and disappeared on a side trail. Then I was alone. I balanced the gas jug on my shoulders above my backpack and carried on. The overcast sky began to lose its late-afternoon glow. The mud stuck to the soles of my sandals until they were as heavy as ski boots. I slipped, swore, pulled off the sandals, and trudged on. Tall grass grew like an endless hedge down the middle of the track. I walked through the end of twilight, expecting to see lights around each new bend, but there were no lights, and no sounds other than the rustling of the forest. I pulled out my headlamp and walked into the night. I cursed the road and the disappearing hitchhiker and islanders in general for going to war instead of keeping up their roads. I cursed myself for not simply waiting a week and catching the supply plane to the Atoifi mission.

Sometime in the middle of the night I saw a faint glow in the forest. I followed it until it became a lamp in the window of a plywood shack. A sign outside the shack announced: Peace Monitoring Council. That was good. The PMC had been formed to encourage militants to give up their guns. Three people answered the door when I knocked: a grandfather, a thickish woman, and a quivering young man. It was too dark to see their faces, but I knew they were good people because they made me a hot cup of tea and offered me a bed and a mosquito net for the night. What a coincidence, they told me when they heard my destination: they would be taking a canoe down to the Atoifi mission in the morning.

The young man, whose name was Patrick, announced he would tell me a funny story from the time of ethnic tension. Once upon a time, Patrick had worked with his best friend, Chris, at the Shell Oil station in Honiara. When the tension began, Patrick joined the Malaita Eagle Force, but Chris joined the Guadalcanal side, the Isatabu Freedom Movement. That was a real scream, said Patrick, because the Eagles had machine guns while the poor IFM boys had to make do with machetes and homemade pipe guns. Patrick insisted that he and his friends had killed at least sixty-eight Guale boys in Marau, thirty-eight in Kakabona, and twenty-five more in Kombule. He met his best friend again after the fighting was finished. "Chris said to me, 'Hey, if you had seen me at the battle of Alligator Creek, would you have shot me?' I told him, of course I would. And it would have been easy, because I had my SR-88, my machine gun, and Chris had to make do with his homemade pipe gun and his prayers! Ha!"

"Prayers?"

"Yes, they were all begging their ancestors to protect them from us. It didn't work. How could magic work against our machine guns?"

"So you guys didn't try using magic?"

"Some of the Eagles did. An old man once came to our bunker with a powerful black stone from Choiseul. He said it would stop the IFM's guns from firing. That didn't work, so we decided to pray to God instead. We prayed every morning before our battles."

"Surely God wouldn't help you kill people!"

"I know, I know," Patrick said, barely able to contain his laughter. "We didn't ask Him to help us win. We said, 'God, we know you are against what we are doing here, but please can you wash us with the blood of Jesus Christ? Can you make us clean again?'"

"Asking for forgiveness even before you sinned," I said. "That's cheating."

"I know, it's crazy, isn't it? *Funi tumas!*"

Morning came, or something like morning. A deep gray glow crept beneath the belly of the overcast sky. It was not bright enough to penetrate the forest along the trail or to transform the oily black hue of the cove we reached after an hour's walk. The sun never did appear in East Kwaio. When I look back and try to remember scenes from the next few days, the mountains, the people, the mission, the machetes . . . all these things return to me in a muddy twilight of charcoal, rotting mahogany, and leaden shadows. It was like moving through Atlantis, a world made heavy and cut off from the truth of things by a hundred fathoms of murky jade.

The peace monitors had arranged for a *kanu*, which was not a canoe but a fiberglass skiff. We slid out through the mangroves and headed south across still water, skirting the inside of a long barrier reef. East of the reef, there was nothing; we were tracing the rough edge of the world. A storm billowed like a sail under the gray roof of the sky, then swept over us. The sea exploded with raindrops. I hid under my windbreaker and watched the shore. As we droned south, the mountains grew taller and pushed out through the coastal plain so that eventually they thrust directly from the edge of the mangroves. Their slopes were not pristine: the jungle was cut and torn like a mangy scalp, a patchwork of cultivated fields, burned patches, and bare red earth.

My great-grandfather was captivated and drawn to these mountains when he sailed along the Malaitan coast in 1892. "I could discern columns of smoke rising here and there in the recesses of the valleys. I pictured the rivers running down from the folded hills, and thought how cool the air must feel far up there above the heated plains by the shore. No white man had ever penetrated these recesses: that was the wonderful thought."

There may have been a grave beauty to the place, but what I felt was an immense hostility, as though the bush itself was urging me to keep my distance. I was not sure if this feeling came from the moment itself or from the history I had read, because the first white men to actually penetrate these hills brought with them a legacy worse than death.

The Kwaio version of this history would have been forgotten outside the bush had survivors not passed the details on to Roger Keesing, an anthropologist who lived among them in the 1960s. Before he died in 1993, Keesing and historian Peter Corris wrote down this story of Malaita's last stand against empire. I carried it with me. *Lightning Meets the West Wind* charted the collision that would define Kwaio culture for a century.

In the old days, wrote Keesing, the Kwaio hills were ruled not by chiefs but by *ramo*, warrior leaders whose power and wealth lay in their ability to collect and distribute blood money. The *ramo* were frequently assassins, quite willing to commit murder in order to exact vengeance on wrongdoers, to enforce the rigid codes of Kwaio conduct, or simply to collect bounty. They were generous givers of feasts and sacrifices to the ancestors, and therefore favored by the spirits. The most powerful *ramo* of all was Basiana, a warm and constant family man who also happened to have executed a score of people. He killed adulterers and thieves. He killed when he was insulted. He killed a cousin because the man had wrongly eaten part of a sacrificial pig. Basiana was proud, stubborn, and ruthless, and he surrounded himself with warriors armed with Snider rifles. The ancestors favored him.

Kwaio life under the *ramo* was not especially peaceful, but the people's good relationship with the ancestors brought certainty and contentment. All this began to change in the 1920s, when the colonial government demanded a yearly head tax—in pounds sterling, no less—from all able-bodied men. Since islanders were still trading in shell money and pigs, the tax forced them to work on white plantations, which was exactly why it had been introduced. The *ramo* saw this as a direct challenge to their rule.

The man charged with collecting the tax was the British district officer William Bell, a tough bastard with a hot temper. Bell had spent years trying to pacify the Malaitan warlords. Those who would not give up their violent ways were caught and hanged. Like Basiana, Bell was proud, stubborn, and ruthless. Like Basiana, he surrounded himself with armed men, though his were a constabulary of Christian converts. And like Basiana, he was thought to positively reek with *mana*. Bell and Basiana knew each other's reputations. They were destined for a confrontation.

Basiana watched as his neighbors to the north and the west were subjugated. He watched them forsake their ancestors in favor of the white man's god. As Bell's power and notoriety grew, the coastal Christians taunted the Kwaio *ramo*. *Missa Bello* will make women of you all, they said.

In 1927 word drifted down the coast that Bell was coming to Sinalagu Harbor to demand not just the head tax but all the rifles in Kwaio. This was too much to ask. Not only were rifles sacred (Basiana's had been consecrated to a warrior ancestor), but Bell had armed the coastal headmen who were loyal to him. The loss of their rifles would render the Kwaio *ramo* impotent and would mean the end of their sovereignty. Basiana called his fellow *ramo* together and made his case for an attack on Bell. Those who had traveled into the white man's world begged him not to do it. "The white people aren't the same," warned a man who had once been interned in the colonial prison. "If we kill them, our homeland will be finished. No child will be left, no woman will be left. They'll destroy everything." Basiana would not be denied his last stand. He reminded the *ramo* of the strength of their ancestors. Weapons were gathered, and priests killed dozens of pigs to enlist the ancestors' support.

Word of the impending attack tumbled down the mountainsides. When Bell arrived in Sinalagu Harbor, his coastal allies warned him to stay on his ship. Just shoot the bushmen on sight, suggested his Malaitan constables. Ignoring them, Bell went ashore, arranged the constables in and around his tax house, sat down behind a table at the front of the building, and opened his ledgers. A long line of warriors carrying rifles, clubs, spears, bows, and arrows appeared on the mountainside above. Basiana's men numbered at least two hundred. They screamed fearfully, but everyone knew that only two or three of their rifles were actually capable of firing, while Bell had a modern arsenal of two dozen rifles and two revolvers.

The warriors formed a line in front of Bell's table. Basiana concealed his rifle between his arm and his torso. He worked his way forward, surrounded by his kinsmen. Bell looked up from his scroll just in time to see Basiana raise his rifle butt with both hands and bring it down toward his head as though he was chopping wood. The district officer's skull exploded. His body went limp. Then the Kwaio warriors swarmed, cutting down Bell's party with a hail of spear, knife, and ax blows. Within minutes, Bell's assistant and thirteen loyal constables were dead. The clearing was strewn with blood, guts, and limbs. Only two of the attackers were killed. It was a glorious victory for Basiana. It was also his last.

Enemies both white and black salivated at the chance to exact revenge on the Kwaio. Hundreds of Malaitans volunteered to help avenge Bell and the dead policemen. Dozens of white planters and traders came forward, too. Within two weeks, an Australian warship steamed into Sinalagu Harbor. A punitive expedition of 50 sailors, 50 native police, 25 white volunteers, and 120 native carriers marched into the Kwaio hills. Villages were torched. Pigs were shot. Chemical defoliant was sprayed onto vegetable gardens. After six weeks the Australian navals retreated to Sydney, leaving the native police—most were Kwara'ae, the Kwaio's bitterest enemies—to administer justice. Now the Kwaio apocalypse began in earnest.

The native police used their new authority and firepower to exact vengeance for grievances going back generations. Dozens of

Kwaio were shot. The female relatives of Bell's killers were gang-raped. Some police hacked off the hands and feet of the dead, piled them on the corpses, then called out tauntingly to the victims' ancestors. Sacrificial stones were defiled. Ancestral relics and drums were smashed and burned. Skulls were taken from shrines and thrown into women's menstruation huts. This humiliation of Kwaio ancestors was the most devastating crime of all. Everyone knew that angry ancestors punished only their own descendants.

Basiana surrendered and was hanged with five of his allies. More than sixty other Kwaio were shot or hacked to death, and thirty died of dysentery in jail. But half a century later, Roger Keesing's informants put the death toll in the hundreds, because after the destruction of their shrines, the Kwaio were effectively abandoned by their ancestors for generations. Sacrifices stopped working. People fell ill. Taro stopped growing. Hundreds of people starved.

The apocalypse was both physical and metaphysical. The mountains still exuded sadness and hostility. No wonder I felt something like anger sweeping down from amid the sheets of hot rain.

The Seventh-day Adventist mission appeared on a bluff above the ocean, its tin roofs glistening like broken glass in the dull light. We tied up to a pier made from a heap of coral rock and hiked up toward the mission and its hospital. The Adventist compound was a jarringly ordered collection of offices, verandas, and hedgerows in complete discord with the tangle of vines and gardens that cradled it. A generator thrummed somewhere out of sight. A line of children in white shirts filed out of a cement-block church.

The screen door of a bungalow swung open, and a white woman emerged, her white dress billowing around her ankles. "Come in! Come in! Your lunch is ready," she bellowed.

I obeyed, and the door slammed shut behind me. The Adventists had been expecting me: I had radioed before leaving Auki, hoping to track down an Australian reputed to have strong connections with the Kwaio. This was not him. This was Geri Gaines, wife of one of the volunteer doctors at the mission hospital. I was transfixed by her. Her face was flushed with the heat. She was tall and broad, and so were her good intentions. We held hands as Geri said grace. Lunch was a hallucination from daytime television. Squeezable bottles of ketchup and processed cheese formed the centerpiece. Geri presented a great mound of Kraft Dinner, which filled the room with an electric orange glow. Then came a plate of chocolate chip cookies. It was heaven.

"We're here for three months—you don't think we're gonna eat yams the whole time, do you?" Geri said, squeezing a glistening slug of cheese onto her plate. "I had our food flown in all the way from El Aye!"

I told Geri I wanted to head into the Kwaio bush. She reached for my wrist and shook her head sadly.

"The pagans," she said. "Such a shame. Those poor people are so close to the mission, but they reef-yoos to change. They reef-yoos to progress. And do you know why? They are too scared of their *devil-devils*, that's why." Anyway, it wasn't a good time to go see the pagans, Geri said. Better to stay at the mission. There would be eight hours of worship tomorrow, it being Saturday.

"But why is it a bad time to see the pagans?" I asked.

"Lordy, where do I start?" said Geri. "First, they've got a dead devil priest to deal with up there. Then there's the Italian mess—"

"Italians?"

"They were fools, as far as I could see. They had it coming to them. And, oh look, here's our David."

David MacLaren looked as though he had been plucked from a Queensland cattle station: all scruffy beard, crow's feet, and sharp blue eyes. He quivered with nervous dingo energy. He glanced at our Kraft Dinner and gave me a knowing wink. Then he closed his eyes and said a whispered grace.

David was my connection. He had been popping in and out of

East Kwaio country for a decade, first to work as chief pathologist at the hospital, then as part of a touring open-heart surgery team, and now to study the place as part of his master's thesis in public health.

The Adventists ran the only proper hospital on Malaita, David said, but they had a problem. They offered medical services for two Solomon dollars (about the price of two coconuts), but the bush Kwaio still could not afford to set foot in the place. Why? Everything about the hospital—its architecture, its procedures, its toilets, its staff—violated Kwaio *kastom*.

Some examples: the hospital was a two-story building, but the ancestors forbade Kwaio men to walk under any structure where women had walked. Men's rooms happened to share the same roof as the maternity ward; this was an outrage, as a Kwaio man should never enter a women's delivery house. The hospital toilets were impressively hygienic, but they were also under that same roof; asking a Kwaio to sleep in such a building was like asking him to sleep inside an outhouse. Then there was the issue of bodily fluids: the Kwaio knew that sink water, which contained human saliva, mingled with toilet water somewhere in the hospital's drains. Fluid from one's mouth could not be mixed with *shit-shit*. No way. If a Kwaio entered such a sacrilegious building, he would insult the ancestors so much that they would withdraw their magic protection: gardens would fail, misfortune would spread through his village, sickness and disease would follow. He would have to sacrifice a dozen or more pigs to placate the dead. A hospital visit could cost a decade of accumulated wealth, not to mention future favors.

David had spent the last three years trying to figure out how to build a hospital wing that the ancestor-worshippers would actually use. He had won the trust and friendship of the pagan chiefs. That's why he could not let me just wander up the mountain. Not now.

"Because of the devil priest," said Geri.

David smiled the smile of a teenager whose mother had embarrassed him. "A *kastom* priest has died," he said. "They will be killing pigs up there, putting on a mortuary feast. All my contacts will be mourning. Nobody is allowed to travel in the district. It's a matter of respect. That's one thing."

"The other?"

"Well, you don't just wander into Kwaio country without the permission of a chief."

"Like the Italians did," said Geri.

"Who are these Italians?"

David sighed. The previous month, he said, a party of white men and women had arrived on the mail plane. They said they were doctors and were here to help. They found a guide and headed for the hills. It didn't go well at all. The doctors didn't heal anyone, but they did break all kinds of *tabus*. The worst thing they did was to carry toilet paper into the villages. It was unused, of course, but the unclean association was a screaming affront to the ancestors. The bumbling Italians made it back down to Atoifi, but a mob of angry pagans cut them off en route to the airstrip. The Kwaio wanted compensation. The Italians tried to negotiate. Big mistake. Machetes were drawn. One Italian was sliced pretty badly—he almost lost an arm, said David. Finally, the visitors agreed to patch things up the Kwaio way. They held a compensation ceremony and took the next plane out.

"You have to understand the pagans are incredibly suspicious of outsiders. They still haven't gotten over the 1927 massacre."

"So what am I going to do?" I asked, simultaneously irritated and vaguely relieved.

"Well, the next plane should come through in four days. You could stay here and talk to our patients," David said.

"We have worship tomorrow," said Geri hopefully.

David watched me grimace. "Or you could get out of the district. Leave the area of mourning, steer clear of anywhere the Italians walked. There is a Christian chief down in Sinalagu who might help you. Peter Laetebo. He worked with Roger Keesing back in the sixties."

"Sinalagu!" Geri sang out. "The youth group is putting on a worship there tomorrow. You could go with them, 'specially if you paid for their gas."

I would have retreated to Honiara the next day if there had been a plane out. I felt crushed by the sodden sky, harassed by the mountains that seemed to want to push the entire mission into the sea. It was all wrong, this place, and also my being here. But the plan was set. I would follow the ghost of William Bell into Sinalagu Harbor, find my heathens, and get the hell out.

I left Atoifi at dawn in an aluminum runabout loaded with ten scrubbed Christians and one portable karaoke machine. We pushed through the barrier reef and headed south. The heavy sky had pressed the ripples out of the sea. Six black dolphins leapt in the distance. We skirted a series of ragged limestone cliffs that eventually ruptured, providing a passage into a vast, diamond-shaped lagoon. The boatman deposited the Adventist youths at the north end of the lagoon, where coral grew in the shallows like giant clumps of rotting cauliflower. Then we headed for the southern corner of the harbor, where the mountains were higher and steeper. The boatman pointed to a low bluff. "Mr. Bell," he said. "That's where they killed him."

He cut the outboard engine and lifted it from the water. We poled through the shallows toward a cluster of huts on stilts. Gounabusu. I hopped out and sank to my knees in muck. The boatman went home. The villagers ignored me completely until I found Peter Laetebo, the chief. He was an ancient and vaguely muddled fellow. He had wrapped a dirty yellow dishtowel around his waist like a sarong, and his belly trembled above it like a deflated balloon. He took me to someone's hut, where we sat on a wooden bench and I tried to explain myself to a rapidly expanding jury. One by one, the village men came in, and I handed out my business card, which read "journalist." The chief smiled and nodded knowingly. On his right sat a burly young man who wore a thick shell money necklace and a Pearl Jam T-shirt; he had bleached his hair blond. Pearl Jam was silent, but I could tell by the way he nodded he was my ally. Things were going quite well, I thought, until the one-eyed man arrived.

He said nothing at first. He just gazed at me with that one angry eye while pus oozed from the other. He wore a bandanna around his head and an army fatigue vest. He slapped his thigh with his machete. It looked sharp. He stroked the hairs on his chin.

"White men are millionaires," he said in pidgin.

"Pardon?"

"I want to know why you *stap* here."

The other men fell silent. I explained myself again and threw in a blurb about promoting tourism or something equally beneficial. I watched the one-eyed man's fingers tighten around his machete.

"This is my land. Those gardens up there on the hill belong to *mifala*. We don't need white men to come and steal the stories *blong mifala*. We don't need another Keesing to make himself rich from our culture."

Keesing? How strange, I thought, as blood rushed to my cheeks. The anthropologist had spent two decades mucking about the bush with the pagans. He didn't get rich, and he was never particularly interested in the Christians down here on the coast. I didn't say any of these things.

The one-eyed man held my business card up with both hands, then slowly ripped it in two. We all watched the pieces flutter to the floor. I thought about William Bell seated at his tax-collecting table, and compulsively I stood up, perhaps shaking just a little. This was a Christian mission village. Christians didn't chop visitors to bits.

"Um," I said. "Sorry. Um, there must be a mistake. I must have made a mistake."

"Yes! You sorry! You should have asked before coming here. You no ask. *Yu mas stap insaed long kanu blong yu and go nao.*"

I had decided that looking at the one-eyed man was a bad idea since I could not keep my gaze from shifting over to that right eye socket, where sometimes a tiny bloodshot sliver of eyeball did appear. I looked instead at the floor, wondering why the chief and the others weren't helping me. What felt like hours passed before the one-eyed man finally stomped down the stairs and trudged away across the dirt.

"Everything is fine, mate," said my ally with the bleached blond hair. He spoke in English with an unmistakable Aussie accent. "I'll take you into the mountains tomorrow. But now, you should come to my house. Right now."

The chief nodded gravely.

My ally introduced himself as Roni Butala. His house was a tin-and-timber shack on the other side of the village, past the South Seas Evangelical Church. I made myself small on Roni's veranda and accepted a cup of tea from his mother. Roni called together a few cousins, then disappeared. The cousins remained. Two of them carried long bush knives. One had a bow and arrow.

"Maybe you should *stap* inside," Roni's mother said nervously.

An hour later, Roni returned with the one-eyed man, who had adopted a more diplomatic aspect.

"Everything is fine," said Roni.

"You are welcome here," said the one-eyed man, whose name was Samuel. "*Yu savve walkabaot.*"

"Thank you," I said.

Samuel offered me his hand.

"Come back inside long house," Roni's mother called to me, urgently now.

I accepted Samuel's hand. His palm was sticky, like wet to-

bacco. He shook mine aggressively. He sneered at me, then retreated.

"We will have to give him some money before you leave," said
Roni.

"Roni!" squawked the mother from the veranda. "Oh, Roni!
Why did you let *fren blong yu* shake the hand of Samuel? This is
bad. Oh, this is bad *tumas*."

"What is she talking about?" I asked Roni. He just rolled his eyes.
But I already knew Samuel's handshake was more than a handshake.
There was a coldness I couldn't seem to wipe from my palm.

That night, Peter Laetebo joined Roni and me on the veranda.
The chief had put on a button-down business shirt. In the lamplight, I could see his facial tattoos shine beneath his white stubble.
They looked like unfinished games of tic-tac-toe. The chief wanted
to *storian*. He had been a pagan priest when he met Keesing, the anthropologist, back in the 1960s, he announced.

"But you're a Christian now," I said.

"*Hem i tru tumas ia*," the chief said, slapping his knee proudly.
"When I was a heathen, life was good, but it was expensive. Every
time my *pikinini* got sick, I had to give up money and pigs to the
devils . . ."

"Ancestors," said Roni under his breath.

"One day *soniboy blong mi* got sick," said Peter. "Fever, belly-
run. I was tired of sacrificing so I brought the boy down to the
mission here. The pastor put his hands on *soniboy* and prayed: not
long, two, three hours, *nomo*. Then the boy woke up and started to
cry. I said, '*Disfala God, hem i tru wan!*'"

Peter had moved his family down to Gounabusu and learned
to follow the new *tabus*. The South Seas Evangelical Church forbade alcohol, tobacco, and betel nut. It forbade any kind of ancestor tribute. Women had to cover their breasts. Those things were a
bother. But Christian life helped the chief to save money: he could
keep all his pigs for himself, and he didn't have to spend weeks in

isolation after sacrifices. So Peter the pagan priest was now a church elder.

Peter couldn't talk for long. His second son was now gravely ill, and the pastor hadn't been able to help. Peter would be sitting at the boy's side for the rest of the night.

"What about you, Roni? Are you a Christian?" I asked when Peter left us.

Roni looked at his mother and hesitated. "We have church in the morning, mate," he said. "I'll take you up the mountain after that."

I went to bed—or rather, to my grass mat—and hoped, silently, that Roni would rescind his offer. I longed to leave East Kwaio. There was a diffuse hostility to the place, something beyond the heat, the stickiness, the constant drip and rot, beyond even one-eyed Samuel's anger. I felt it spreading through my joints like a poisonous ache. I felt it in the damp night air as I lay awake on the floor of Roni's house. I felt it through the sleepless night, and then I felt it amplified by the sound of a church bell, which began clanging long before dawn.

My legs and feet had been scratched countless times during my trek across the island. What began as nicks had suddenly developed into spectacular abscesses. Purple blisters spread out under my skin. They were streaked like marble with faint intrusions of pus. An inexplicable boil had risen on my little toe and was threatening to erupt. My head throbbed. What was it I wanted from the pagans? I couldn't remember. What could they possibly have to say about the spiritual crisis of the Solomons? I couldn't imagine.

Roni's mother greeted me on the veranda. "Oh, no!" she said when she saw me. "Oh, Roni! *Mi tellem yu finis for no lettem Samuel for touchim disfala fren blong yu!*"

Roni put a hand on my forehead. "Fever," he said. "Now you *must* climb the mountain with me. It will take *kastom* medicine to fight a curse like this."

I wanted to tell Roni that it was not Samuel's handshake that had made me sick. It was the bad air, the unwashed hands, the mosquitoes, the septic sludge that dribbled into the harbor, the sickening heaviness of the air. It was climate and biology that had got to me, just as it had got to Europeans for centuries. The Australian navals who had charged into the Kwaio bush looking for Bell's murderers in 1927 experienced the same thing. Many were carried back down to their ship on stretchers, covered in septic ulcers, shivering with malaria, and dripping with diarrhea.

Just to spite Samuel, we put on clean shirts and attended Sunday mass, which was a show of pure evangelical anarchy. Hands waved. Eyes rolled. The people reassured their god. They shouted that he was the greatest, the mightiest. "Hallelujah!" they wailed. "Hallelujah!"

Roni and I slipped out midprogram. We followed a trail that zigzagged up the mountainside, through sweet potato gardens, limestone rubble, and fallow patches choking with woody brambles. The slope was steeper than the tin roof of the church. The air was dead calm and cruelly hot. My clothes were soaking wet.

"You were loud in church this morning," I said to Roni. "So you are a Christian."

"When in Rome," he said, gazing up into the forest.

"Come on, Roni, which side are you on?"

"I am on the side of my ancestors, that's which side."

Roni had grown up in Gounabusu. He was a smart kid. He had won a scholarship to Massey University and spent four years in New Zealand. That's why his English was so good. The Kiwi girls loved Roni, but he was startled by their *kastom*. One white girl invited Roni home to meet her parents in the suburbs. When she put her arm around him and told her father, "This is my boyfriend," Roni screamed and fled. Later, the girl explained to him that in New Zealand it was an honor to be introduced to your girlfriend's father. Roni told her: "If your father was Kwaio, he would have taken a knife and killed me."

Roni had studied plant science and fraternized with the granola crowd. He returned to Malaita as an environmentalist. He also carried a new sense of Kwaio otherness and took to wandering up into the hills, and into the past. He smoked and storied-on with the patriarchs and pagan priests. He grew dreadlocks—not matted like Bob Marley's but braided as he imagined his ancestors' had been. (Roni's dreads were gone now. His mother had finally ordered him to cut them off. She was worried the ancestors would recognize Roni as one of their own and try to influence him.) Now he was helping to rebuild the traditional school that Keesing had once established on the mountainside, a place for the pagans to learn to write down the names of their ancestors, to pass on their *kastom*, and to study mathematics, so they would know when the Christians were trying to cheat them.

"So you really are a pagan," I said.

"I went to Christian school. I believe in God. I know he is powerful. But if I had to choose," he said, "I would choose the ancestors."

"I don't understand. If you believe in the Christian God, then you must believe he is more powerful. That's what the church teaches."

"Look. Up there," he said, pointing to a nearby ridge. Most of the land had been cleared, but a clump of trees had been left on the crest. "Those forests are *tabu*. That's where people keep their ancestors. Now imagine you lived here. When you died, your children would take your skull and put it in the *kastom* hut so your grandchildren could make sacrifices to you, and so you could stay with your own land forever. That's our *kastom*. That's what I want."

We pushed on, climbing up into the shadows of the rain forest. Roots splayed out from great tree trunks like webbed feet. Vines trailed overhead. Condensation dripped from ferns. We splashed up a creek bed, past tiny clearings thick with taro and papaya. We climbed into the soft belly of a slow-moving mist. It was cooler there. I forgot my headache, forgot the malevolence of the mountain, didn't think twice when a face appeared through the leaves, then disappeared with a rush of breath.

We rounded a bend and stepped into the iron age. The clearing was all blackened palm stumps, smashed limestone, and fresh-churned mud through which pigs rooted vigorously and women dashed, bare breasts swinging. The women ducked into the doorways of thatch huts and watched me from the shadows. I could see the glowing embers of their tin pipes. The face from the mist appeared at the top of the clearing, a teenage boy in soccer shorts, now wielding a machete the length of his torso. Beneath him, sitting on a white rock, cross-legged, stoking a pipe and smiling like a garden gnome, was Roni's friend Diakake Doaka, who was introduced as chief but may have been more of a priest, and who liked to be called Jack. He had the same worn fishing hat as Henry Fonda in *On Golden Pond*. Jack may have been an eloquent orator in the Kwaio tongue, but he had an even worse grasp of Solomons pidgin than I. Much of what I pass on here is Roni's translation of our conversation.

Jack was pleased to see Roni. He was particularly relieved to see me. He told me he had had a dream about me the previous night. "The grandfathers told me you were not welcome in Gounabusu," he said. "You must never sleep there again. The Christians will try to poison you."

Jack seemed gratified when I told him that I was ill and that I was keen to see the *kastom* doctor Roni had promised me.

"Soon," said Jack with a satisfied chuckle. "The *lamo* is on his way."

In his book *Kwaio Religion*, Keesing wrote that the Kwaio worldview is reflected in the social geography of their settlements. The men are literally on top. Jack's village matched Keesing's description. The highest point in the village was dominated by the priest's hut, where sacred things were kept. (There were skulls inside, but I didn't see them. Being sullied by my time in Gounabusu, I wasn't allowed to so much as peek in the doorway.) It was a quaint cottage, the only one in the village surrounded by plants and a bamboo fence. Next down the slope was the unmarried men's clubhouse. This was my favorite: a fort raised on stilts six feet off the ground that looked like the kind of playhouse an investment banker might build for his kids. It had a neat pitched roof and a timber floor, on which were scattered pieces of a radio. (A functioning radio would have been useless anyway, because the price of batteries had tripled since the tension began.)

In the middle of the village were a couple of communal huts, where women cooked and children rolled in the dirt. Smoke rose from one thatch roof like steam from a wet lawn. The communal huts had special rooms just for pigs. "Our *pik-piks* are important," said Jack. "We love them almost as much as our sons. No good suppose somebody steal 'em." Farther downhill were the women's communal sleeping huts, which were austere. At the bottom corner of the village, where all the mud and pig piss eventually trickled, was a tiny hovel, not much bigger than a doghouse. A shy girl peeked out from behind. I tried not to gawk at her. This was the place where women waited out their monthly menstruation time.

David MacLaren had explained this geography to me and insisted that it shouldn't be taken literally. The Kwaio didn't really think that women were lowly and impure and that men were more holy. No, they both had their own sacredness, and the menstruation hut was a kind of earthly mirror image of the priest's house. But everyone knows that sewage flows downhill. And here in Jack's village, it was the women's place to wallow in it.

The village was only a hundred days old. Apparently, the community—which consisted of an extended family of about twenty—had moved to avoid a spiritual catastrophe. A man had fallen ill at their last settlement. He was near death when Jack received a dream in which the ancestors revealed the cause of the illness. A woman had urinated, or perhaps begun her menstruation cycle, in one of the village huts. Jack knew that the grandfathers' displeasure about this defilement could only be relieved by moving and starting again. So here they were in the fresh mud.

Jack's wife—nobody told me her name—was using a stone to smash a heap of *gnali* nuts she had collected in the forest. They tasted like almonds. Mosquitoes rose in the late-afternoon haze. Jack and his wife were highly amused to see me spread insect repellent on my legs. "*Waet man weak tumas*," I explained, and Jack nodded in agreement. I was miserable. My joints felt as though they had been battered with a pig club. The boil on my toe had ruptured obscenely. I wrapped it in duct tape. Where was the damn *kastom* doctor? It was not that I imagined any sort of magic would heal me. I wanted to see the *kastom* doctor in the same way a tired mountaineer wants to see the top of Everest. The doctor's arrival would mean the beginning of my journey back out of East Kwaio.

"I think you have a good life here," I lied to Jack.

He nodded and explained that life in the Kwaio bush was good because he and his family still obeyed the rules that a giant snake had imparted to the ancestor Ofama, 125 generations before. Respect the ancestors and their shrines. Don't steal pigs or women that aren't yours. Don't kill without a good reason. Take care of your own ground, your pigs, and your taro gardens. Be tidy. Don't use your house as a toilet. All quite reasonable. Oh, and men must never eat from a plate used by women. Men should live and shit uphill, women downhill. Women and the things they touch should never, ever, gain more altitude than men. Men's bathing water should be diverted so it doesn't mix with women's pollution somewhere downhill. Priests should offer extravagant sacrifices of burned pig to the ancestors, and the meat should be eaten by the priest alone. Etcetera.

My feminist friends nod when they hear these stories. They tell me that *kastom*, myth, and *tabu* are tools of the patriarchy, of powerful men pushing everyone else down, especially women (i.e., in the menstruation hut).

That may be true, but I was less interested in the politics of the rules than I was in their mythical origins. The bishop of Malaita had introduced me to the theories of French linguist Maurice Leenhardt, who had lived on New Caledonia between 1909 and 1926. Leenhardt concluded that Melanesian myths were not fictions plucked from the ether so much as they were an expression of lived experience. By this I believe he meant that, though Melanesians could not control their natural world through technology, their myths provided tools to help them adapt to it. Every day they saw how the order of the world depended on the standards of their conduct.

In some ways, Leenhardt's theory seemed to fit here in East Kwaio. When the ancestors were honored and their rules obeyed, life generally went well. But when the rules were broken, people got sick, crops failed, and women became infertile. Sometimes natural calamities occurred without warning, but the Kwaio always seemed to find a reason (a shrine disturbed, for example, or a house fouled by urine) to connect these events to the ancestors' wrath. Things could be made better only by offering a sacrifice to manipulate the forces of the supernatural realm in their favor, or at least to placate them.

I couldn't see how the edicts of Melanesian ancestors differed from the exacting rules that Moses had handed down to the Israelites in the Book of Leviticus, or the bizarre prohibitions—no consumption of fish without scales, for example—still maintained by the Seventh-day Adventists. Humans crave structure. We crave rules. Where few are required, we extrapolate; we tease them out of our myths. Obey, or the gods will exact vengeance. Obey, or you will burn in hell. Obey, or the taro will rot in the ground.

All Jack Doaka had to do to reinforce his faith was to look at the world beyond the Kwaio hills. It was going to hell in a hand-basket. Jack had no doubt that all the great evils of Solomon Islands life stemmed from Christian transgression. War? That's what Christians did; it's what the government—which was really just an arm of the church—brought to East Kwaio in 1927. Sexually transmitted diseases? They were spread by Christians who defied the old sex *tabus*. Poverty? That came from dishonoring the ancestors, which Christians were always keen to do. Christians were greedy. They chased money and forgot their place in the world.

Not only had Christians rejected their grandfathers in favor of one from a faraway island—how crazy was that?—but they had followed the missionaries to the coast and given up their ancestral lands. This was the biggest crime of all, said Jack. Most Christians, he said, couldn't even find their own land anymore. How could there be peace when men were living on other men's land? "The grannies warned me that one day the people would rise up and start killing each other over the land," said Jack. "See what happened to the Malaitans who didn't listen, the ones who left the land of them and went off to Guadalcanal. *Bigfala trouble nao!* We don't have those fights here, because we listen to the grannies and we stay close to them. We stay on the land *blong mifala nomo.*" It was clear that the Christians' luck had run out, said Jack. They had completely fallen out of favor with the ancestors, and now they were paying for it. They had no power. Just look at Peter Laetebo, the chief down in Gounabusu.

"What about him?" I said. "God saved his boy's life. That's why he became a Christian."

Jack thought that was hilarious. While he cackled and wiped tears from his eyes, Roni explained the joke. Just yesterday, Chief Peter had paid Jack a load of shell money so that Jack would sacrifice a pig for the sake of his other sick son. The young man was sick because he had gone and cut down a tree near a pagan gravesite. The ancestors were naturally furious.

"Years ago, Peter could have made this sacrifice himself," said Jack. "But now that he is a Christian, he is unclean. He has lost all his power. He has to come ask *mifala* if he wants a favor from the ancestors."

So much for spiritual fidelity. Roni gave a satisfied smile. He said that Peter was so impure, he wasn't even allowed to enter the pagan villages. But Roni could. The pagans knew *he* wasn't a real Christian.

Jack said he did not mean to be disrespectful. He was sure that Jesus was a strong ancestor. It was just that he was an ancestor from another island; it was natural that his power would be weak here on Malaita. The only Christians Jack knew who actually wielded power were the *tasiu*. Yes, said Jack. The Melanesian Brotherhood. They had *savve*.

I cannot remember the *kastom* doctor's face. Later, Roni explained that this was part of his magic. I do remember that he was a tall bony man and that he wandered out of the forest carrying a black umbrella and a woven handbag full of betel nuts and lime. He did not introduce himself. Nobody said hello to him. He reminded me of a crow. The doctor squatted on a log and watched us silently for a time. He husked a betel nut with his teeth. He pulled out a bamboo container from which he spooned a finger of lime into his mouth, along with the betel. He chewed until the pink juice dribbled down his chin. finally, he let out a bored sigh, lifted himself up, and strode toward me on those long, scaly legs. He paused in front of me, cocked his head, and cooed softly.

"Take your shirt off," translated Roni.

I took my shirt off, then realized the whole village had come together to watch the spectacle. The only people not paying attention were two teenage boys, who were engrossed in picking through each other's scalps and biting to death whatever it was they found.

I sat still. The doctor paced around me as though inspecting a show dog. He nodded and hummed knowingly. He ran a hand along my shoulder blades. I shivered. He kneaded the skin on my shoulders and along my spine. That was quite nice. Then I felt the doctor's breath on my right shoulder blade. I couldn't see him, but my nostrils quivered at the mulchlike scent of betel nut on his breath. I could feel both his hands cupped against my shoulder, and I could hear the rush of air as he sucked and blew through them. As the exhalations came harder and faster, I could feel spit striking my skin and I could hear the terrible cough and gurgle of the doctor's effort, which reached a troubling crescendo and then ceased with a loud pop.

The crowd gave a communal "Ahhhh."

"What? What?" I said.

"Lookim!" said Roni, pointing to the doctor, who had re-treated a couple of yards. The doctor was retching and holding his throat. Then he let out a tremendous cough, and something came flying out of his mouth, much as a hairball might issue from the throat of a cat. He picked the projectile out of the dirt and showed it to me. It was a tiny wooden disc. It was red, but dusted with lime.

"That is what made you sick," the doctor said quietly. "*Wanfala* rubbish man down in Gounabusu put this inside your skin." He bit a corner off the disk. "There. Now I have killed the *swear*.* You'll feel better tomorrow."

---

* *Swear* is the Solomon Islands pidgin word for "curse," a translation that re-veals the cultural gap between Melanesians and Europeans. If swearing—or cursing—at people is the same as wishing them ill, then it makes sense that Melanesians view those words as synonyms. It also shows their inherent belief in supernatural power. For example, a British trader who yelled "God damn your eyes!" at an islander wasn't actually attempting to blind the man. He was just swearing. But for Melanesians, an invocation is an invocation. There is no difference between a curse and a *swear*.

The doctor warned me not to spend another night down in Gounabusu. His magic would not protect me from my enemies in the Christian village, he said. Then he extended his black umbrella and strode off into the forest.

The rain finally came, and so did night. We took shelter in the communal hut with the women, who served us unseasoned taro steamed inside lengths of bamboo. We ate with our hands. Everyone mumbled and joked quietly. I lay down on a wooden rack uphill from the women and watched them poke at the coals of the little fire glowing on the dirt between us. I could hear pigs grunting softly behind a leaf wall. I began to feel better. Not from the doctor's cure, I told myself. Oh, no. The doctor and I both knew that his little bark disc had come not from under the skin of my back but from his handbag. It was still caked in lime. This was not the miracle I had been waiting for. Still, I did feel strangely comforted and unthreatened here among Jack's clan. The air felt lighter than that on the coast. The mountain, when you were on it, was not hostile. Despite the outward chaos of pigs and mud and burned forest, I felt an ethereal, ordered calm. The wounds on my calves were beginning to dry out in the smoky air. The ache began to subside.

It struck me that the mountain Kwaio led a peaceful life. It was paganism without the bite.

"This is a far cry from the days of blood feuding and those *ramo* assassins," I whispered to Roni. "So peaceful."

He translated for Jack.

"*Ramo* . . ." said Jack. "*Ramo* . . . Ah, *lamo!*" The Kwaio, I remembered, substituted "l" for "r" when they spoke.

"*Ramo!*" exclaimed Roni, and they both laughed.

"What's so funny?" I asked.

"You think the *lamo* are gone? Every village still has one! If someone seduces one of the daughters here, or steals a pig, or murders someone, Jack will gather a bounty of pigs and shell money so he can pay the *lamo* to go kill whoever did it."

"Tell me more!"

"Why didn't you just ask the *lamo* when he was here?" said Roni.

"Wha—you never introduced me to a *lamo!*"

Roni translated, and Jack laughed so hard tears came to his eyes.

"The *lamo* was here all afternoon, but you ignored him, so he just healed you and went home," said Roni.

The doctor was the *lamo*. The doctor was the assassin.

Six months after I left East Kwaio, a new administrator arrived at the Atoifi Adventist Hospital. He hiked out into the forest to measure a plot of land. He did not know that the land was the subject of an ownership dispute. A *lamo* met the administrator in that field and cut off his head. The Kwaio have always been passionate about their land. The severed head was recovered. The assassin was not.

17

Raiders of the Nono Lagoon

*I shall define cannibalism as a cult construction which
refers to the inordinate capacity of the Other to consume
human flesh as an especially delectable food.*

—GANANATH OBEYESEKERE,
"Cannibal Feasts in Nineteenth-Century Fiji,"
in *Cannibalism and the Colonial World*

The believer never forgets his first miracle. Mine remains utterly
clear. It came to me high on a forested ridge above the skull grot-
toes, the sacrificial slabs, and the vast cradle of New Georgia
Island's Marovo Lagoon. That's where I disobeyed the chief of
Mbarejo and performed my ritual in the dead calm of afternoon. I
made trees shake and birds take flight. I transformed the muggy
stillness into a maelstrom of tearing wind, groaning tree trunks, hot
raindrops, and churning mud. Let that be my story. I did make it
rain, and for a good cause, too.

It was never my intention to explore the lagoons of the Solomon

Islands' Western Province. The *Southern Cross* had ventured as far west as New Georgia in 1866, but the Anglicans never had the gumption to leave any teachers there. "New Georgia has been known to the Mission chiefly as an island inhabited by bloodthirsty head-hunters and cannibals," wrote my great-grandfather in explaining the mission's reticence.

I was carried west by a moment of serendipitous frustration. A few days after returning from Malaita to Honiara, I was assured of the imminent departure of both the *Eastern Trader* and the MV *Temotu*, and had hauled my pack down to the port, ready for the five-day journey to Santa Cruz and my Nukapu.

"You go when?" I asked the mate of the *Eastern Trader*.

"*Taem disfala Temotu hemi i go,*" he said.

"You go when?" I asked the engineer of the MV *Temotu*.

"Maybe next week," he said.

"Bloody liar," I fumed. "You have said the same thing for a month."

He just laughed.

A curtain of rain swept across the pier. It lifted the betel husks and the garbage, carrying them in slow-moving streams around my feet. I had had enough. I would not be shackled to Honiara any longer. I marched to the next pier.

"You go when?" I asked a sailor who was leaning on the rails of the first ship I saw.

"*Mi go wea?*" he replied.

"No," I said. "I don't care where you go. I'll go anywhere as long as it's today."

"*Cranky waet man,*" he said. "*Mifala go neva. Sip, hem bagarup.*"

I tried the *Compass Rose*, whose steel deck was fully loaded with oil barrels and rebar.

"You go when?" I asked a fat woman sitting with her children on the open deck.

"Good question," she said.

I tried the *Isabella*. It would leave for Santa Isabel the following morning.

Then the *Baruku*. It would leave for somewhere someday.

Then the *Tomoko*, a once sleek ferry that looked as though it had been pelted with rocks. The *Tomoko*'s engines were rumbling. A sooty cloud was erupting from its smokestack. People were tossing babies, bags of rice, and grass mats into arms that reached out from its long passenger decks. Those arms were as black as beetle wings, the color of New Georgia skin. If the *Tomoko* was going anywhere, it was heading west, to New Georgia. Santa Cruz was east, but I didn't care.

"You go when? You go when?" I hollered. The bowline went slack.

"*Mifala go nao!*" a voice yelled back, and a muscular hand dropped down from the upper deck. I reached for it and was pulled into a crowd of steaming bodies.

"First class! First class!" I shouted. The owner of the hand that had pulled me aboard led me through a passageway—the floor was a slippery paste of oil, spit, crushed insects, and a disturbing slurry that seeped from the ship's head—and then, to my shock, through a door that read: VIP Cabin. It was a miracle. One bunk was piled high with old computers. The other was mine. I smashed six cockroaches, blew air into my mattress, lay down, and let the ship carry me away.

Through the porthole, I watched the sea and the sky merge into night. Tarpaulins swayed. Doors knocked. Cockroaches crept into the folds of my clothing. The ship rolled me gently to sleep.

I was awoken not by the light and bustle of dawn but by stillness. The *Tomoko* had stopped moving completely. The cough and rattle of the engine had settled to a restful hum. I listened. Finally, there came a shout in the distance, followed by a hoot from the bridge. Then, splashing water. I felt my way out onto the deck. A searchlight shot from the bridge into the blackness. It was reflected back by a dozen pairs of eyes, which drifted close and became men in slim dugout canoes. They paddled alongside the ship and passed baskets of yam, taro, and bushels of betel nut up over the rails. Flats of tinned meat and sacks of Delite Flour were passed down. The trade was carried out in murmurs until the *Tomoko*'s engine rumbled to life again. The ship pushed forward. For a while, the market men clung to our side, their canoes pulled along like lampreys on a great shark. Then we left them behind.

As the stars faded, islands took shape around us. To port: dark coves wrapped in jungle, ridges climbing toward clouds and the red edge of dawn. To starboard: a low band of shadows stretched into the distance like sections of a long, crumbling wall. We had entered Marovo, longest of the lagoons that surround New Georgia and its smaller neighbors like a series of enormous moats, protected from the open ocean by a sixty-mile string of barrier islands.

I was intrigued by these lagoons specifically because my great-grandfather had *not* ventured here. The region was considered too dangerous for the *Southern Cross* in 1892. My great-grandfather formed his opinion of New Georgia on his visit to Santa Isabel, a half-day's sail to the east, which he described as a "hunting ground" for raiders from New Georgia. "They are, perhaps, the worst of all cannibals, and great is the dread in which they are held by all who live in these waters, whilst the effect of their raids has been that, of the hundred miles of Ysabel, eighty are practically uninhabited. The people have either been wiped out and eaten, or else they have migrated to safer quarters." The Isabelan survivors, who lived in a constant state of dread, sought refuge in tree houses or in hilltop fortresses.

By 1892 the New Georgian "savage" had taken on a mythic aspect in the eighteenth-century European imagination, thanks to the shocking tales seafarers related on their return from the lagoons. These days, postcolonial theorists can't agree if many early accounts of head-hunting and cannibalism in the South Pacific were based on fact or European imagination. Revisionist historian William Arens proposed in *The Man-Eating Myth* that the cannibals who always seemed to inhabit the edges of the Western world were largely the product of intellectual conjuring. He argued that explorers, missionaries, and anthropologists constructed their cannibals using secondhand stories and the glue of their own primordial fantasies. The cannibal was a projection of European psychoses rather than an accurate representation of history. Princeton anthropologist Gananath Obeyesekere later deconstructed so-called eyewitness accounts of great cannibal feasts in Fiji to prove that those stories were fictions written to satiate a public hungry for a taste of tropical savagery.

The revisionists aren't suggesting that head-hunting and cannibalism never happened, but rather that cannibal tales reveal more about their believers than they do about the people they describe. Europeans wanted to believe in headhunters as much as they wanted to believe in their own heroes. Both provided psychological fodder for empire-building.

The colonial historian Austin Coates used head-hunting lore as justification for British intervention in the Solomons: islanders needed to be ruled to prevent them from killing each other off. But a perusal of early reports reveals that it was the arrival of Europeans that precipitated the worst violence.

For all the supposedly unchecked carnage, some historians suggest that the New Georgians may have established a steady state of feuding, trading, and head-taking before white men arrived. Yes, the New Georgians were sure that human heads contained concentrated *mana*, and that the raising of a canoe house, the launching of a war canoe, the honoring of ancestors, all required skull offerings. But raids were annual affairs, carefully planned, steeped in ritual, magic, and communal work. Expeditions took weeks of planning and travel, and involved barely a few hours of fighting, the grand finale of a yearly cycle of preparation, feasting, carving, gardening, and trading.

It was a shocking, yet quite sustainable, way of life until white traders began arming their allies with axes and guns. Although European governments had agreed to ban the sale of firearms to islanders in the 1890s, apparently only Germany, which controlled Santa Isabel, enforced the ban. The gun-toting tribes of New Georgia were rendered superhuman compared to their unarmed prey on Santa Isabel, whose tree forts were not much protection against lead shot. That was one factor. The other was European tinkering with the supply and demand of skulls. The Royal Navy punished unruly lagoon dwellers by smashing skull collections that had taken centuries to accumulate. This caused a crisis of *mana*. In response, the Roviana chief, Ingava, put together the greatest war machine the region had ever seen—hundreds of warriors, hundreds of breech-loading Snider rifles, and at least two European whaleboats—then spent much of the next decade replenishing his stock of skulls.

Amazingly, the lagoon population only really began its downfall *after* the Royal Navy had put a stop to all the raiding. The pioneering anthropologist W. H. R. Rivers noted a spectacular drop in birth rates among communities on the Vella Lavella and Eddystone islands in the first two decades of the twentieth century. People had stopped getting married and having children. Rivers concluded that this reproductive lethargy was, in fact, triggered by the ban on head-hunting, which was essential to the fabric of religious and community existence. Without head-hunting, islanders simply lost their zest for life. They grew bored and listless. Communities were dying from *tedium vitae*. The only hope, he felt, was for Melanesians to embrace Christianity with the same passion and vigor as they had their old beliefs. Rivers, who did much of his traveling aboard the *Southern Cross*, would likely have suggested the Church of England as a cure, but it was far too late for the Anglicans to set up shop in New Georgia; Methodists and Seventh-day Adventists had gained a foothold in 1902, and their charismatic worship turned out to be just the heartfelt substitute for cannibalism that Rivers had prescribed.

A century later, it was clear that New Georgia had got its groove back. There was no shortage of children in the village of Seghe, the *Tomoko*'s first landfall. We pulled up to a coral rock jetty, and all hell broke loose. Passengers tumbled over the rails and scrambled away from the ship as though it were on fire. It might as well have been. The head had been overflowing like a fountain all night, transforming the ship's passageways into a frothy slough of gastrointestinal horrors.

I bought a coconut in the market that had sprung up at the foot of the jetty, and sat under a tree, sipping the sweet milk, and I let the *Tomoko* pull away without me. The market disappeared, too, carried away on the backs of women with shining skin and frizzy hair bleached surreally blond by the sun. Seghe fell silent. I picked up my pack and wandered through the palms.

There was a line of plywood shacks strung between the sea and a vast lawn, which steamed in the morning sunlight. That lawn, it turned out, was all that remained of the airfield the Americans had built during the war. There was a red shack beside the field. I went inside and found the air agent yelling into a radio phone. The only point of interest in Seghe, he told me, lay in the lagoon at the end of the runway, where there was an American fighter plane from the war. It shone in the depths like a great silver fish.

"You could fly back to Honiara," he said. "The plane will be in this afternoon."

"Skulls. Maybe I could look for skulls," I said.

"There's a girl you could have. Over at the village rest house," he said.

"Or crocodiles. I could look for crocodiles," I said.

He shrugged and pointed through the chicken wire of his window to where a few men were lying under a tree. "That boy will help you. He has a *kanu*. Hey! John Palmer!"

John Palmer was the tallest Melanesian I had ever laid eyes on, topping out at about six-foot-six if you included his hair: his head was shaved except for an island of braided dreadlocks on the crown. He had bound the strands together so their splayed ends resembled the fronds of a palm tree. He wore army fatigue shorts. He had the wide eyes of a child, but to be accurate, he was not a boy. He was at least twenty-five.

The air agent told John he should quit whatever mischief he was up to and take me away to look for skulls and crocodiles. I could come back to Seghe and catch the plane out in a week.

John suggested I come stay with him on his island. If I had strong legs, he could also show me the Nonotongere.

"Nonotongere?" I asked.

The air agent interrupted. "Crocodiles, fine. Skulls, fine," he barked, then poked me in the chest with his finger. "But don't you lead John Palmer astray. Don't you put his Christian soul at risk. Leave that stone alone." I left it for the moment.

I was suspicious of John Palmer. I wasn't sure why he was so willing to help me. "You want money?" I asked.

"*Yu savve pem petrol long kanu blong mi*," he said hopefully. Gas money.

"And . . ."

"And nothing."

John left to hunt for fuel, and I waited with the boys by the airstrip. In the afternoon a Twin Otter buzzed in, released a trio of Asian men in gum boots and polyester business suits, then took off again.

"Loggers spoiling everything," said one unhappy onlooker who introduced himself as Benjamin. There was a time, he said, when he thought he could make a living from ecotourism—in fact plenty of people in the lagoon had the same idea after the World Wide

Fund for Nature told them how special the place was back in the nineties. The United Nations had been on the verge of declaring Marovo a World Heritage Site. People constructed bungalows with stoves and raised beds for tourists. Benjamin had opened his own lodge over on Vangunu. But then the tension came, and the government withered, and the tourists disappeared, and the Malaysian Chinese showed up with their suitcases of money.

One by one, the lagoon's chiefs had been selling their forests in return for cash and tin roofing and outboard motors, and the red scars had crept up the hillsides, and the guts of the forest seeped into the lagoon like blood, and the coral choked and turned white in the silty half-light, and fishnets began to come up empty.

Sometimes people didn't want their chiefs to sell off the forests. They burned logging trucks and stole chain saws. Back in the nineties, islanders had tried to work with groups like Greenpeace to start village-based "ecoforestry" ventures, but the foreign loggers had guns, guards, and friends in high places. At least one eco-activist got his neck broken. Onetime prime minister Bartholomew Ulufa'alu tried to clamp down on corruption and unsustainable forestry in the nineties, but all that ended when the Malaita Eagle Force arrived on his doorstep with machine guns. Now things were back to normal. "The loggers' work is even easier now that the government is broke," said Benjamin. "They bribe the government agents and the chiefs, then cut as fast as they can."

New Georgia's wealth, its *mana*, was being sucked away and delivered raw to mills in Malaysia and Japan. Meanwhile, Benjamin's eco-lodge was empty, so he had started a canteen beside the airstrip, where he sold crackers and warm beer to the loggers.

A woman from the village came to warn me about John Palmer. She said he was the sort of boy I should avoid. He was a rubbish boy. He ran with the rebels from across the water in Bougainville. And worse. "What kind of worse?" I asked. "Just worse," she said, staring at the dirt, then stomped off without another word.

John returned after dark with the last two jugs of gas in Seghe. We jumped in his *kanu* (another flimsy fiberglass runabout) and headed west to Nono Lagoon. The stars were out, but their light was nothing compared to the halo of phosphorescent sparks that flowed around the bow. Our wake glowed behind us like the tail of a comet. There were other lights, too: yellow nebulae, waving and pulsing under the surface of the lagoon.

"Divers," said John. "Collecting *bêche-de-mer*."

Sometimes John would ease the throttle and shine his light into the clear water, and then it was as though the belly of the lagoon had been split open and its entrails had floated up in great bubbles, stopping just short of the surface. Coral. Thousands and thousands of pounds of pale green and purple coral. Within the folds I could see the *bêche-de-mer*, the mottled sea slugs that had excited Chinese palates and lured traders to these waters for two centuries. Some were as big as footballs.

Islands drifted past like shadows on shadows. Then a violent constellation of incandescent orange emerged from behind a curtain of palms. It was a ship, anchored in the middle of the lagoon. It must have been fifty times bigger than the *Tomoko*. Floodlights shone down from two steel cranes. The lights illuminated a stack of raw logs on the deck below. The cranes jerked and twisted frantically, like great metallic birds arranging a nest of sticks.

We rounded a point, and the curtain of islands closed again. We steered toward a single spark of light, which grew into the warm glow of an oil lamp sitting on the porch rail of a cottage. We tied up to a heap of rocks and were greeted by six shirtless young men. They all wore dreadlocks, and they all smoked long cigarettes rolled from magazine paper. John introduced them as his *brothas*, which didn't tell me much because that might mean "brother" or "cousin" or "uncle," or some more distant relative. These *brothas* were Sam, Laury, Oswold, Allen-Chide, Namokene, and Ray. The island was called Mbatumbosi, but John preferred to call it Bad

Boss, because that name made it seem tougher. It did feel a bit like a gang hideout at first. The brothers smoked and wrestled and lay about in hammocks. There were no women, no sisters, no scolding parents.

"We are alone," said Allen, as he brought our dinner—a pot of plain rice—to a boil on a gas stove on the porch.

"We are free," said Ray.

"We are raiders," said John.

"Raiders," I said encouragingly, "like your ancestors?"

"No, mon. Raiders blong luv. Olsem Casanova!"

John explained the modern art of raiding. The brothers would take their *kanu* over to the hamlets that dotted the edges of their lagoon, and they would whisper beneath the young women's windows: "Come out, come out and play." And the girls did crawl out their windows and disappear with the brothers into the shadows. The Methodist village of Nazareth made for poor hunting, but the girls on Mbarejo, which was Seventh-day Adventist, were always eager.

"So you are creepers," I said, recalling the men who had harassed Sabina back on Vanua Lava.

"Yes!" said Allen.

"No!" said John. "The girlies, they come to us. They tell their daddies that they are going fishing on the reef. Then they paddle straight to Bad Boss."

Ray said that it was the marble trick that attracted the girls more than anything. The boys had learned the trick from Japanese fishermen. John had one marble. Ray had two. What you did, explained John, was smash a glass mug and file down a small piece of the handle until it was perfectly round and smooth. Next you took an old toothbrush and filed the end of it to a sharp point. Then you got your brother to pull out a pinch of skin on the shaft of your penis, so you could poke a hole through the skin with the sharp end of the toothbrush. You used the toothbrush to push the marble into the hole. In with the marble, out with the toothbrush, a splash of Dettol disinfectant, and voilà, you had transformed your penis into a sexual novelty. John unzipped his fly and, squirming with pride, exposed just enough of his penis to prove they weren't lying. There was indeed a roundish lump just under the skin.

"*Lookim*," Ray said as John pushed the lump with his finger, "*hem roll all-abaot!*"

Then we all bowed our heads, and Ray said grace beneath John's framed portrait of Princess Diana.

The brothers may have been raiders. They may have been vagabonds. They may have been naughty. But they were not living alone on Bad Boss by choice. John's parents lived in Honiara and so had he, before the tension.

The problem, he said, was the color of his skin. John was tall and lanky, like his great-grandfather, one of the lagoon's first white traders. But John's skin wasn't white or black or even a Guadalcanal shade of peat brown. So the Guadalcanal militants wouldn't believe John shared their blood. They chased him and beat him. Then, when the Malaita Eagles took their revenge in Honiara, John got a second round of beatings. That's why he was hiding out on Bad Boss. Not because his father had caught him hanging out with Bougainvillean exiles. Not because he was in hot water for hiring a car and helping his friends in the Bougainville Revolutionary Army round up a trunkful of machine guns. No, said John, he was a refugee. It had been three years since he had sat in a car or tasted chocolate.

We passed days languidly on the lagoon. We paddled through the estuary of the Choe River looking for crocodiles, but there were none to see. We took John's boat out through a gap in the barrier islands to spear minnows for lunch. We climbed among the limestone cliffs on the barrier islands. The rock was an amalgam of petrified coral and giant clamshell, and impossible to walk on with bare feet. We found the first skull under a cracked slab. It was surrounded by fractured bones, doughnut-sized rings of carved rock and bits of shattered clamshell jewelry. I picked up the skull. It was warm. A spider skittered along its jaw. Startled, I let the skull slip from my hands. It struck the ground and lost a tooth.

"No problem," John said. "This is not one of my grandfathers. This is someone my grandfathers killed, probably some weak *fala* from Roviana."

Back on Bad Boss, John led me to three skulls tucked into a shady ravine behind his house. He picked up one and lovingly rubbed the mildew from its forehead. Its eye sockets were cracked and imploring. This, said John, was one of his great-grandmother's people. Those folks were tough, but apparently not tough enough. They had migrated west to Bad Boss to escape the marauding tribes of Roviana Lagoon. Then they were chased away again.

"So you come from a long line of refugees," I teased John over dinner.

He assured me that his ancestors had killed many people. They had raided villages from Roviana all the way to Isabel. And besides, the Tagitaki were no ordinary enemies. They were giants who wielded clubs so heavy it took six ordinary men to lift them. That's why the ancestors fled. The Tagitaki had once lived on the mountain ridge across the lagoon from Mbarejo. That ridge was *tabu* now, said John.

"Because of the ghosts of the Tagitaki?"

"Ha! Of course not."

"Then why?"

"Because of the Nonotongere."

I had heard that name before.

Once upon a time, long before men hunted for heads, said John, a giant serpent had prowled the lagoons. The snake was thicker than a sow and as long as the airstrip at Seghe. One day, the snake fought with a giant lizard. It didn't go well for the snake. The lizard ripped it to pieces. Parts of the snake's body now littered the foothills of New Georgia, but its head lay on the crest of the ridge where the giant headhunters once lived. That was the Nonotongere. It had retained all the giant snake's *mana*. If you disturbed the snake head, shouted at it, or even so much as blew on it, the devil inside it would answer you with a meteorological hissy fit. It would bring wind, rain, and thunder.

"Nonotongere! Didn't the air agent in Seghe tell us to stay away from it?" I said.

"Maybe," John said and smiled mischievously. "Would you like to go say hello to it?"

John was not one for following rules. He told me he was not afraid of the devil stone. Sometimes he hiked up the ridge and blew on it, just for the sheer joy of watching rain sweep across the lagoon below, knowing that the drizzle and cool breeze would enliven the young women. He imagined all those damp T-shirts clinging to all those young breasts.

"Mmmm, yes, Nonotongere, *hem gud tumas*," said John, closing his eyes, drawing deeply on his cigarette.

Another magic stone. Melanesians were like my great-grandfather: they waxed as mystically about their *mana* as Henry Montgomery had about the Holy Spirit. But good luck if you wanted proof from them. I did not bother to pester John for a demonstration of the Nonotongere's power. I was tired of pushing, testing, failing. But that night in my dreams, my mosquito netting was transformed into the glowing miracle cloud from Henry's Irish garden. There were the ghosts of my ancestors again, moving through the rosebushes, which had grown into frangipani and palm. There was the old stone church, the light of the visitation, and the old man collapsed beneath it, sobbing in gratitude, embracing the floor, whose speckled jade tiles were like the scales on the back of a great, sleeping serpent.

John lifted my mosquito net and shook me awake before dawn. He whispered in my ear: *"Day blong Nonotongere!"*

Under an overcast sky, John, Allen, and I motored over to Mbarejo to pick up Jimmy, a jittery, distracted fellow with one functioning ear. We needed Jimmy because he was on good terms with the chief of Mbarejo, who owned the mountain where the Nonotongere waited. We stopped at a waterside canteen and bought supplies for the expedition: three sticks of tobacco and a pad of notepaper for rolling. Then we headed for New Georgia.

There was a logging camp in the bay across from Mbarejo. The camp sat in the middle of a dismaying smear of red-brown mud. It looked as though the hillside had caught some necrifying skin disease, and its flesh had rotted right down to the muscle. Trucks roared out of the forest one by one, but the mud near the lagoon was so viscous they had to dump their logs on the top of the hill. Bulldozers dragged the logs through a deepening trench of slick clay down to a bark-strewn pier. A gang of kids slipped in and out of the trench, cheering each passing log.

The chief of Mbarejo had given a Malaysian company permission to log the mountain. John wasn't sure how much the loggers paid the chief, but the old man had been handing out canoe engines, chain saws, and other bits of cargo to his *wantoks* for the past year. John had managed to score some tin roofing. He said he felt slightly guilty; he knew the loggers were spoiling the lagoon, but it was nice to have a tin roof on his house. And anyway, what choice was there? Everyone knew the Malaysians had paid the government and would get the logs whether the lagoon people wanted to sell them or not.

We tied up to a rock near the pier and found the chief up to his fat ankles in mud. John negotiated. Jimmy gazed at the sky, which was thick and disapproving, and cooed at it.

"Fine, fine. I give you permission to see our *kastom* sites," the chief bellowed over the roar of the bulldozer. But don't you disturb that devil stone. Don't you dare!"

"I promise I will respect your *kastom*," I said to the chief.

"*Kastom?* I am *wanfala* Christian, not *wanfala* heathen," he replied. "That stone means nothing to me. But look at this mud! We don't want any more rain around here. No more rain, do you understand? Don't you so much as touch that stone!"

The chief trudged over to Jimmy and yelled in his good ear. Jimmy yelped like a kicked dog. The chief pointed at the mountain and yelled some more. Jimmy leapt in the air and charged up the log trench. We followed. At the edge of the camp, we were intercepted by a distressed-looking Chinese man in gum boots. "You not from Greenpeace? You not hippie?" he said to me. I shook my head.

"You not taking photos of logging?"

"No, no, of course not."

"Our security man, he will go with you."

We all climbed into a rusted pickup, John, his brother Allen, Jimmy, the security man, and I. Everyone insisted I sit in the front seat, so I did. The truck driver's name was Foo. He told me he had a wife back in Kuala Lumpur. Every year, he got a month's vacation and took his wife to a casino hotel in Tenerife. He despised New Georgia. I told Foo a Cantonese phrase I picked up in Hong Kong, something like "*Lohk gau si*"—It's raining dogshit. That made him laugh.

We slid through the muck, past a platoon of young men with chain saws on their shoulders, who looked miserable. Instead of shell money, the men had engine gaskets and chains and sprockets strung around their necks and wrists.

It wasn't the missing trees that struck me the most. It was the ground. The red earth had been unbound, freed from its protective weave of roots and bush. It was crumbling, collapsing, sliding all around us; now seeping away like hot lava, now spilling over the roads; filling the gullies like wet cement, overflowing from creek beds, leaving the mountain thin and wasted like the victim of a sorcerer's life-sucking curse.

We had driven for fifteen minutes when Jimmy banged on the roof of the cab, and Foo stepped on the brake. Through a hole in the floor near the brake pedal, I saw the tire lock and skid. I remembered another common Cantonese saying: "*Sihk yah ng-jouh yah, jouh yah dah-laahn yah*"—You consume everything but make nothing, and you make a mess of anything you touch.

Foo laughed again, sadly this time. "A mess," he said. "Sure. A real mess." Then he drove away with the security man.

The rest of us followed Jimmy up through the slash, which was as dry as kindling and crusted with baked-on mud. The forest, when we reached it, was cool and damp. We bushwhacked toward the ridge crest. The guys swung at the undergrowth with their machetes. I remember the rocket-ship trees and their splayed roots. I remember the soft leaves that left welts where they brushed my ankles. But I can't remember much else about that forest, because I was trying to keep up with Jimmy, who was charging through the bush, oblivious to our screams for him to slow down. His hoots and squawks echoed through the canopy. Finally, he paused alongside a tremendous, spiraling tree trunk, spray-painted with the letter T in orange. The mark stood for *tabu*. The loggers could cut down the forest until they reached that mark. Directly below the T was a heap of ruins: a tumbled-down wall, a stone terrace, and the remains of an earthen oven. Most of these rocks were the remains of the city of the Tagitaki, shouted Jimmy above the silence.

A faint path wound along the ridge crest. We followed it until we reached a roughly polished sandstone slab and a heptagonal pillar, about the height of a lectern. This ruin was John's favorite. He said the slab was for special occasions, those times when the Tagitaki managed to bring home one of their enemies' children. When the Tagitaki caught a baby, they would keep him for a while, fatten him up on taro and *gnali* nuts. After a few months, the giants would get together and play catch with the toddler. That helped soften the meat. Then they would lay the child on that sandstone slab, slice him open, and eat him raw. Nobody seemed to know what the pillar was for.

My friends in New Georgia loved their baby-eating stories even more than colonial historians did. Everyone had one. They made me wonder if the cannibal-myth doubters had ever bothered to consult Melanesians about their historical revisionism. It was hard to dismiss them when the locals themselves were such adamant believers in the savagery of their ancestors.

But why did New Georgians treasure their baby-eating stories? The simplest answer would be that the stories lent their tellers a kind of primordial cachet. For John, they were a reminder that his forebears had been kick-ass warriors, and that the only tribe tough enough to chase them were baby-gobbling giants. But I think the horror stories served another function. Just as white men had used cannibal stories as a kind of moral armor to justify their interventions, the Christianized New Georgians had employed them to reassure themselves that the new way was the best way, that they were following a better path than their ancestors. They served to remind the lagoon people of the darkness that lurked within their own souls, the darkness that required vigilance. If the cannibal story is mythical—which is to say that its main function is to hint at truths of the human soul—then its historicity is of secondary importance. The key to mythical truth is not bones and ruins, but belief itself.

This is the tug-of-war between historical and mythical truth, and it occurs amid tales of horror and magic alike. The stories my great-grandfather brought with him to Melanesia—the miracles and resurrection of Jesus, the almightiness of God, the fires of hell, the glories of everlasting life—these were the shimmering images that had convinced islanders to turn their backs on their ancestors, just as they had convinced our own forebears to relinquish their Nordic gods.

It's faith, not veracity, that gives stories their power. And thus charged, stories confer power back on their believers, whether that power is simply the strength of certainty, spiritual clarity, or something more. In Honiara, people assured me I would be in no danger from black magic, even if a sorcerer waved a handful of *mana*-charged cobwebs in my face, because my disbelief was stronger than *kastom* magic. But when you fall toward mythical thinking, when you rub up against the rough edges of it long enough, it can enter you like a virus, and the world changes. There is more danger, but there is more possibility. Events present themselves symbolically. They wrap themselves in magic rather than coincidence, and their circumstances assume direction and purpose.

So faith is a decision, but it can be precipitated by certain conditions. A story, say, about the connection between a mythical snake, a lump of rock, and a storm, is presented. Context, something like a battle between natural goodness and industrial logging, provides a foundation. The landscape might reflect these things: it might be ravaged, or it might seethe with its own fragile power. The air might take on a certain quality, perhaps a kind of pregnant heaviness. There might be an eerie silence. These things might prepare you.

They might lead you to the readiness I began to feel as I followed one-eared Jimmy up the ridge, through the jungle, past the ruined fortresses of the giants, toward the leaden sky.

I paused to wring the sweat from my T-shirt, only to realize that Jimmy's grunts and whoops had ceased, and the forest had gone suddenly silent. The silence wasn't complete. It was punctured by the whine of chain saws in the distance and occasional squawks from longbills up in the canopy. Nothing moved. The gray sky glowed. The forest waited expectantly. The stillness was crushing. Ready.

I found Jimmy, John, and Allen in a glade at the top of the ridge. They were crouching near a mound of cut stones. "Nonotongere," said John, nodding toward a hunk of weather-blackened limestone in the undergrowth.

For all its notoriety, the snake stone should have been as big as a house. It was not. It was about the size of a medicine ball. From a certain angle, with the shadow beneath its angled jaw, with its angry temples and blunt snout, the stone did look like the head of a snake. A hole the thickness of a broomstick had been carved through its cheeks. The hole ends could have been eyes. I reached out and ran my fingers along its jaw. The rock was warm.

"Careful! Careful!" sputtered Jimmy.

"Sorry," I said, and stood up.

John looked at me and winked. *"Bae-bae yumi checkem olgeta skull,"* he said to Jimmy's good ear, and we tromped to the far side of the clearing where the rocks had been piled into a squarish vault. On top of the vault were several thick slabs, sprinkled with bits of broken shell. Jimmy hacked away at the shrubbery around the vault. John caught my eye again and winked. I got it.

"I'll make lunch," I said.

I stepped back to the snake head, keeping an eye on Jimmy and his machete. I crouched down. It's not like I would be risking an earthquake. Nobody would be hurt. I pursed my lips, blew a quick puff of air across the snake's snout, then jumped to my feet.

A shriek rose from the far side of the clearing.

"What's wrong?" I shouted.

"We just knocked some bones. Jimmy, he's worried," said John. Nobody but me seemed to notice the trembling in the canopy, the gentle rustling of leaves, the faint breeze that whisked through the glade and disappeared into the stillness of the afternoon.

We ate in the cradle of a rocket tree. Allen cut up some papaya. I opened a can of spaghetti and a packet of shortbread biscuits I had brought from Honiara. Jimmy collected some *gnali* nuts and hammered them open with a rock. John cut some leaves and spread our food on them. We used the biscuits to scoop up the spaghetti.

"If the chief is a Christian, why is he so protective of the Nonotongere?" I asked John.

"Because chief works for the Chinese," he said. "Suppose we make rain: then the whole operation must shut down, and chief won't get paid."

"No! *Hem i becos chief hem i no likem for yumi sick from olgeta devil,*" said Jimmy, who was fidgeting nervously again, cocking his good ear toward the vault as though someone were calling to him. *"Nogud yumi tochim olgeta bones. Yumi mas go out from disfala place!"*

Jimmy couldn't see the Nonotongere from where he sat. It lay behind our picnic tree. I excused myself to pee. But I didn't do that. I snuck behind the tree and knelt down by the snake head. I cupped that warm stone in my hands—gently, tenderly—then I took a deep breath and blew a lungful of spaghetti-scented air into the snake's eye hole. I took another breath and blew even harder. I blew until I was dizzy, and then, as soon as I could stand, I stumbled back to our picnic. John watched me sit down and gave me a conspiratorial grin. Jimmy was trimming his fingernails with his machete. I reached for a piece of shortbread, then hesitated. My eyes met John's. We were ready.

The change came without warning, like a great wave breaking over the glade. It roared through the trees and flattened the brush. Leaves swirled and raced like swallows, then fell like green snowflakes. Tree trunks groaned. Longbills peeled from the highest branches like shingles torn from a roof and flew away, down into the valley. I could see the sky through a break in the ravaged canopy. The overcast was no longer flat. It was not distant. It did not glow. It was purple and heavy. It was collapsing, first in great sagging boils, then in translucent curtains, now in dirty gray stalactites, liquid spears of plunging pressure, all falling with the weight of exhilaration and relief.

Jimmy got to his feet, began to shout and moan, then dashed toward the stone vault.

"What is he doing?" I said.

"He is telling the ancestors he is *sori tumas*," said John. "Jimmy thinks he brought the rain. But it wasn't Jimmy. It was you!" John grinned from ear to ear. It was the smile of a teenage shoplifter, a lagoon Casanova, a first-time car thief.

"*Yumi go nao!*" wailed Jimmy as the first drops of rain exploded on his forehead.

"Yes, we go!" John shouted. "No good the devils find us and follow us home!"

"We go!" shouted Allen.

"We go!" shouted I.

The rain came thick and hard. It exploded on the forest canopy like thousands of firecrackers, then poured through in tiny rivulets. The air vibrated with the impact. Water cascaded from broad leaves and tree trunks and rock walls. It collided with itself, gathered in glorious torrents, and gushed down the trail.

Drenched, we charged down the ridge, splashing through the runoff, leaping deadfalls and sacrificial stones and lines of panicked black ants. We burst out of the forest into the logging slash. The road was not a road anymore. It was a river. It bubbled like hot chocolate. Trucks stood abandoned. A line of young men trudged toward a hut in the distance. They carried long-blade chain saws on their shoulders and left a trail of rainbow-swirled gas stains in the puddles behind them.

The rain streamed down my face, and I could not wipe the smile from it. I knew I was beaming like a fool, because John looked at me and burst out laughing himself. But he didn't know the truth behind my smile. It wasn't because we had disobeyed the chief like a couple of rascals. It wasn't because we had tricked Jimmy. It wasn't because I had conjured a tempest from the eye of the Nonotongere. (A storm! I had made it rain! Don't tell me I didn't!) It wasn't because, for the first time in weeks, the deadening heat and the fog of lethargy had loosened their grip on me, and I could run and breathe and feel my skin again. It was because, in that moment, I let myself imagine that empire had not stolen all the *mana* from New Georgia, that for a few hours or days, or perhaps just for those few seconds, magic could halt the crushing engines. The trucks were stuck. The fallers and the drivers were under cover, smoking and making plans to paddle back to their families. Foo was dreaming of Tenerife. The chief of Mbarejo was pacing back and forth in the mud, cursing. And there was mud between my toes.

If you summon a storm, and your call is reinforced by an idea about the power of a stone or a god or a spirit, and then the storm does fall on you, surely you should honor the moment with faith and not bury it in skepticism. Surely you should wrap it in mythical truth, rather than explain it away. The Nonotongere drew the tempest down from the sky. I would let that be my story. It was a good one to believe, much better than the one with John complaining that it rained every afternoon on New Georgia. So I accepted it, and I was made ready for more.

18

Under the Langa Langa Lagoon

The supernatural power abiding in the powerful living man abides in his ghost after death, with increased vigour and more ease of movement.

—R. H. CODRINGTON, *The Melanesians*

Word moved quickly across the lagoon. By the time I stepped ashore in Seghe, the air agent had heard that John and I had climbed the ridge beyond Mbarajo. He knew we had played with the forbidden Nonotongere. For one thing, the airstrip had been rendered useless for the better part of a day by the deluge. He was terse with me, but he did sell me a ticket, and I flew back to Honiara with a planeload of loggers and their bodyguards.

We raced through the clouds, which seemed different now. Everything was different after my storm: mist, rocks, and trees were infused with personality, willpower, potential energy. The world vibrated with *mana*, and I could feel it—I could almost see it flowing through the air. I was terrified of losing my new vision. I wanted to feed it.

The promise of magic walked the very streets of the capital. The Melanesian Brotherhood's headquarters were just west of Honiara, so the *tasiu* were everywhere in the city. I saw them each time I returned. Some wore the same humble black-and-white uniform I had seen Ken Brown wearing back in Vureas Bay. Others, the novices, wore electric blue robes with red sashes. They walked barefoot or in flip-flops. Their brass medallions glinted in the sunlight. They held hands and giggled like schoolchildren. I was in awe of them, and yet somehow not ready to confront them. I suppose I was worried their magic would not stand up to my challenge. I wanted a sure thing. And so I looked to the ocean.

The islanders who were recruited by the *Southern Cross* assured the missionaries that the most powerful locus of magic was the world beyond their island shores. The creatures that lived in salt water always held the most *mana*. Alligators, sea snakes, bonitos, and frigate birds: any of these animals might be inhabited by a *tindalo*, the soul of a dead man. The most sacred sea creature of all was the shark. Sometimes, before a man died, he announced that he would return by sea; his *wantoks* knew the deceased had come home when they spotted a shark remarkable for its size or color. Mission students told Codrington that a chief on Savo, off the coast of Guadalcanal, regularly swam out from his beach to make sacrifices to a shark, and that shark would come to him and gently accept his offers of food. The people loved and respected their ghost-sharks, but no people loved them more than the saltwater men of Malaita's Langa Langa Lagoon. In the old days, a Langa Langa shark caller could summon a favorite shark to sink enemy canoes. The shark would drag the victims back to shore so they could be chopped up. Langa Langa priests regularly called sharks to their island. In exchange for bits of pork, the shark ancestors would allow young boys to ride across the lagoon on their backs.

People still told stories about the shark callers. A fellow I met at the Mendaña Hotel bar told me that he was once fishing far out at sea with a Langa Langa man when their outboard engine conked out. This might have been the end of them, but the Langa Langa man took control. He jumped into the water and performed a strange swim-dance. Then he ordered my friend to go to sleep under the deck cover. "I didn't sleep," he told me. "I lay there and listened. Soon I felt waves breaking off the bow. We were moving quickly through the ocean—it was as though we were being pushed by an engine. After an hour, I got up and looked around. We were back in the harbor! Then that Langa Langa man, he swam to shore, collected some coconuts, brought them back to the boat, chopped them up, and threw them in the sea. That's when I knew it was his shark granddaddy who had pushed us home."

Shark magic seemed like a sure thing. I told my friend Morris at the moribund national tourism office that we should promote sacred shark tourism; he could supply the shark priests with pig guts so they could toss them in the water and convince their ancestors to entertain paying customers. I would be the first. Morris insisted that Christianity had put an end to shark worship back in the 1970s. The descendants of the shark people now sipped the blood of Christ instead of slaughtering pigs and dumping the entrails in the sea, so naturally the sea spirits had abandoned them.

"But don't be sad," said Morris. "The MV *Temotu* is back in port, haw haw! You will be leaving for Santa Cruz next week." Morris seemed to be right about the *Temotu*. The ship's purser even agreed to sell me a ticket to Nendo. Five days to go, he promised.

But I was sure that Morris was wrong about the shark callers. I had found my connection. Her name was Veronica Kwalafa, and she ran a faith-healing clinic near the Quality Motel. (God had given Veronica the power in a dream back in 1987. He had shown himself as a bright star—just like the one the prophet Fred had seen before his return to Tanna Island. For $4, Veronica would hold your hand or massage your back, and because she had something like a television in her head, she could see your troubles and tell you how to fix them.)

I had met Veronica weeks before. She had assured me there was one shark caller left in the Langa Langa Lagoon. He was her brother, of course, and he was the boss of the underwater world. He could talk to the sharks. He would wade into the shallows and caress them like pets. The sharks used their magic to help him walk for hours on the ocean floor. Veronica had said she'd take me to the shark caller if I promised to tell the world that her services were available via mail and that people with any kind of sickness could contact her through Mary Manisi, PO Box 93, Honiara.

I promised. But whenever I returned to the faith-healing clinic to seal our deal, Veronica's door was locked, and so it was on my return from New Georgia. I jumped up and down, slammed my palm against the hot paint, but Honiara never rewarded impatience. So I did what everyone with disposable income and time to kill did in the capital: I went to get smashed at the pool bar of the Mendaña Hotel.

That's where I met the saltwater men. They were stone drunk and not doing a good job of keeping their heads off the table. I knew they were from the lagoons of Malaita because, when they did lift their heads, I could see geometric engravings on their cheeks.

They called to me: Could I please ask the bar manager to turn up the music? He would listen to a white man. The music was already loud. It was playing the New Guinean hit *"Mi Dae Long Yu"*—I'm dying for you. The Malaitans sang along:

O daling, mi misim yu,
O daling, mi luvim yu,
O daling, mi dae long yu.

I pulled up a chair and told the saltwater men about the shark caller of Langa Langa Lagoon. They said they belonged to Lau, a lagoon on the northeastern tip of Malaita.

"The church wiped all the sacred fish from Langa Langa, and from our lagoon, too," said the most sober of the three. His facial scars reminded me of the Nazca lines. There were two concentric circles with streaks shooting out from them like sunbeams. "It's *tabu* for people to try to talk to sharks. Dangerous for the soul. We are Christians now."

"Ah, so then you wouldn't mind a little shark's fin soup."

"Don't say that! The sharks are our ancestors."

The scarred man looked at me sternly. "*Yu blong wea?*" he asked.

"Canada."

That brought a chorus of disapproving grumbles.

"We once had strong *kastom* at our home in the Lau Lagoon," the scarred man said. "An octopus. He took care of our ancestors. If they were lost at sea, he would bring them home. If they were drowning, he would save them."

"What was its name?" I asked.

"We cannot tell you that. It's a secret. Anyway, the octopus is gone now. Gone! And it was a *wantok* of yours, one man-Canada, who stole him from us."

All three men were fully awake now. "Maranda," they said together.

"Maranda, this thief, now he is showing our octopus to tourists in Canada," said the second man.

"He is making lots of *sellen* from our ancestor," said the third, rubbing his thumb and forefinger together in front of my nose.

"What do you mean? He took the octopus on a plane?" I said.

This was apparently a wildly stupid question. The men laughed. I bought more beer. And the story came.

The sacred octopus was inhabited by an ancestor of the villagers at Foueda, an artificial island constructed from hunks of coral out on the Lau reef. The octopus had indeed been helpful to people, but he demanded sacrifices in return for his patronage. Sometimes the octopus would crawl right up out of the sea into a man's canoe to let him know it was time for a sacrifice. He would crawl onto land, too. If you left a basket of food outside your door, the octopus would plunk himself down on top of it and engulf that *kai-kai*. He would change the color of his skin from red to black to show he was pleased. He preferred pig guts to fruit. To communicate with the octopus or sacrifice to him, you had to know his secrets. The only men who knew these things were the Lau *kastom* priests who had been handing down the sacred knowledge for centuries.

The octopus's troubles started when the Christians arrived. The missionaries called the octopus a devil. Young converts refused to learn the sacred *kastom* knowledge. The priests were left with no one to whom they could pass on their sacrificial rituals. The last of the priests were growing old when the white man named Maranda climbed ashore on Foueda. The priests refused to let him into their ancestral sanctuary, but Maranda was resourceful, said the scarred man. He tied a tape recorder to a stick and poked it over the wall of the sanctuary while the priests performed their sacrifices. That's how he stole all their secret incantations. That's why, when Maranda got on his boat and went back to Canada, the octopus followed him. Now the people of Foueda had no octopus to protect them from the perils of the sea.

"But what about the *kastom* priests? Why couldn't they stop the octopus from leaving?" I asked.

"Dead," said the scarred man. "All gone now."

"And there are no new priests to take their place?"

"There can be no priest without the secret knowledge."

"So there are no priests."

"Don't you see?" he cried. "*Maranda* is the only octopus priest!"

"But Maranda, he was not so smart," slurred number two. "He spoiled his sacrifices. He made the octopus very angry, so it made him sick. And it killed his wife."

I eventually tracked down the alleged octopus thief, who turned out to be the acclaimed cultural anthropologist Pierre Maranda, now professor emeritus of anthropology at Université Laval in Quebec City. Maranda and his wife *had* lived among the people of the Lau Lagoon from 1966 to 1968, and they had recorded the sacred knowledge.

I e-mailed Maranda an account of my conversation with the saltwater men. In his response, Maranda admitted falling deathly ill after his first fieldwork in the lagoon. After he got sick, he said, the islanders made a sacrifice on his behalf, and he did recover, "which made them very happy." Maranda insisted his illness was not a curse but a bout of malaria. As for his wife, she didn't die until more than a decade after the octopus's disappearance. Maranda told me he had assured the Lau people that he did not have their octopus in his swimming pool, but to no avail.

Perhaps Maranda doesn't deserve to be characterized as the trickster-villain of the Lau myth. In fact, he may have done them a lasting favor. He insists that the *kastom* priests encouraged him to record their secret prayers, and for very good reason. When Maranda returned to Foueda in 1975, Laakwai, one of Foueda's two high priests, lamented that the old *kastom* was "finished." The priest's sons were refusing to take on his duties after his death. They had caught the Christian bug. The other high priest, Kunua, had the same problem. Ten years later, both priests had given up hope. Laakwai dove under a woman's canoe, knowing he was committing a fatal reversal of high-low energy. Kunua purposefully botched a ritual. Both men died within weeks. It was suicide by metaphysical transgression. Thus, Maranda had become the sole keeper of Foueda's sacred knowledge and the default *kastom* priest, a legacy he holds to this day in his office on the far side of the world. I suspect Maranda's relationship with the myth is more than academic. When I asked him the name of the sacred octopus, he was no more forthcoming than the saltwater men in the Mendaña Hotel bar. The name, he said, was a secret he could only divulge to a Lau successor committed to honoring the ancient *kastom*. He's still looking for that man.

My encounter with the saltwater men filled me with an even greater sense of urgency. With beer on my breath and sea spirits on my mind, I stumbled back across town to look once more for the faith healer, Veronica Kwalafa.

The door to the healing clinic was open. I walked in to find no lights on and the ceiling fan cruelly immobile. The power was out. I could hear Veronica humming quietly behind a curtain at the back of the office, where she had shown me the tools of her trade (a crystal ball, a Bible, and a Hello Kitty ruler).

Veronica's husband, Philip, was fast asleep on a wooden desk in the reception area. I cleared my throat. He didn't stir.

"You promised to take me to the shark boss, and then you disappeared," I said.

Philip lifted his head. It took a moment for the arc of saliva between the desktop and his slack lower lip to break. Veronica appeared. I liked Veronica. She was soft. Her white hair had the texture of candy floss. I did not like Philip. He was a lazy slug of a man. Veronica did the healing. Philip guarded Veronica's box of money. She was big enough to crush him, but she called him Daddy.

"We are very busy. We cannot guide you to Langa Langa," said Philip.

Sweat rolled down my back. I imagined taking my chair and breaking it over Philip's head. It was the heat that made me feel such things. I ignored him.

"I want to help you," I said to Veronica. "I want to show the world that your brother still has the power."

"He does! He does have the power," she said.

With five days to go before the *Temotu*'s departure for Santa Cruz, I didn't have much time, but I did have a plan. Solomon Airlines advertised daily Twin Otter flights to Auki. Malaitans could afford to fly; they had all that compensation money to spend. I could fly, too. I had my credit card. It would be a treat for Veronica, who had apparently been too honest to make a compensation claim after the civil war.

"Wouldn't you like to go see your brother?" I said to her.

"Oh, yes," she said.

"We'll fly to Auki together tonight. I'll pay. Then we can look for your brother in the morning. But the thing is, we can only stay for four days."

How could she resist?

"Daddy," she said quietly, "what do you think? Should I go?"

Philip ignored her. He was doodling on a scrap of paper and sucking his lower lip like a spoiled child. He was jealous of Veronica.

"Daddy?"

I was beginning to despise him.

Finally, Philip looked up at me. "You say you want me to go with you to Langa Langa? I'll go. Yes, I'll go."

I was too horrified to speak. Veronica studied the floor. Philip assured me that four days would be more than enough time for the shark boss to produce his shark.

Our plane did not leave for Auki that evening. The pilot had disappeared. The following morning, I returned to the airport with Philip. A Twin Otter was waiting on the tarmac, but still no pilot. We caught a cab back to the pilot's house to wake him up, but in our absence, another pilot arrived at the airport and flew our Twin Otter to New Georgia. I could feel the hours, my shark hours, rushing past me. The sun crept across the sky. The heat was not like heat at all. It was more like a great weight pressing down from the sky and squeezing you until you oozed fatigue and sweat like honey from a sponge. My skin itched. I could feel the previous day's SolBrew seeping through my pores. I swore at some people in the departure lounge. Philip swore, too. He told the air agents we were on an important mission. Then he asked me for some spending money so he could buy a carton of cigarettes for his in-laws in Langa Langa. He smoked those cigarettes as we sat in the betel-stained terminal.

"I have three days now, and I'm running out of money. Maybe God doesn't want me to go to Langa Langa," I said.

Philip pawed my shoulder and gave a phlegmatic chuckle.

"If we had just taken the boat, we would have reached Malaita by now," he said.

In the afternoon, by stunning coincidence, both a pilot and a plane appeared on the runway. The plane was an Islander, which was a step down from the usual Twin Otter: more like a go-cart with wings. There was room for six of us. From my front-row seat, I gazed down over the pilot's shoulder at the cockpit, which resembled the console of my brother's 1968 VW Bug, in that it seemed to be held together by a collage of duct tape. But the plane flew well enough. A half-hour later we skidded to a halt on a grassy corner of Malaita, and a half-hour after that Philip was leading me through the market to Auki Harbor, where I had landed on the *Kopuria* three weeks before. We headed for the rubble jetty where the saltwater people landed their boats. We bartered for space on a fiberglass *kanu* with ten other people and their groceries. We headed down the coast at a walking pace, pushed by a twenty-five-horse outboard, which screamed in protest.

The Langa Langa Lagoon began just south of Auki, and stretched for twenty miles along Malaita's mountainous west coast. Its surface was absolutely calm, protected from the chop of the strait by a string of reefs. Gnarled chunks of storm-tossed coral poked out of the sea like rotten teeth. Mangroves covered the shallows, their roots splayed above the water like the bare legs of so many thousand old women, leafy skirts hauled up past knotted knees.

The saltwater people must have wanted very badly to live away from Malaita. In the absence of natural islands, they had built their own from rocks dredged from the sea bottom. There were dozens of artificial islands. Here was a pedestal with barely enough room for one shack. There, an abrupt plateau the size of a baseball field, rising head-high above the tide line and brimming with bungalows and palm trees. There were docks and long piers. There was a soccer pitch! It was a rough-edged Venice, all fashioned from the bones of the reef.

Why did the saltwater people go to all this work when dry land lay a half-hour paddle away? Some say they fled the hills because they weren't tough enough to defend themselves from the Kwaio warlords. The other, equally compelling reason was that there were no mosquitoes out on the lagoon.

We zigzagged from wall to craggy wall so passengers could leap across the murk to their villages. Nearly every island had a cathedral-sized barn in which rose the frame of a half-finished ship. The saltwater people were the Solomons' boat builders; half the wooden ferries that chugged in and out of Honiara were born on the shores of Langa Langa. But now, with Jimmy Rasta's boys terrorizing the sound, nobody was in any hurry to finish a ship, so the half-completed craft languished like the skeletons of beached whales, their great beams and ribs bleached as white as bone from years of waiting.

The day was fading. We pulled up to a muddy beach. There were a few huts among the mangroves, but this settlement could hardly be called an island. Most of the huts stood on stilts, and the high-water mark showed as a filmy ring around their ankles. Unfinished rock walls, foundations, and pathways stood just barely above the patchwork of sand and mud. Philip led me across the island, handing out cigarettes as he went. Crabs skittered out of our path like rats into sandy burrows.

I spotted the shark boss sitting in the shadows of an open cookhouse. I knew it was him, even before I got close enough to see his eyes. And it wasn't just because he had Veronica's frizzy white-blond hair. He glowed. His leathered skin was translucent, as though the light of the fading sky were shining right through the gridwork of tattoos on his face. He wore a broad smile. I remember his eyes were as blue as those of my ancestors. (But Melanesians have eyes the color of burned almond—how could his have been blue?) He was surrounded by children. A wooden tray on the bench beside him contained hundreds of rough red discs. He was carving shell money.

"I knew you were coming," said the shark boss, whose name was Selastine. "Last night I saw you in my dreams."

I was encouraged.

"Yes, I saw you sleeping in Auki," he continued.

"We slept in Honiara last night," I said.

He paid no attention. "I know why you are here, and I will help you. For how many weeks will you stay?" he said.

"Weeks?"

"You have come for the shark, no?"

"Yes, that's it. For the shark. But I have to leave in three days."

Selastine looked at Philip and chuckled. "It takes many days, many pigs, to call the shark to shore," he said. "You must buy pigs. We must sacrifice. You must stay for weeks. Months."

"But Philip said . . . "

And then I stopped. Philip was already tucking into a dish of Selastine's fish and taro, refusing to look up and acknowledge my glare. The bastard had duped me. His promise that four days was enough to catch a bit of shark magic was a big, fat lie. He had simply wanted to fly in an airplane. He had wanted a vacation. He had wanted to sponge off his in-laws. That's why we were here. I imagined sharks tearing into his bulging stomach.

"I must leave in three days," I said, quietly, and then mumbled something pathetic about Bishop Patteson and Nukapu, about having to catch the boat to Santa Cruz.

"No worries. We can still *storian*," said Selastine, looking at me sympathetically.

I felt dumb with disappointment and anger. I wanted to thrash Philip, or at least to humiliate him in front of his in-laws. But mostly I wanted to cry. My frustration was deep and wide. It was about more than Philip's deception, more than tricks with sharks. It pulsed through me. It was fueled by the readiness that had come to me during the tempest on New Georgia, but it was bigger than that. It stretched across oceans, years, generations. It was a longing for something just out of reach. It was a story wanting an ending.

"I should just leave. I should leave right now," I said.

"*No kanu long naet*," muttered Philip through a mouthful of mashed taro.

"You stay," said Selastine softly. "We can fish out on the reef. We can dive."

Evening settled on the lagoon and the village. A half-moon crept up through the mangroves. I pulled out the food I had brought and piled it on the bench. Instant noodles, bread, peanut butter, and a bag of candies. Selastine handed out the candies to his grandchildren, of which he had dozens. His daughter set a pot of water to boil on the fire. She served us noodles topped with peanut butter.

I didn't speak. Selastine began his tale. I only jotted it down later, when I realized that the story was part of his gift to me. I may not have all the details just right. But the truth of myth isn't in the details.

Once upon a time, a young woman of Lalana Point got *bubbly*, which is to say pregnant. She was unmistakably *bubbly*, and there was no sign of any father, and her shame was great, so the woman left her village and traveled around the lagoon. When the time finally came to give birth, she settled in Binafafo, where she had twin boys. The first of these twins was not a boy but a shark, so the woman filled a giant clamshell with water and slipped the shark-boy into it. Her second child was a regular boy.

When the brothers were old enough, the woman let them play together in the shallows of the lagoon. She would throw sticks into the water, and the boys would fight over them. The shark-boy grew. So did the man-boy. So did the sticks their mother threw for them. One day, when the brothers were fighting over a stick, the shark-boy bit the man-boy's hand right off. The man-boy swam to shore and bled to death. His mother was angry and bereaved. She told the shark-boy, whose name was now Bolai, that the only way to atone for his terrible deed was to swim into exile over on Guadalcanal.

Bolai did as his mother told him. He swam west across the strait, and when he reached Guadalcanal, he immediately gobbled up three boys. That was at Bobosa River. The people at Bobosa were understandably cross, so Bolai swam up the coast to Logu. He ate some people there, too, and the Logu people vowed to kill him, so Bolai swam on to Simui, where he ate a few more children. The Simui people built a barricade of trees and sticks to trap Bolai in their lagoon. When he tried to swim through it, his leathery skin was shredded by the sharp sticks. The people caught Bolai and carved him up. Now it was his turn to be eaten. They gave his head to an old woman, who built a fire in order to smoke-cure it. But just as the fire crackled to life, the woman noticed that tears were falling from the shark's eyes. She took pity on the poor shark head, especially when it told her its sad story.

"Don't cry for me, old woman," Bolai said. "Just go and gather the rest of my bones from the village. Bring them back to me. Then you go up into the bush and watch what happens down here tomorrow morning." The woman obeyed, and sure enough the next morning, a giant wave rose up and swallowed the village of Simui. Bolai pulled together his bones and created a new body for himself. It was huge, and as black as cooking charcoal. Bolai swam all the way back to Langa Langa, where he told his mother that he had made amends for killing his brother. She was pleased. She told Bolai to stay in the lagoon forever, and to be a good boy and cause no more harm to his own people.

"And that," said Selastine, "is why no one has ever been eaten by a shark in Langa Langa. Bolai is in control of the whole lagoon."

"And Selastine, he is the one who knows the shark. He is the shark boss," said a voice from the shadows. I realized the entire village had gathered around us.

"Yes," said Selastine. "The power of the shark stops inside me. I can use him. I call him to help me dive in the salt water. I can dive to fifteen fathoms. He gives me air. I can stay under the salt water for ten minutes!"

Selastine had a roomful of corroded treasure he had pulled from the wreckage of sunken ships near a reef far off the coast. Nobody else could get at the ships because of the sharks that guarded them.

"Aren't you afraid?"

"No, no. Bolai protects me. He swims around me, guides me. He likes to rub his belly against mine. He is bigger than all the other sharks. Longer than this house."

The shack was as long as a limousine.

"Why you?" I asked Selastine.

"Because the shark's mummy was my ancestor. Only I know Bolai's secrets. Only I know how to sacrifice to him properly. And I pray to him, too."

"Where?" I said, thinking there might be a shrine.

"What do you mean, where? I pray in the cathedral. The Catholic church."

"I can't imagine your priest is happy about that."

"He doesn't mind. He knows the shark is not a devil. He knows he is my ancestor and that he gives me good power."

By now the women had disappeared. The old folks were receding into the blue-gray half-light beyond our oil lamp. Their cigarettes flickered like stars on the horizon. Philip had long fallen asleep, his jowly face collapsing into his chest. I was not so angry anymore.

A few teenage boys still lingered. They clambered over the half wall of the cookhouse and whispered. Selastine turned to me and spoke with the gentle voice of a holy man: "*Yu savve swim long solwota?*"

We took a couple of the boys and pushed Selastine's canoe into the lagoon. The boat consisted of three mighty planks pegged together a long time ago. There was room for twenty people in among the fishnets and sloshing fish-gut water.

The lagoon was still except for the dip and slice of our paddles. The half-moon illuminated the thin veil of clouds that had spread itself across the entire dome of the sky. The hills of Malaita were the color of licorice. The lagoon flashed with amoeba-shaped patches of reflected light, a glimmer here, an urgent flutter there. Hot white sparks erupted from each paddle stroke.

We glided to a halt. The water became like the sky. The stillness of the night was broken only by distant percussion. It began as a crude thumping, like the sound that grouse make in the Canadian bush. But the thumping grew and was joined by more thuds and thunks. It became a kind of melody, rising and twisting, flowing across the water from some distant hamlet. I recognized it as the sound of a pipe drum band, of boys striking bamboo tubes with the soles of their rubber flip-flops, as they had after the bishop of Malaita's cathedral service.

Selastine stripped to his underwear and pulled on a pair of goggles, the kind you could buy for a couple of dollars in the Chinese stores back in Honiara. His white hair shone like a halo.

"Wait," I said. "Why did Bolai have to go and eat all those people on Guadalcanal?"

The boys giggled.

"Because his mother told him to," said Selastine.

"Why the hell would she do that?"

"To make better the death of his brother."

"I don't understand. How could that help?"

"This is Malaitan *kastom*," he said. "If you want to avenge a death, you don't go and kill another person in your village. You have to go to another place to do it."

"But the shark-boy was the one who killed in the first place!"

"It doesn't matter who killed. What *kastom* requires is a life to avenge a life. If you killed my brother, for example, I would not need to come back and kill you. Anyone's life would do. And I wouldn't have to do the killing myself. I would pay someone to do it."

"Like a *ramo*?"

"Yes, that's it. Bolai was our first *ramo*. This is *kastom*."

It didn't seem much different from the cycle of payback that had exploded during the tension and that was still crippling the plains around Honiara. Payback was tradition. It was *kastom*.

Selastine picked up his speargun and pointed his flashlight into the water. There was nothing to see. He looked at me.

"You come now!" he shouted, then leapt into the water, disappearing in a cloud of bubbles and phosphorescent sparks.

"*Yu garem glass-blong-diver. Yu swim. Hem fun!*" said one of the boys.

I pulled on my mask and crawled over the gunwale. The water was warm. I poked my head beneath the surface and gazed down into the abyss, where there was nothing. I pulled myself close to the canoe and imagined bad things.

The calm was broken suddenly by the leap and crash of something big.

"Long-fish. Hunting," said a boy. "You go! You go!"

I imagined myself as seen from below: a soft bundle of exposed flesh. I flattened myself against the canoe, wrapped my legs around the hull. All this talk of indiscriminate revenge killing had filled me with a nauseating sense of vulnerability.

Another explosion of water, this time near the bow of the canoe. It was Selastine. He was like a breaching whale. He gasped and sucked at the air. "*Gudfala* moon! *Gudfala* night! Come now. Follow my light," he said. And then he took a long heave and slipped away again, leaving an expanding circle of silver ripples in his place. I saw the flashlight beam across the hull of the canoe, turn toward the deep, and then descend until it was engulfed by a silty mist.

One of the boys pushed down on my head with his paddle blade. He hammered on my knuckles, making it somewhat less comfortable to cling onto the boat. The boys thought I was afraid. Of course I was afraid! I was swimming with the bloody lord of the sharks. But the humiliation made me let go.

I took a breath, pushed off from the canoe, and reached into the void with both hands. The effect was mesmerizing. Every movement, each handstroke, was followed by a momentary burst of blue-green light, as though I had released a handful of fireflies. I circled beneath the canoe, which, with its paddles pointing out, resembled a great black dragonfly hanging in the sky. I waved and curled my hands, kicked above me until my body was surrounded by a whorl of stardust, like the sorcerer's apprentice in *Fantasia*. I was laughing when I surfaced, and so were the boys, who knew what I had seen.

And I could stop here. I could let this be enough. But there should be more to this story, shouldn't there?

I do remember there was more.

I realized Selastine was still underwater. How long had it been? One minute? Five?

"Selastine," I said, and the boys just laughed. "*Hem go walka-baot. Hem fising.*" I peered down and saw nothing. I took a great breath and dove, kicking at the sky, pulling at the deep, peering through the blackness.

There is a panic that comes when you hold your breath for too long. It's about oxygen, of course, and the thought of all that water pouring into your lungs. I saw the faintest glow, a foggy circle of light beneath me, and I struggled against my buoyancy, but the panic turned me around. I kicked for the surface and emerged far off the bow. The boys paddled toward me. I grabbed the gunwale and took ten deep breaths, then dove again. I exhaled slowly this time. I ignored the phosphorescent sparks that peeled from my fingers. I saw the light and kicked hard toward it. It grew into a jaundiced whorl of seaweed and sand. Perhaps there were coral rocks. I couldn't tell. A great, obscuring dust storm of silt was sweeping through the lagoon. I kicked farther and saw that the light was coming from a man, from Selastine. He was sitting cross-legged on the ocean floor, not moving, just sitting there. Occasionally, a bubble escaped from his mouth and floated like a nervous jellyfish up toward the steel glare of the night sky. The panic returned, obscuring my vision, screaming for me to surface, even as I struggled to make sense of the scene, which was somehow right and not right at the same time, and confusing, because I knew I should have been scared, yet I was not.

Selastine was not alone. Between the halo of his flashlight and the impenetrable void, in the gray murk between certainty and imagination, I saw something like a great drifting shadow. It was sleek, as long as a car and as black as cooking charcoal. And it was circling the shark boss, slowly, slowly, and if I could have pulled myself down just a little deeper I would have been able to give it a shape, but even as I gaped I was beginning to rise slowly back up toward the surface and the shark boss was becoming a blur, and his pool of light was shrinking and the great shadow was melting into the murk.

I wasn't certain at the time what I saw. I never spoke to Selastine about it. When he bobbed to the surface a moment after me, he just smiled and said, "*Gudfala* moon! *Gudfala* night!" again, and I agreed. We paddled to the shallows and splashed around a bit, while the pipe drum band thumped away beyond the distant mangroves. We returned to the fire and drank hot water mixed with milk powder.

Selastine asked me to stay a week, so we could fish and dive on the reef. I told him I couldn't. I told him I was bound for the Santa Cruz Group, to look for Bishop Patteson's ghost on Nukapu. He understood. Then he asked for my diving mask, and I gave it to him.

When I returned to Honiara, I didn't think about the circling shadow, not even when my friend Morris asked me about Langa Langa. Did I see the shark spirit? Did we have a tourist attraction? he asked. No, I told him. No, I told all my friends, though each time I told my story, I felt it could have been more complete. And then, late one evening after the lights had failed and the rascals had fled the city, after the conversation of a dozen men had trailed away around me and there was no sound but the rustling of palms and the whirring of cicadas, as the perspiration seeped down my back and the circle of listeners drew close, I let myself say yes. Yes, I saw a shadow in the deep. Yes, it was big and it was as black as cooking charcoal, and every sweep of its tail fin raised a storm of silt from the lagoon floor. Yes, that shadow had circled ever so slowly around my friend the shark boss, who was sitting cross-legged on a bed of crushed coral. And the story became whole, and I grew more certain every time I repeated it. Now there is no doubt. Yes, it was a shark. Yes, it was Bolai. Yes, an ancestor could still be summoned from the darkness. I would believe, and it would be true because I believed.

Myth, like love, is a decision. What it answers is longing. What it demands is faith. What it opens is possibility.

19

The Brothers and Their Miracles

And the Lord said unto him, What is that in thine hand?
And he said, A rod. And he said, Cast it on the ground.
And he cast it on the ground, and it became a serpent;
and Moses fled from before it.

—Exodus 4:2–3

When I returned from Langa Langa and found neither the *Temotu* nor the *Eastern Trader* in port, I was not surprised or particularly upset. I went straight to Chester Rest House, a hostelry run by the Melanesian Brotherhood. There were no guards at the rest house, nor was it wrapped in barbed wire like the Quality Motel. But it was the safest place to bunk in Honiara. A rascal wouldn't dare risk God's anger by crossing the *tasiu*. I did not go to Chester for protection, but to get closer to the brothers and to their magic. I was ready for both.

The rest house stood in a grove of flowering trees on the hillside above the port. There were papayas in the garden and frangipani blossoms scattered in the dirt. There was a cement porch on which the brothers lounged, smoked, chewed their betel, and guffawed at the world. These brothers were not at all like *Tasiu* Ken, the stoic dispenser of curses I had met on Vanua Lava. They nestled in each other's arms like children at naptime. They shrieked like birds when amused. They liked to tease the Sisters of Melanesia, who lived in a house just down the hill. Chester became my home and the brothers my friends.

A dozen *tasiu* lived in a communal household next door to Chester. Seven times a day, a bell would ring and the brothers would disappear to the chapel inside their house to pray. That's what made the brothers powerful, people said. All that prayer. My first friend, little Brother Albert Wasimae, showed me the chapel. It was the size of a bedroom. There was a small wooden cross on the altar, and a picture of a pale, white Jesus wearing his crown of thorns. Also on the altar:

Two chicken's feet, bound together and caked in dried blood. The feet were a killing charm, surrendered by a man on Malaita.

A plastic vial of ground coral. You could kill a man, or at least give him insomnia, if you blew that powder at him.

A tongue of shriveled gingerroot, wrapped in a brittle leaf. You could use that root to spoil someone's brain.

A bullet, whose power was obvious.

Brother Albert told me that all of these bad things had been rendered impotent by prayer and a sprinkling of holy water, which was kept in glass jugs on the floor. The bad things had been gathered in the course of the brothers' Clearance Mission.

I had heard about this Clearance Mission. It was not the same as evangelical work; it was a campaign of direct action against black magic. The *tasiu* would tour the countryside, making surprise visits to villages where people had complained of curses and sorcery. When they arrived, the brothers ordered the entire community to come to church. All the residents were then obligated to wrap their hands around one of the *tasiu*'s walking sticks and tell the truth about their own use of magic. People knew that *kastom* spells were no match for those walking sticks, just as the Egyptian pharaoh's magicians had not stood a chance against the staff of Moses. They handed over whatever charms they had. A liar would simply be unable to let go of the walking stick until he told the truth. The test left the worst ne'er-do-wells in convulsive fits. Sometimes, said Brother Albert, if the confrontation was with a *kastom* devil, the clash could be so explosive it would break a walking stick in two. So the *tasiu* carried spares.

There was a corkboard by the door of the chapel. Tacked to it were dozens of notes written by people who wanted the brothers' help—or rather, God's help, which they hoped the *tasiu* would direct their way. People asked the brothers to pray for their careers, their marriages, their children's success in school exams. Some had attached money. A politician's wife complained that her husband spent too much time campaigning: could the *tasiu* pray for the politician to come home, or at least send money? One writer lamented that his daughter was having trouble becoming pregnant and explained that this was likely the result of a curse cast by angry in-laws. Another pleaded for the brothers to save him from the "green leaf with satanic power."

People in the Solomon Islands had looked to the *tasiu* for hope and for miracles for almost eighty years. Their journey, like that of Abraham, began with a vision and a message from God.

It was 1924. Ini Kopuria, a beefy young corporal in the Native Armed Constabulary, suffered an injury while trying to arrest a bad man. His leg was torn open, or perhaps it was broken. Nobody remembered the details. It was the message that mattered. As he rested in hospital, Kopuria had a visitation from Jesus. "Ini," said Jesus, "you are not doing the work I want you to do." It took Kopuria several months to realize that what Jesus really wanted was for him to organize a fraternity of native missionaries to carry the gospel to all the places where people still clung to their heathen ways.

The bishop of Melanesia, John Steward, ferried Kopuria around the islands aboard the *Southern Cross* so that he could recruit volunteers. By the end of the year, Kopuria had enlisted six. The volunteers returned to Kopuria's farm at Tabalia, on the northern tip of Guadalcanal. They cleared the jungle and built a house for their headquarters. They called each other *tasiu*. They took vows of chastity, poverty, and obedience to the church. They adopted a uniform, which consisted of a simple black loincloth and a black belt, underneath which was wrapped a white sash. This was the birth of the Melanesian Brotherhood.

The brothers traveled in pairs, trekking barefoot to the most remote pagan villages in the Solomon Islands. They did not behave like other missionaries. They were humble. They worked in people's gardens, slept in people's homes, and spread the word gently. They also carried walking sticks, which they used to exorcise evil forces from bodies and places. Even in the early days, islanders recognized that the *tasiu* carried a tremendous amount of *mana*. People said they could heal the sick and perform miracles. They were not afraid of devils or ancestral spirits. Their *mana* was similar to the power held by *kastom* priests, but it did not come from traditional spirits or ancestors. It came from God. What made the *tasiu* holy was their prayer, their devotion, their vow of poverty, their separation from material striving. People respected the clergy. But they revered the *tasiu*. Everyone knew that God worked through the *tasiu*, and that crossing them was akin to crossing God.

Everyone knew that when the darkness closed in on Honiara, when the city and its shanties were claimed by chaos, fear, and dumb violence, it was the Melanesian Brotherhood—not the police, the government, or foreigners—who brought back the light. In 2000, when bullets were whizzing back and forth between the barricades that surrounded Honiara, the brothers camped for four months in the no-man's-land between the Malaitan and Guadalcanalese militants. The *tasiu* negotiated for the release of hostages, they calmed bands of vigilantes, they sheltered refugees. They carried the bodies of the dead back to their relatives. They exhumed corpses from shallow graves so that murder victims could be identified. They marched into militant camps to press for peace.

"In the name of Jesus Christ we appeal to you: stop the killing, stop the hatred, stop the payback," went their official letter. "Those people you kill or you hate are your own Solomon Islands brothers. Blood will lead to more blood, hatred will lead to greater hatred and we will all become the prisoners of the evil we do."

Their prediction was accurate. After hundreds of people were shot, chopped, or tortured to death, hundreds more were wounded, and tens of thousands of people displaced, it was generally agreed that the country had indeed become a prisoner of hatred. The killing did not ease up until the *tasiu* made their most famous stand, out past the airport on the Alligator Creek Bridge. Everyone knew the story: how the *tasiu* had walked right out onto the concrete stage of the bridge with their walking sticks; how, shielded from the bullets only by their holiness, they created a human barrier between the ignorant armies. The fighters saw that the *tasiu* were not hurt by their bullets. They saw that God disapproved of their violence. This was the beginning of the end of the war.

After the peace agreement was signed, members of the Melanesian Brotherhood led the ex-militants and their convoys of stolen trucks into Honiara and presided over the peace celebrations. For all their dashing back and forth amid the bullets, not a single *tasiu* was killed during the conflict. Most people agreed this was a sign of their special relationship with God.

Now, when people in Honiara wanted to forget their sad stories and push back the darkness a little, they talked about the Melanesian Brotherhood. The *tasiu* had pulled a demon from so-and-so's soul. The *tasiu* had used a dash of holy oil and a tap of a walking stick to extract a sickness-inducing stone from a man's wrist. The *tasiu* had rescued a bloodied victim from Harold Keke's boys and taken him to their base at Tabalia, where God had made him strong again, then sent a single thunderbolt to illuminate the faces of the man's rescuers.

Everyone's favorite *tasiu* story was one about the snake gun: The Peace Monitoring Council had been attempting for more than a year to retrieve arms from all the ex-militants. But the boys liked their guns and did not want to give them up. The police weren't much help, largely because members of the Royal Solomon Islands Police had stolen their own guns and distributed them to *wantoks* in the first place. The situation seemed hopeless. So a few months before my arrival, the government had asked the Melanesian Brotherhood to take over the job of disarmament. The *tasiu* formed a special unit to go out and ask for the guns back, in God's name.

The disarmament unit had already collected several hundred guns when news came of a shootout on the outskirts of Honiara. The *tasiu*, not the police, went to investigate. They drove to the house of the man responsible. He denied everything. The lead *tasiu* told him, "We know you were shooting a gun at your neighbors, and if you don't give us that gun, we will just have to wait here until you change your mind." They waited. The man sweated nervously in the sun. Minutes passed, maybe hours. Finally, a shadow appeared on the man's dirt floor. It slithered out into the sunlight. The man's son said: "Daddy! Daddy! Look at the snake!" The man tried to ignore the shadow, which continued to writhe threateningly in front of him. One *tasiu* said, "Don't touch it." Then he reached down and grabbed the snake by its head. The serpent stopped writhing. It became as hard as metal. The *tasiu* lifted the snake in the air, and it was transformed back into the machine gun it had always been. This is the kind of story they tell now in the Solomon Islands.

I was fascinated by the way the brothers had grafted the traditional concept of *mana* onto Christianity. Like the old *kastom* priests, the *tasiu* were credited with directing supernatural forces, but their power came from the same God I had learned about in Sunday school. I had been taught to see biblical miracles as educational metaphors. But the brothers had taken the Anglican God and wrestled him back down to earth, where he was behaving much like a Melanesian ancestor spirit, much like the god of my own ancestors. Here he was, allowing his power to be directed by incantations and walking sticks. Here he was, getting involved and taking sides, just like in the Old Testament.

I was drawn to the *tasiu*, though for weeks I had felt unfit to befriend them; surely they would sense my skepticism and know my questions were insincere. But my time in the lagoons had changed me. Now I was ready. I wanted to witness the spectacle of the clearance and disarmament missions. I wanted to see the brothers make those sorcerers squirm in church. I wanted to see them turn guns into snakes, or at least to see them strike the fear of God into the hearts of men like Jimmy Rasta. But the brothers in Honiara had no idea which of their outstations were conducting clearance raids. We learned of clearance victories only after the fact (some ginger collected here, a sorcerer humbled there). The disarmament crew was more easily caught. They were based in the bishop of Melanesia's old house. I went there and found them watching videos of old American cop shows—"to improve our investigative skills," they explained.

One member of the team promised to take me along on a mission. Brother Clement Leonard was a great bear of a man with enormous hands and ruby-stained lips. "You stick with me," he said. The brother had so much betel crammed into his cheek, he could only slur. "I am your connection. I am your source. I will help you."

"There is urgency," I said. It was true. I was running out of money and time. But the urgency was about more than that. I was worried that my memories of lagoon magic might fade. I was worried that I would lose my new way of seeing.

"I understand," said Brother Clement. But he must not have understood, because I didn't see him for days.

I could not get close to things. The adventure was always yesterday. The action was always beyond the horizon. In fact, receiving news of any action in the Solomons was a bit like looking at the night sky; you knew a star had been real at some point because its light reached you, but you also knew that spark was thousands of years old and that the star's fire might by now have died entirely.

I was waiting out the midday glare at Amy's Snack Bar on Mendaña Avenue one afternoon when a tallish man with delicate pale skin strode by. I noticed white skin in Honiara because, like everyone else, I kept an eye out for my own *wantoks*. (After months alone, I was beginning to grasp the *wantok* concept. Nobody understands you like someone from your own island, or even better, like someone you can talk to without resorting to pidgin, which is nobody's mother tongue.)

The white man wore glasses and had an unruly shock of light brown hair. He was smoking. That wasn't remarkable. This was: he wore a black shirt, black shorts, and a black-and-white sash around his waist. I had never thought of asking the *tasiu* if there were any white men in their order. I couldn't imagine someone from my world falling so completely into the realm of miracles. I pushed my way onto the street and chased him down.

"Awright?" he said when I caught him. His accent, to my untrained ear, suggested south London, salt-of-the-earth, but he had the bearing of an Old Etonian.

I knew of the brotherhood's vow of poverty, and I had seen their diet of root vegetables and mush, so I suspected the white *tasiu* would accept an invitation to dinner at the Hong Kong Palace, where the spring rolls were served with ketchup but the beer was cold.

"Brother," I said, after we had polished off a couple of Sol-Brew, "what the hell are you doing in that uniform?"

He laughed. "Sometimes I wake up and think I must be bonkers," he said, wolfing down the last of our chop suey. "I'm forty-two years old, and I have no estate, no house, no money, no car, no material symbols to mark my existence . . ."

"You are an ascetic," I said.

"Actually, yes."

Richard Carter was born in Guildford, a cathedral town just south of London. His father was an Anglican priest. He had studied English and drama. He had always been a Christian, at least in a postmodern sense. He had thought that God was a good idea, that Jesus was a very good teacher. Christianity had seemed a useful religion.

The young man's view of the cosmos changed after he moved to Indonesia, and then to the Solomons in 1987. He came to teach at the Church of Melanesia's Selwyn College. He saw things he had never seen in England, things that convinced him, just as they had convinced the Victorian missionaries, that the struggle between good and evil was something that could be seen and touched. Carter was ordained a minister in 1992. From the beginning, he was drawn to the *tasiu*, and they to him. He was captivated by their lives, by their meekness, by the tenderness and nobility of their community, by the holiness he saw in their poverty. The brothers must have seen a similar holiness in Carter; they invited him to join their order, and he became Brother Richard. Soon he was rewriting Christian parables as Melanesian dramas, which the brothers performed on tour throughout the islands.

"But what about the miracles?" I asked. Did he believe in the fantastical *mana*-ization of the brotherhood or in all that funneling of divine power through walking sticks and holy water? Had the islanders wiped the rational skepticism from his English soul? I wanted him to shout *yes*.

But instead he smiled cryptically. "I have become more receptive to the mysteries of faith, to things that can't be explained simply . . ."

"Bending bullets?"

"No, I don't believe in bending bullets. But believe me, somehow this community of young men is able to do things that other Melanesians can't. And it's all through the grace of God. The brothers don't spend three or four hours a day in prayer for nothing, you know. Here, let me tell you a story.

"In my early days, I was on the *Southern Cross*, heading for the Reef Islands with the brothers. We heard on the ship's radio that a man back at Taroaniara, the ship's base, was possessed by some kind of evil. The poor guy had been foaming at the mouth, that kind of thing, and finally he had died. Well, by some miraculous coincidence, our first landfall in the Reefs happened to be this man's home village. We went ashore. The old folks gathered around and told us that the dead man had recently been selected as their next chief. But not only that: they said that anyone they had ever chosen to be their chief had been afflicted by a death curse— there had been possessions, sickness, freak accidents, all kinds of stuff. It had been going on for decades. You could feel the darkness in the village. We were faced with an ancestral curse so strong it had cast a pall of darkness over the place. So the brothers sat down and decided to perform a clearance.

"The next morning we conducted a rousing service about the power of light over darkness. We reminded people that in the presence of God, evil is a nonreality: it cannot exist. We made a procession around the village with big pots of holy water. We went from house to house, driving out evil and praying while the brothers marked crosses in the sand. A lot of this 'driving out' involves using primeval symbols, you know: water, fire, or marks in the sand to express spiritual truth. Anyway, this exercise was incredibly powerful. More and more people joined the procession. They followed the brothers around. They started singing hymns to the rhythm of *kastom* songs. Then, after the ceremony, all the people who had been pie-faced, dark and gray, they were suddenly light and cheery and laughing. You could feel the oppression lifting like a great weight from their shoulders! There was a physical sense of release from darkness. I felt it, too, the darkness dissolving away. And, you know, the village has never been bothered by that curse again."

"And this is your miracle?"

"Yes, it is. I would probably explain those events differently than the Melanesians would. But their fears were real. The darkness that held them was not something you could simply dismiss. It was killing people, and the brothers helped put an end to it. I have no difficulty coming to terms with the miraculous aspect of what happened there."

No thunder. No blinding clouds. No ghosts. Carter's tale didn't match up to my own miracle stories at all. It did not seem like proof of anything more than the power of psychology. I wanted to ask him how miracles worked, what demons looked like, how he thought evil and goodness might interact with atoms and molecules in order to change events in the material world. What about the guns that melted into snakes, the helpful crocodiles, the walking sticks that hung in midair? Did he believe these things really had happened or not?

"Why can't you just let the stories be?" he asked.

"Because I would like to know they are true."

"Ah," he said. "You want proof."

"I made it rain by blowing on a *kastom* stone," I offered, hoping he would see that I was a believer, too. What he saw was my hunger, my childish urgency.

He sighed. "Look, our knowledge of truth, the truth about that which is life-giving and eternal, it exists beyond the bounds of rationalism. Faith carries us closer, but in the end we can't describe it. We just don't have words for it. At the end of the day, we are reduced to telling stories about that mystery. That's what I know."

"But guns turning into snakes . . ."

"Did Jesus actually walk on water? My answer would be, yes, he did, in his disciples' memory of him. He did in their faith experience. The walk on water could not be captured on video or analyzed by a scientist, and yet it was profoundly true for those who witnessed it."

The white *tasiu* refused to be pinned in the magic debate. He drifted between metaphor and an amorphous mysticism. It took many hours of conversation, months of reflection, and the death of our friends to understand his message. What I now think the brother was saying was that stories are containers for spiritual truths. What I think he was saying is that it was the apostles' faith in such miracles that enabled them to surmount fear and chaos in order to lay the foundations for their church. The miracle was made true because it was believed. But did the miraculous moment lay in history, in imagination, or somewhere in between?

The Canadian scholar Northrop Frye argued that it was a mistake for biblical scholars to attempt to divine the boundary between historical and mythical truth. Frye, who was a United Church minister, insisted that the key to understanding the Bible was to see it entirely as a work of metaphorical literature. Some parts of the New Testament may be historically accurate, but they are accurate only by accident. The Bible's writers—none of whom actually met Jesus—were not at all interested in historical reporting because they were tackling the much more important task of imparting a grand metaphor. And that metaphor was the life of their Messiah, who was, as they say, the *word* made flesh.

"Jesus is not presented as a historical figure," wrote Frye, "but as a figure who drops into history from another dimension of reality, and thereby shows what the limitations of the historical perspective are." The Bible, he concluded, was *more* true because of its counterhistorical nature.

Frye could just as easily have applied his theory to Melanesia. If people used myth to express spiritual truths, then it made sense for miracles to be attributed to the *tasiu*, who embodied everything that Melanesians had come to see as holy. People felt their goodness, their glow. Stories about the *tasiu* began with observed events, but, as Frye would have it, these were not always enough to convey the force of the holiness that people felt. So the storytellers dramatized the observed moment with symbolism. A lightning strike. A helpful crocodile. Whatever. They did what storytellers have done since the beginning of time: they embellished in order to elevate their formless truths and place their stories in the mythical realm.

The key to finding God, Frye said, was imagination.

My great-grandfather would have been appalled by Frye. He insisted that a man had no business serving as a religious teacher if he denied "the plain facts of the Gospel record." Biblical miracles were rock solid. The incarnation and the resurrection of Jesus were nonnegotiable. But how did Henry Montgomery know these things? Where did his certainty begin? I searched through his writings for answers, and what I found was an infuriating smugness: "Our faith rests on a revelation from above. God has spoken to us, and we have heard His voice and have been assured that it is the voice of God Himself," he wrote in *Life's Journey*, a series of essays published in 1916. In other words, God was true for Henry *because* he believed, because he had faith. In one essay he personified Faith as a feminine spirit. He gave her a voice. Faith pitied and chided skeptics, reminding them that she was above proof, "but I am more certain to your heart and life because I am seen by better eyes than your bodily eyes. Your soul and spirit have eyes too. That is how you see me and accept my message from God."

All this was infuriating, and seemed unfair, too. Henry Montgomery got his proof. He got his miracle, in the form of a personal visitation from the Holy Spirit that Easter morning in his Irish garden. All I wanted was more of the same. I wanted the *tasiu* to make their walking sticks hang in midair for me. I wanted them to beguile crocodiles. I had not yet considered that my great-grandfather was a teller of mythical stories. I had not yet considered that his miraculous visions, and my own, could be expressions of the soul's other way of seeing. I was not yet ready to consider the idea on which Frye and the white *tasiu* likely agreed: the measure of a miracle's truth was not the accuracy of the event so much as the quality of the faith it inspired.

Brother Richard said that magic did not count as a miracle unless it led to God. That is why he was so worried about the Melanesian Brotherhood. Faith in the power of the *tasiu* and their walking sticks was verging on idol worship. People were forgetting that those walking sticks were merely symbolic. Some members of the order had even begun to believe they could direct supernatural power. All this talk of guns turning into snakes was causing them to develop a sense of invulnerability and spiritual pride. It was a trap, and it could only lead to more fear and superstition. What the islanders needed, said the white *tasiu*, was a new kind of story, one that would lead them closer to the transcendent vision of the New Testament.

I did not see the *tasiu* bend bullets or cast out demons. I did not see them turn machine guns into snakes. But I did see something of their power, which was not as I imagined. And I did see the beginning of a story that would carry them through a great darkness and back into the light, a story in which the brotherhood would give up their *mana* but be utterly reborn. And like the New Testament, like the myth of Bishop Patteson, that story would be about suffering as much as it would be about rebirth.

I was sitting on the veranda at the Chester Rest House one morning when the MV *Temotu* appeared like a great white lie in the port. I saw her tie up to one of the cement piers. Then came the *Eastern Trader*, following like a mongrel after its master. I ran down to swear at their crews. Where the hell had they been? West, they said. When would we be leaving for Santa Cruz?

"Tomorrow," said one sailor with a chuckle.

"Tomorrow, someday—or tomorrow, the day after today?"

"Tomorrow, tomorrow, of course."

I was about to leave when I spotted a burly *tasiu* climbing over the ship's rails; it was Clement, the gun brother who had promised to be my source. He was lumbering toward a Toyota Hilux with a white flag mounted on the roof of the cab. The flag had a black cross stitched to it. There were more *tasiu* inside the truck. It was the disarmament gang.

"Where are you going?" I demanded.

"CDC-1," said Brother Clement. "Criminal activity. We're on a mission."

CDC-1 was part of a giant swath of plantations east of Honiara once run by the foreign-owned Commonwealth Development Corporation. During the tension, the company had evaporated and its Malaitan workers had been run off the island. Now the people who considered themselves to be the traditional owners of the plantation lands were fighting over the spoils.

"I'm coming with you," I said.

"Yes, you are coming!" said Brother Clement, as though he had planned it all along.

We stopped at the Sweetie Kwan store, where I bought bread, peanut butter, and sticks of tobacco for everyone. Then we were off: stereo blasting, cigarette smoke pouring from the windows, betel spit flying.

The driver, who would not tell me his name, threw on a New Caledonian reggae cassette.

"We will call him Driver X!" said Clement, who sat in the front seat, chewing and toying with his medallion. The necklace was strung with hundreds of tiny dolphin's teeth. I sat in the backseat, flanked by Brothers Floyd and Nicolas, who sang and giggled and tickled me until I had to slap them. Another brother huddled in the truck's box. I recognized him as Francis, the white *tasiu*'s best friend. Francis had soft skin and straight hair, marks of Polynesian, rather than Melanesian, ancestry. He was born in faraway Tikopia. I couldn't see his eyes through his wraparound sunglasses. He was very quiet. I concluded that he was not so important.

I wish that I had known then about the fate Brother Francis would meet on the Weather Coast. I wish I had known then that he was the beginning of a new story and the end of my own.

Driver X threw on a Bob Marley cassette and cranked up the volume. We rocked out of town, past the rusting remains of World War II Quonset huts, past the garbage mountains and the hundreds of betel nut stands, past Jimmy Rasta's bottle shop and the airport. We crossed the Alligator Creek Bridge, which seemed to have forgotten the battle that had been fought across its span. Grass was beginning to sprout through the concrete.

We howled like teenagers. We sang along with the music: *Let's get together and feel alright.* There was trouble ahead, but we were blameless. It was a road trip. I felt as though we should have been drinking Slurpees spiked with vodka and throwing beer cans at street signs. None of the *tasiu* was over thirty.

There was no traffic after Alligator Creek, but sometimes we saw people on the road, hiking with gas jugs or plastic baskets on their heads. Driver X slowed to pick them up, but Brother Clement stopped him.

"No! Official business! Very important! Very dangerous!" bellowed Clement.

"Commando unit! Strike force! Bruce Willis!" shouted Floyd.

"Army! Army!" chanted Nicolas, poking me beneath the ribs and saluting. "*Yumi stap insaed long army!*"—We're in the army.

Brother Francis just smiled and waved at the foot travelers. We didn't stop for anyone.

Soon the countryside changed. There was nobody left on the

road—which had once been a paved highway but was now disin-
tegrating, clawed by great forests of grass and fern and woody
shrubs pushing in from both sides. We passed the bullet-riddled
shell of a gas station and later a health clinic, also abandoned. The
journey began to feel less festive.

The next bridge required four-wheel drive. It had been
bombed to stop the Malaita Eagles from getting too far out of Honiara, but the bombing had been halfhearted. The bridge had not
been destroyed but had simply sagged into the riverbed. The midday air thickened. It dripped with bad memories and a hazy,
shapeless malevolence. The brothers stopped singing.

We approached what looked like a lemonade stand. Its occu-
pant, who wore a camouflage sun hat, stood up, rubbed his eyes,
and motioned for us to stop. Clement spoke to him in mumbles,
and the man waved us on.

"Which side is he on?" I asked.

"This week, he is Gold Ridge," said Clement.

A junction in the road and another guard hut. Men leaned
against what looked like a giant outhouse, erected in the middle of
a side track. Its walls were solid and windowless except for a hori-
zontal slit in one wall, from which a gun barrel pointed. The shack
gave off a puff of smoke, and then it lurched forward. The shack
was not an outhouse. It was a homemade tank. Its gun barrel
shifted and remained trained on our truck as we rolled away again.

The situation on the plantations was not simple, Clement said.
Sometimes the plantation villages fought with each other. Sometimes they fought with a faction based at Gold Ridge, in the hills
near the abandoned mine. The previous day, a boy from Matepona,
a village just past CDC-1, had been kidnapped by the Gold Ridge
militants. The police were still too afraid to cross Alligator Creek,
so it was up to the *tasiu* to perform the rescue.

We stopped at a clutch of tin-roofed bungalows hopping with
children and clucking chickens in order to pick up the boy's father.

He was a weak-looking man with gray hair and glassy eyes. His name was Johnson.

"Where is Junior? Where is my boy?" he said somewhat rhetorically, since by this point we had established that the Gold Ridge boys had kicked the shit out of Johnson Junior, then taken him back to their base. Why had they kidnapped him? Johnson had no idea. His was a good Christian family. Clement tapped his feet impatiently.

Johnson, his wife, and his brother hopped in the back of the truck with Brother Francis, who smiled at them but remained silent. We headed east, past another roadblock, past rows and rows of neglected oil palms, their shaggy tops casting mottled shadows on the jungle that had begun to rise, unchecked, beneath them. Bushy vines climbed up the palm trunks, arcing into the sky above the fronds. I once heard someone describe the Solomons as a green desert. Now I understood. Like the shifting sands, the jungle was always creeping closer, seizing on weakness, threatening to bury human industry in suffocating mounds, in an impenetrable, seething desolation of electric green.

We pulled into a clearing. There was a sign: Tetere Police Post. But there were no police. The lawn was overgrown. A crowd of men waited in the shade of an oak tree.

"The Gold Ridge boys," said Brother Clement.

Our arrival was not a surprise. That was obvious, because the Gold Ridge militants had hidden their guns. (People were careful around the brotherhood. If a *tasiu* saw your gun, he would insist that you hand it over.)

The militants shifted nervously, glaring at Johnson like wolves assessing a wounded buck. Their leader was a fat man with silver aviator glasses.

"Now we will straighten things out," Clement whispered to me.

"Welcome, *tasiu*, welcome," said the leader. "This is just a family problem. We are sorry to bother you."

"Yes, said Johnson, who was slouching deferentially behind Clement. "Just a small problem. I just want my Junior back."

"And we want our machine gun back," snarled the leader.

"And no more bombing," said a sinewy young man behind the leader, pausing to spit a great hork of betel into the grass no-man's-land between us.

Machine gun? Bombing?

It was difficult to understand the exchange that followed. The militants were furious, and Johnson was vague. But gradually it became clear that Johnson and his boy were not as meek as they seemed.

Apparently, a gang from CDC-1 had blocked the road between Gold Ridge and Honiara—roadblocks were a convenient way of extorting cigarettes and petrol from travelers. That was a month ago. The Gold Ridge gang was upset about this, even though they had blocked plenty of roads themselves. They made a retaliatory sweep through the plantations, beating the odd settler and stealing the odd pig. But when they hit Johnson's compound, Johnson and his Junior fought back mightily, wrestling an SR-88 assault rifle from one of the attackers and sending the Gold Ridge gang running. Then Johnson Junior acquired some explosives and bombed a bridge on the Gold Ridge road. That's why the Gold Ridge boys had hunted him down, and why he was now bleeding in a shack behind the police station.

Nobody shouted. Johnson whimpered. At first the militants spoke in hushed, pleading voices. Clement tried to negotiate, but even as the militants deferred ("Thank you, *tasiu*, yes, *tasiu*, we are sorry, *tasiu*"), they grew more agitated and shuffled forward. They hissed like snakes and quivered with quiet outrage. The militants stopped chewing their betel. Clement chewed faster. A drop of red foam boiled at the corner of his mouth. Perspiration beaded on all our faces. The tension was nauseating. I wished I had not come.

And then Brother Francis stepped forward. He wore a shy

half-smile. He pulled off his wraparound sunglasses to reveal the eyes of a daydreamer. He did not look at Johnson or at the militants. He gazed at the trampled earth as though looking right through it, then toward the deep green folds of the highlands, then up at the sky, and then he bowed his head. The militants seemed transfixed by his movements, like charmed snakes. The bickering trailed off. Brother Francis spoke softly, and his voice was like a breeze blowing through the yard, rustling through the dry grass, easing the weight of the humid afternoon. I could barely hear him. At first I thought he was reasoning with the militants. But his murmurs were too melodic for that. I realized he was praying when I noticed two dozen other bowed heads. The militants unclenched their fists. The leader removed his aviator glasses. An immense calm fell on us all.

And that was it. Within minutes, the problem was settled.

We drove back to Johnson's house, where his wife and his sister served us great lumps of taro in coconut milk. Johnson beamed. "You know, my boy didn't blow up the bridge," he said cheerily. "He just made a little explosion to scare those Gold Ridge boys away."

"*Hem stret brotha*," said Clement. "But we need the gun."

"The gun?" said Johnson, smiling weakly.

"The gun," said Clement, rolling a fresh wad of betel around his gums.

Johnson hummed and hawed. So did his brother and his wife. But they knew the game was up. Finally, someone produced a battered SR-88 assault rifle from inside the house. There was no ammunition. We took the gun with us. The agreement back at the Tetere police post had been for everyone to return the following day. The *tasiu* would bring Johnson's gun. The Gold Ridge gang would bring Johnson Junior—alive. There would be an even trade, and then they would all make a picnic together. In fact, when the brothers returned the following day, they picked up

Johnson Junior but informed the Gold Ridge boys that they were keeping the SR-88 so they could dispose of it in God's name. Who could argue with that? The militants didn't.

We sang all the way home, and we stopped at the middle of the Alligator Creek Bridge so I could take a photo of the brothers. I wanted them to hold the gun above their heads. They refused, but they did pull out their walking sticks. I keep that photo on my wall. There is Driver X, running along the bridge railing. There is Brother Nicolas, beaming, and Brother Floyd, barefoot. There is Brother Clement, with his walking stick and his white sneakers. And behind them, squinting into the light, his lips pursed into that shy half-smile, is Brother Francis, whose face and name have now been seared into my memory.

How could I have known that it was my job to remember more than I remember of Brother Francis?

How could I have known that he would go off to challenge the greatest darkness his country had ever seen? Would I have warned him? And if I had warned him, would he have sailed to the Weather Coast anyway?

I didn't yet know the significance of the moment. I didn't yet know that after all the talk of miracles and magic, it was Brother Francis who would offer an answer that obscured all the rest. I didn't yet know Brother Francis's place in the story, or my own. That knowledge would take months to come, and by that time Brother Francis would be dead.

The last time I saw Brother Francis, he wrote in my notebook: Believe.

20

Nukapu and the Meaning of Stories

Behold, I shew you a mystery; We shall not all sleep, but we shall all be changed, In a moment, in the twinkling of an eye, at the last trump: for the trumpet shall sound, and the dead shall be raised incorruptible, and we shall be changed.

—1 Corinthians 15:51–52

The story on which Brother Francis would base his life and his death was the one that had guided Melanesians for more than a century. It brought my great-grandfather to the archipelago, and it had drawn me, too, from the moment I discovered that packet of sand back in Oxford. I had found a dozen different accounts in libraries in Oxford, London, Sydney, and Canberra. Some were the scribbled testimonies of sailors. Some were written years after the fact by amateur evangelical historians. Some were fanciful reconstructions. The story captivated me, but it also bothered me, because the earliest versions of it were constructed and put to work even before Bishop John Coleridge Patteson's followers had figured out just how and why the first bishop of Melanesia was murdered on Nukapu. But the story of Patteson's martyrdom did not require facts to survive. It lived independently of them. It was bigger than facts. That is why I call it a myth.

My great-grandfather gave his version in *The Light of Melanesia*. The things Henry Montgomery wanted remembered were these:

Patteson had always followed his god. As a boy, young Coley longed to say the Absolution in church, because he saw how happy it made people.

Patteson was royally blessed. As a student at Eton, Coley was nearly crushed when he stumbled in front of the oncoming wheel of the royal carriage, but he was saved by the outstretched hand of young Queen Victoria—"How much depended upon that happy moment!"

Patteson was the rightful successor to Selwyn, founder of the Melanesian Mission. He showed uncommon bravery, but also gentleness, in his South Pacific adventures. More than once, wrote my great-grandfather, Patteson was confronted by a native with arrow on the string and bow drawn tight. "Shoot away!" Patteson would shout. "It is all right," and his pluck and his smile would disarm his opponent.

Other accounts indicate that while Patteson escaped certain death many times, he could not always save his disciples. In 1864, Patteson was chased from the shores of Santa Cruz by a crowd of three hundred agitated villagers. He reached his whaleboat and used the wooden rudder to shield his crew from the hail of arrows. But the oarsmen were pierced like pincushions. One took a bone-tipped arrow in the chest, another through a cheek. Fisher Young and Edwin Nobbs, lads who had sailed north with the bishop from their home on Norfolk Island, were both struck, but they kept rowing until they returned their master safely to the *Southern Cross*. Patteson nursed the boys' wounds, but he knew tetanus would take them both. Patteson later wrote to a cousin: "On the fourth day that dear lad Fisher said to me, 'I can't think what makes my jaw so stiff.' Then I knew that all hope was gone of his being spared." Young was buried on Vanua Lava. Nobbs was consigned to the deep.

People said the bishop, who thought of the boys as sons, was never the same after that. It was as though he knew of the fate that awaited him on Nukapu.

Friends urged him to return to England, but he was determined to crack the pagan shell of the Santa Cruz Group. For nine years he tried to land there, and for nine years he was repelled. His work was made increasingly dangerous by the presence of labor recruiters among the islands. The natives found it hard to distinguish between the *Southern Cross*, which carried their children away to mission school, and the blackbirding vessels, which carried strong young men off to work on plantations.

"The exasperation of the Natives is very great," wrote Patteson. "Kidnapping is going on fast. Many quarrels have arisen; Natives are retaliating; And they can't always discriminate, you know, between a friendly and an unfriendly white man."

The bishop sailed toward Santa Cruz in 1871 in an atmosphere of foreboding. The *Southern Cross* had just completed a loop north through the Solomons to collect the evangelists it had deposited two months previously. The missionaries' reports were alarming. Natives had killed all the crew on at least two labor-recruiting vessels. At San Cristobal (now Makira), the captain of the Fiji-based labor-recruiting ship *Emma Bell* bragged to missionary Joseph Atkin that Santa Cruz would be his next hunting ground.

All this bad news weighed heavily on Patteson, who expected to die on the islands but did not wish more of his followers to die along with him. The *Southern Cross* sped toward Santa Cruz but was becalmed near the volcanic sentinel Tinakula, whose peak smoked and glowed like the fires of Sinai. The bishop fell into deep meditation. The crew mused that he was praying for the poor souls who still remained in ignorance and darkness. My great-grandfather recounted Patteson's diary entry for that night: "On Monday we go to Nukapu. I am fully alive to the probability that some outrage has been committed here. The master of the vessel whom Atkin saw, did not deny his intention of taking away from these or from any other island any men or boys he could induce to come on board. I am quite aware we may be exposed to considerable risk on this account. I trust that all may be well, and that if it be His will that any trouble should come upon us, dear Joseph Atkin, his father's and mother's only son, may be spared."

The bishop would be denied that last wish.

The wind picked up, and at midday on September 20, the *Southern Cross* hove to outside Nukapu's barrier reef. No canoes ventured out to greet the ship, so Patteson, despite his trepidation, decided to go ashore. The crew lowered a whaleboat, and Patteson set off with four rowers: Joseph Atkin, Stephen Taroaniara from Baura, and two youths from Mota. They paddled to the reef, where they were intercepted by several canoes from the island. The Nukapuans were friendly, but the low tide made it impossible for the whaleboat to cross the reef, so the bishop accepted a ride to shore in one of the canoes. The rest of the canoes remained with the whaleboat and its rowers.

The strangers chatted across the water. The missionaries and the Nukapuans watched the bishop land on the island and disappear into a hut. Then one of the Nukapuans stood up in his canoe and raised his bow.

"Have you got anything like this?" he asked.

What a strange question. Of course the missionaries did not carry weapons.

Then he shot the first arrow.

"This one is for New Zealand!" shouted another warrior.

"This one is for Mota!" shouted another.

"This is for Baura," shouted another.

And so on, until the air was full of arrows.

The missionaries beat a frantic retreat, but not before Atkin had been struck by an arrow in the left shoulder and one of the Mota boys had taken one in his right, and someone else had an arrow through his straw hat. The arrows were each a yard long, heavy and tipped with shards of human bone, designed to break in the wound and fester. Taroaniara was hit six times: one arrow broke his jaw; another pierced his chest. The Nukapuans yelled and laughed at the fleeing missionaries, but they did not give chase.

When the whaleboat reached the *Southern Cross*, five arrowheads were pulled from Taroaniara's body, but the sixth had lodged too deeply in his chest to be extracted.

As soon as his own wound was cleaned, Atkin climbed back into the whaleboat with four men and went to look for the bishop. When the tide rose, they crossed the reef and scanned the shore with a telescope. They saw a pair of canoes put out from Nukapu. Near the middle of the lagoon, one paddler dropped a rock anchor. The men retreated to shore, leaving the anchored canoe behind. Atkin and his fellows rowed toward it cautiously and peered inside. There was a large parcel wrapped in a fine woven mat. Poking out from one end of the parcel was a pair of feet in striped socks. They unrolled the mat to find the bishop otherwise naked. The right side of his head had been shattered. There were more light cuts here and there on the body, but it was clearly the blow to the head that had killed him.

And this: the Nukapuans had attached a palm frond to the mat, over the bishop's breast. Five of the frond's leaves had been knotted. Five wounds. Five knots. It must have been a message.

And this: the dead bishop was said to have been wearing a placid smile, which was also widely interpreted as a message.

As soon as Patteson's body had been lifted into the whaleboat, a hundred islanders poured onto the beach and let out a collective scream. The missionaries retreated to the *Southern Cross* and put her sail to the wind.

The next morning, Bishop Patteson's body was consigned to the deep within sight of Nukapu. It took six days for tetanus to take hold of Joseph Atkin's nervous system. Taroaniara died two days later. The two were buried at sea before the ship reached Mota.

Codrington, who was now the mission's de facto leader, begged the government not to retaliate, but the HMS *Rosario* was immediately dispatched to Nukapu to bomb the island and burn its village. The ship's commanding officer reported that the foray incurred "severe loss of life."

Anglicans around the world mourned, but they also rejoiced. The church finally had its first episcopal missionary-martyr, a shining archetype of Anglo-Catholic sacrifice. Patteson's story was represented on stained-glass windows, carved into the stone of Exeter Cathedral, and writ into Victorian children's books, place names, and Sunday sermons.

Years passed before the missionaries returned to the island and learned the details of Patteson's death, but that did not stop them from wrapping the tragedy in symbolism and political intent within weeks. The attack had not been an act of spontaneous passion. The Nukapuans, they noted, did not decapitate the bishop, nor did they eat him, as islanders had done to the Reverends Williams and Gordon on Erromanga. The Nukapuans knew the bishop was a big man among Europeans. They treated his body with respect, right down to its presentation in that woven mat. So why had they killed him? The murder was a message, and that message was crystal clear, at least to the missionaries. Five knotted palm leaves. Five wounds. Five islanders must recently have been killed or kidnapped by labor recruiters. This was more than revenge: it was a demand for white men to stop the kidnapping.

"There is very little doubt but that the slave trade which is desolating these islands was the cause of this attack," announced Codrington. "Bishop Patteson was known throughout the islands as a friend, and now even he is killed to revenge the outrages of his countrymen. The guilt surely does not lie upon the savages who executed, but on the traders who provoked the deed."

The missionaries, who had long fought with labor recruiters for the islanders' attention, now lobbied in England and Australia to restrict the blackbirders. Churches and newspapers across the empire joined the outcry. Queen Victoria expressed her disapproval, and early in 1872, the British Parliament finally passed a law to regulate the trade—all this before anyone knew exactly what had happened on Nukapu.

When the *Southern Cross* returned thirteen years later, some Nukapuans told the missionaries what they wanted to hear.

"Let us follow the bishop ashore," my great-grandfather's version went. "We saw him last in the chief's canoe crossing the reef, and at length landing on the beach. It seems that he went into the house of which I have spoken, and laid himself down flat on his back, with his head on a Santa Cruz pillow, and closed his eyes. The place was full of people. Behind him there sat a man who had in his hand a wooden mallet. With this he struck the bishop on the top of his head. Death was instantaneous. It is said that he did not even open his eyes."

That much, all the Patteson stories had in common. But there are many stories and many more details.

The truth is, nobody ever said conclusively why and how the bishop was killed. The mission's accepted version is that the murderer was a relative of one of five men who had been kidnapped and taken to Fiji on a labor vessel. The murderer was banished from Nukapu for his outrage. He drifted from island to island like Cain, until he was finally shot by a chief on Santa Cruz. And those kidnapped men? One died on Fiji, but the other four stole a boat and followed the stars west, back to Nukapu. Of course, these details were related to the missionaries through interpreters, and the shell-shocked islanders were unlikely to contradict a tale that had already gained popularity among white men. This mission-friendly story also happened to give everyone a convenient scapegoat for the crime. But as Australian historian David Hilliard noted more than a century later, it did not explain the obviously premeditated attack on the crew in the *Southern Cross*'s whaleboat. And in fact, it was contradicted by the first missionary to actually live on Nukapu and become fluent in the local language. Actaeon E. C. Forrest was told that Patteson was killed over nothing more than a breach of etiquette. He had given a present to the wrong chief at the wrong time. This version did not carry the symbolism and power of the earlier myth. Perhaps that is why it was not included in the official version of the Patteson story. Regardless, it made Nukapu shine even more mysteriously for me.

I couldn't shake the sense that the island was the place where myth and history intersected. If I could just cross that reef and wade to its shore, if I could feel the island's certainty, I might be able to divine the space between all the old stories, and in that space find some truth about the god that my ancestors had carried around the world. I wanted an answer that felt as real and as powerful as the *kastom* miracles of the Nono and Langa Langa Lagoons had felt for me.

My maps insisted that Nukapu was a real place. There it was, a tiny speck on the northern fringe of the Santa Cruz Group, caught in the cartographer's grid, 166 degrees east of Greenwich, 10 degrees south of the equator, 430 miles east of Honiara, beyond a blankness of sea and the deep blue canyon of the Torres Trench. People in Melanesia all knew of Nukapu for the act of violence that marked the frontier between the age of the ancestors and the age of the new god. They knew it as the epicenter of the myth that bound them to their church. But nobody seemed to have been there. The island had begun to feel like more of an idea than a real place. Weeks had passed since the captains of the *Eastern Trader* and the MV *Temotu* had first promised a quick departure for the Santa Cruz Group. So it was with no great expectations that, on the morning after my adventure in CDC-1, I packed my air mattress, stocked up on cookies at the Sweetie Kwan store, and sauntered down to the port, as I had done a dozen times before. I didn't get my hopes up, even when I saw diesel smoke curling above my two ships and the pier between them seething with bodies.

A fierce, betel-stained drunk lurched out of the crowd toward me. "*Yu go wea? Fren! Fren! Yu go wea?*"

What eyes! What breath! What teeth! The man was a complete mess. I gave him the standard brush-off: "*Jes walkabaot.*"

He grabbed me by the hand before I could escape. "*Yu no rememba mi?*"

There was something about his face, those broken teeth, the foam gathered around the edge of his lips. Of course! This was the man I had been harassing for weeks. It was the captain of the *Eastern Trader*.

"My friend, we are all fueled up," the captain spat excitedly. "*By yumi go long Santa Cruz! Olgeta cabins booked-up nao. Sori! Sori! But yu savve slip insaed cabin blong mi!*"

The thought of bunking with the captain was horrifying. I knew the decrepit *Eastern Trader* would only be sailing if the MV *Temotu* was leaving, too—that way there would be a quick rescue if the old girl foundered at sea. But was the captain drinking in celebration or fear? I shook free of his grip and lost him amid the hundreds of Santa Cruzians and big-boned Polynesians who crowded the pier. There was a desperate excitement in the air. Everyone was flush with compensation money. People climbed over the *Temotu*'s rails, tossing aboard sacks of rice, rolls of chicken wire, and jugs of petrol. I joined them.

The *Eastern Trader* gave a wail and pulled bravely away. We all assumed the *Temotu* would follow, and there was much joyous smoking and spitting, at least until a loudspeaker crackled and hissed to life. "*Wantoks*, this is your captain," a voice boomed. "We should go now. We are ready to go now. But we cannot go now. *Mi sori tumas*, but human life is too precious to risk. We will try again at ten a.m. tomorrow."

What had happened was this. The police had finally mustered the courage to confront Jimmy Rasta's boys over their pirating of the Langa Langa ship *Sa'Alia*. There'd been a shootout on the beach east of Honiara. The police had won. Five of the pirates had been captured and taken to jail, but Rasta had returned to his compound for cocktails, and everyone knew that when Rasta hit the booze he got angry, and when Rasta got angry he tended to steal ships and bludgeon people with the butt of his gun. The seas would be much safer when he was hung over.

The loudspeaker crackled again: "I want to warn anyone who would steal any of the personal belongings left on this ship, especially the person who has lifted the calico, that we *tasiu* are here as God's witnesses. Think hard. If you want to enjoy the rest of your life, do not steal on this ship. God will punish you." It was Brother Clement.

When I returned to the port the next morning, the voice of the *Temotu*'s captain was echoing off the warehouse walls. "If you don't come on time, *wantoks*, how can we leave on time? I'm serious now! We're going home! Brothers and sisters, we're going home!"

I climbed aboard. The ship's pastor read a prayer, finishing it with an imploring, "Lord God, *olgeta laef blong mifala stap insaed long hand blong yu*."

God, our lives are in your hands. The tone of the prayer didn't do much to inspire confidence in the ship itself.

The lines were loosened and tossed aboard. The engine rumbled. I went to check on my berth. I had fought with the ship's agent until he had agreed to assign me a first-class berth. This, I now discovered, gave me the right to occupy a painted rectangle of floor, roughly the size of my inflatable air mattress, in a cabin with sixty other people. I had left a blanket on my square to mark it. Now the blanket was buried under a heap of bagged rice, Chinese noodles, grass mats, and plastic buckets.

I squeezed between two families: on one side, a mountainous Polynesian matriarch whose children crawled over her breasts like ants on their queen, and on the other, a prematurely seasick woman with a gaggle of teens who took turns wiping the drool from her chin.

Brother Clement appeared, and I remembered his vow of poverty. I invited him to my painted square for a picnic of crackers and peanut butter. He fell asleep on my inflatable mattress and stayed there for a day. I curled up on the linoleum with the Polynesians.

I realize I have complained about my ocean passages, and I would like to tell you that this one was different, that I sat with my legs dangling over the bow, experiencing the mariner's camaraderie and the exhilaration of the sea. But that's not how it was at all. My passages were getting exponentially miserable.

We were welcomed by the bruised folds of an approaching storm shortly after leaving the shelter of the strait that separates Guadalcanal and Malaita. As usual, the head overflowed. As usual, the wind picked up. As usual, the waves grew beneath us, lost their form, and became a mishmash of monstrous lumps, like giants writhing under a blanket.

The *Eastern Trader* turned back at Santa Ana, last of the islets that trailed from the eastern tip of Makira. For the first time on my journey, there were no islands left on the horizon. The optimism of our departure evaporated. The cargo mountains collapsed, and the babies began to howl. The cabin was transformed into an infernal day care of screaming tots, glassy eyes, swollen breasts, and bile.

Occasionally the *Temotu* corkscrewed, sending cargo and babies and vomit buckets tumbling across the cabin and unleashing a chorus of "*O, Jisas Krais! O, Jisas Krais!*" The cries sounded like accusations, as though God were letting us down horribly. "*Tasiu!*" people shouted after one nasty lurch, as though Brother Clement could calm the tempest. But he snored through the night and into the morning, oblivious, on my mattress.

We crashed through another afternoon and evening. I could not sleep. Near midnight, I climbed to the top deck to watch the ship's dogsbody wrestle bucket after bucket of trash over the rails. "We must not carry this mess with us to paradise," he shouted, "so we must feed the sea, my friend. Ha ha! The sea will consume it!"

I watched the garbage disappear into the night. The storm had exhausted itself. A light appeared on the horizon just off the bow, a faint crimson glow. It grew and became not a fire but a damp reflection of fire, like a red spotlight projected up onto the belly of the clouds. My heart raced at the sight. The light could only be Tinakula, the volcano around which the Santa Cruz Islands were scattered like the remnants of an ancient eruption. Tinakula! The volcano had inhabited my dreams for years.

Tinakula has guided explorers and missionaries to their deaths for nearly half a millennium. Like poor Alvaro de Mendaña, who discovered, named, and sweated to death in the poorly named Graciosa Bay in 1595. Or the mysterious comte de la Pérouse, the French navigator who had ably explored much of the North and South Pacific, but who was never seen again by Europeans after he left Australia's Botany Bay in 1788. Nearly forty years later, relics from la Pérouse's two ships were discovered on Vanikoro, a day's sail southeast of Tinakula. Islanders reported that their ancestors had slaughtered most of la Pérouse's crew and retired their skulls to a local spirit house.

Then came the missionary martyrs. First to die were Nobbs and Young, Patteson's beloved protégés. But a decade later, the

British commodore James Goodenough, protector of the Melanesian Mission, sailed past Tinakula and waded ashore at Carlisle Bay on Santa Cruz. He walked from one village to another, leading to much confusion among the warring natives as to whose side he was on. The locals attacked, and Goodenough recognized his diplomatic blunder. He ordered his men not to bomb or burn the village, then he died from his wounds.

"To step ashore at Santa Cruz! To sleep among people so famed for outrages committed in moments of excitement! The very thought was inspiring," gushed my great-grandfather after landing on the island in 1892. I felt the same way as the glow of Tinakula drifted toward the stern of the *Temotu*. We were turning, following the great shadow that had grown from the sea to starboard. This was Nendo, Mendaña's Santa Cruz. The calm water that soon steadied the ship was Graciosa Bay, where the Spaniard's adventures ended. We steered toward a constellation of quivering flashlights. A hundred people waited for us on a rubbly pier.

Nobody wanted to unload cargo in the rain, so we stayed in Graciosa Bay for two nights. I slept at the village rest house. So did the captain and crew of the *Temotu*, because there was a gas stove at the rest house, and a woman who was a cousin of a crew member and could therefore be ordered to cook.

I ate with the ship's crew. We found warm beer. The crew drank to get drunk. I drank to stop the world from swaying. It felt like we were still at sea.

"You go to Nukapu? I'm half-Nukapu!" said a thin man with an enormous, stretched mouth. He might have been the ship's engineer. "And I can tell you I am a proud man. It was my people, my blood, who killed Bishop Patteson."

"Then perhaps you should be ashamed."

"Aha! Wrong. You know, the bishop predicted that he would die on one of our islands. And he said he would die for us. My people helped him achieve his destiny. We made him a martyr."

"Stronger in death . . . ," I said.

"Yes, much stronger in death!"

"Just like Obi-Wan Kenobi," I said.

"Yes! Just like . . . *hao?*"

I told the crew the great tale of Obi-Wan Kenobi, the Jedi master from *Star Wars*. I liked the film because it was unambiguous. Kenobi was the wise man of the story and the keeper of sacred knowledge, like Patteson. I told the crew how Kenobi had confronted Darth Vader, the personification of darkness, in a duel. Kenobi did not win by slaying his opponent. No. He warned the Dark Lord: "If you strike me down, I shall become more powerful than you can possibly imagine," and then he raised his light-saber above his head and allowed Vader to cut him in half. But there was no blood. Obi-Wan Kenobi's body simply disappeared. The martyr's spirit lived on to inspire and guide the forces of goodness. There was also the part about the Force, which I explained was something like *mana*.

"Oh, yes, our story is like that exactly," said the engineer. "Patteson is more powerful now than ever. You know what we call the spot where he was killed? We call it 'the Clinic.' Because if you are sick, you just go to the bishop's cross and pray, and you will be healed. Ah! And when cyclone Namu hit in 1986, the only place that wasn't drowned on Nukapu was the Clinic. Everyone gathered there and was protected from the waves."

The residents of Nukapu are now so proud of their place in history they stage a feast on each September 20, the anniversary of the bishop's murder. The next party would take place in four days. If I could reach the Reefs and find a canoe, I could get to Nukapu in time for the martyr's anniversary, suggested the engineer.

"And what do you know of Mr. Forrest," I asked. I knew his answer would be *nothing*, and it was.

I cannot let this story continue without Actaeon E. C. Forrest, the fly in this mythological ointment. It was Forrest who revealed that Patteson's murder may not have been a message to Queen Victoria to stop the blackbirding. It was Forrest who reported that the murder was nothing more than an overreaction to an episcopal faux pas. And according to *The Light of Melanesia*, it was Forrest, not Patteson, who saved Nukapu. But his story and his name have now been crumpled up and tossed into the dustbin of mission history.

I must tell you the tale of a misfit whose life did not match the missionary template. Actaeon Forrest was a man of faith and a lay missionary who came to the Santa Cruz Group sixteen years after Patteson's death. My great-grandfather was in awe of him. He described how Forrest had heroically survived ambushes and assassination attempts. How Forrest had repeatedly dashed out between two parties of warring natives, determined to halt the whistling arrows and make peace. How Forrest had braved the seas by canoe to initiate the pacification of the Reef Islands, despite having once been capsized and stalked by a giant horned sea monster. How Forrest had survived by pluck and wit, built a school on Santa Cruz, and finally begun to win over the hotheaded natives. "This gallant man," wrote Henry, "single-handed, is fighting our battles here in perils among waters, in perils among arrows, in perils among fever, and in loneliness." It was Forrest alone who had begun the Christian conquest of Santa Cruz.

A photo in *The Light of Melanesia* shows Forrest standing with a group of Cruzian men. The men are naked except for what look like woven handbags hanging in front of their genitals and, of course, their spectacular shell jewelry: wide hoops through their ears, moonlike discs strung from their necks. The men are stern and muscular. Forrest is bookish and shy among them in his white, three-quarter-length trousers and rolled-up shirtsleeves. He looks like a schoolboy hoping desperately to be chosen for the cricket team.

Forrest's name was not wiped from *The Light of Melanesia* simply because my great-grandfather published it before his downfall.

The rest of Forrest's story has survived only in bits and pieces. I found scraps of it at Lambeth Palace, in the private correspondence of colonial administrators and church leaders. In 1896 the third bishop of Melanesia alerted the archbishop of Canterbury that Forrest and another teacher had fallen into very great sin. "They were both found guilty of indecency with the native boys," wrote the bishop, who elsewhere lamented that Forrest had shown a damning lack of remorse: "He says that [the natives] do not think much of his offence; if so, his work during the 9 years he has been here has been worth nothing." Charles Woodford, the resident commissioner of the Solomon Islands, wrote that tales of Forrest's "sodomy" were a matter of common report among steamship crews.

Forrest was dismissed from the mission, but he refused to leave Santa Cruz and began a trading business. The missionary conqueror of Santa Cruz soon became the mission's greatest foe. Woodford wrote in 1899 that Forrest, who had more influence among the natives of Santa Cruz than any other living white man, had bragged about reducing the number of mission schools in Santa Cruz from six to one.

The bishop of Melanesia was concerned about a scandal. He wanted Forrest out of his diocese. But Forrest had become so popular among the islanders it took Woodford five years to convince anyone to testify against him. Finally, Woodford had a couple of men from Ulawa sign depositions accusing Forrest of cajoling them into bed some years previously. Woodford edited the depositions, then he declared Forrest "dangerous to peace and good order" and signed a warrant for his arrest.

Forrest was arrested by a passing sea captain, but he escaped from custody immediately upon arrival in Sydney. Using his cutter, *Kia*, he established a trading base in the Torres Islands, south of Santa Cruz—just beyond Woodford's jurisdiction. Forrest settled down and adopted a young man, whom the natives referred to, apparently without judgment, as his "wife." He lived in relative peace for nearly a decade. But this was the Victorian era. Once the albatross of unspeakable sexuality had been slung around Forrest's neck, he was doomed. It did not help that he warned the natives on his island not to be lured aboard labor-recruiting vessels. When the recruiters complained to the government about this, they never failed to point out that Forrest's wife was clearly no woman.

Forrest had one friend left in the mission, the Reverend W. J. Durrad, who also lived in the Torres Group. When one of Durrad's servants complained that Forrest had sought his cooperation in an "act of indecency," Durrad informed Forrest that he intended to report the matter. It was now certain that if Forrest did not take drastic action, he would spend years behind bars. He wrote an apology for having troubled the New Hebrides resident commissioner. He left instructions for his debts to be paid through the sale of his boat. He left gifts for his crew. He left his land and personal effects to his "adopted son," Barnabas Ditwia of Loh. And then he drank poison. The investigations into Forrest's character and his involvement with the Melanesian Mission were suspended, and he began to sink into the murk of history.

There was no place for Forrest in the Nukapu myth because evangelical myth offers no room for nuance or sex. In order for the Nukapu story to sanctify the mission and give Melanesian Christians their martyr archetype, it needed to remain immaculate, asexual, and incomplete.

Sex: according to one English historian, it was very much a driving force behind empire-building, particularly in the repressive Victorian era. In the book *Empire and Sexuality*, which I carried to Santa Cruz in my knapsack, Ronald Hyam argued that imperial expansion was as much a matter of copulation and concubinage as it was Christianity and commerce. He pointed out that while Victorians exported their prudish sexual mores around the world (banning polygamy in Melanesia, for example), those who carried the torch of empire were frequently refugees from psychosexual tyranny at home.

Melanesia was fraught with temptation, which the missionaries were not always able to resist. So it was that Charles Brooke was dismissed for some unnamed sexual impropriety just three years after he watched Patteson's paddle toward death. Arthur Brittain and C. D. G. Browne were sacked for their lack of self-control in the 1890s. And adolescent sex was "rampant" at the mission school on Norfolk Island: thirteen Melanesian recruits were suspended for sexual misbehavior in 1899 alone.

Forrest had first defended himself by saying the islanders were not offended by his conduct. That was probably true. Early anthropologists reported accounts of homosexual behavior all across Melanesia, notably on Malaita, and on Malekula in the New Hebrides, though the church soon rendered it *tabu*.

I can't help being drawn to Forrest, whom I have decided to remember through the fog of history not as a sinner but as an irrepressible gay adventurer. Perhaps I am drawn to him for the tenacity with which he survived after being abandoned by his colleagues and peers—everyone who shared his skin color. More likely it is because in all my months among the islands, through all those long nights, amid the sad whoosh of wind and waves, among men who would stand close, grasp my hand in their own strong hands for hours, and gaze into my eyes without reservation or intent, I knew how Forrest must have felt. That loneliness. That longing. I could understand how Forrest, who had tried to reach for the infinite, was yet pulled by the desire for something closer, something like, but yet unlike, himself. It was the wrong desire for his times. It was even more wrong now that Melanesia had been transformed into a twentieth-century holdout of Victorian sexual mores. But still it was there, and I felt it acutely. The loneliness that wanted more than a firm handshake. The longing that did not seem to fit into any Christian myth and which was monstrous in the eyes of Melanesians. So the ghost of Forrest traveled with me in Santa Cruz, as present as Patteson and Codrington and my great-grandfather. But I was careful to keep my own romantic longings secret, and I did not press Forrest's case among the crew of the *Temotu*.

We pulled out of Graciosa Bay at dawn. Everything had changed. The ship was nearly empty. The cargo was gone. So was Brother Clement, and so were all the vomiters. We followed the coast of Nendo, then turned north at a bearing nearly parallel to the swell, which had found its shape again.

I was standing by the rail on the ship's bow when John, the ship's dogsbody and garbage-dumper, gripped my arm, pointed north, and squealed. "Look, Charlie!" he panted. "It's paradise, Charlie! Don't you see it?"

There was nothing to see but a frothy white line on the horizon. It looked like the first hint you get of the Rocky Mountains when driving west across the prairies: a ragged fringe of glaring peaks and cumulonimbus clouds. I peered and peered and saw only that mirage of snow. But by afternoon a faint, dashed line had begun to appear amid the glare. It thickened into tufts of palm. The snow became surf. A wall of foam, a thousand white bouquets of spray, exploded along a reef that stretched as far west as I could see.

John began to leap up and down like a child. A dozen other men climbed to the bow, and they, too, were all leaping and jigging on the shifting deck. They were Reef Islanders, and they were coming home.

The Reefs were as much shoal as they were island. It was as though a vast jigsaw puzzle of coral had been shaken, and a few pieces had shifted and slid atop the rest. Some, with their palms and breadfruit and papaya trees, resembled flower baskets perched on black stone pedestals. The rest were like giant clumps of moss. None was higher than the mist that billowed from the breaking surf.

The sun fell. The palms were seared gold. The lagoon and the sky melted into shades of scarlet. John pulled a lever, and the anchor rattled into the sea. Canoes came from every direction, like iron filings toward a magnet. I caught one to Pigeon Island, last of the old copra trading posts. The traders kept a room for travelers decorated with matching sheets and drapes. Avocado, 1969. They had a generator, which fueled Mozart's Twenty-ninth Symphony in A.

On my map, the Reef Group resembled a jellyfish swimming east. Its head was a brainlike cluster of islands with great tentacles dragging behind. Some of those tentacles began as islets, but they all disintegrated into light blue tendrils and streamers, coral reefs that disappeared, appeared, zigzagged through the sea until the longest finally trailed off more than twenty miles west. Nukapu lay on its own, far beyond the last shoal. It was not an easy place to reach. Fortunately, anyone heading for Nukapu was likely to first come to the trading post for fuel. I waited for two days, and they came: three men and a boatload of mosquito nets. They were health workers conducting an antimalaria campaign. But they had also heard of the impending feast on Nukapu, and they liked the idea of free food. They agreed to take me with them if I paid for the gas.

We left at dawn. The boat was a wide aluminum sled with a forty-horse outboard engine. The lagoon was so broad you could barely see its western fringe. But it was as warm and as calm as a bathtub. Sometimes the water was so flat and so clear that skimming across it felt like flying above a surreal blue desert. It glowed like the sky. Sometimes the coral colonies rose beneath us like giant muffins, clouds, or castles, with parrotfish swirling around their ramparts like flocks of birds. Sometimes the lagoon showed the curve of the earth. Passing islands did not retreat into the distance but sank beneath the ice-smooth horizon. Sometimes I saw people walking on that liquid horizon, casting nets far from any canoe or island like so many fisher messiahs. But when we approached, we found them ankle-deep, teetering on the fringes of barely submerged mesas of coral. Sometimes the water was so shallow we had to cock the engine, climb out of the boat, and push, and then the reef was a miniature forest of grasping fingers, white twigs, and brainlike stones. Orange anemones moved like animated shag carpet. The coral sliced into my ankles, and a flurry of tiny fish the color of Bunsen burner flames rose to chase the trail of my blood.

We approached the northern lip of the lagoon and cut the engine again. The men used an oar to push through what looked like a field of sunken caribou antlers. Then the lagoon floor was cleaved open by a deep crevasse. We followed it as it widened into a canyon and then a valley, and finally a deep blue infinity. The sun and the stillness of the day had pressed the southeast swell into a benign, undulated smoothness.

We passed Pileni, where Henry Montgomery had landed with Forrest. A single cloud hung above it like a white umbrella. A few miles beyond Pileni was what appeared to be the last island in the world, a lonely white dune, bare except for a low fin of scrub and oak. The swell curled into long arcs around its reef. We skirted the reef, and I scanned the island for signs of life.

"Nobody *stap long disfala aelan*," said one of the mosquito men. What a thought. A desert island. I realized that I had not spent a night alone in four months.

We switched fuel tanks and continued northwest. By midday the horizon had been wiped clean of everything except Tinakula, which we could see if we stood up. The journey began to feel like a descent into a dream. The world was delicate and ethereal. It lost its solidity. We rode up gentle blue hills and down again.

These were our way marks:

A sunbathing turtle.

A leaping porpoise.

A flock of black gulls.

A single cloud grew in the sky to our west. We aimed for it. After an hour, palms rose out of the swell. Nukapu.

It looked just as it should, like the lithograph I had seen in the Melanesian Mission's annual report for 1878. Like a scrap of shag carpet. Like Gilligan's Island.

It was eerily familiar: There was the reef, which we poled across, and the lagoon. There was the sandy shore. There were the thatch huts, and there was the smoke that had twisted up from cooking fires for a millennium. There, on a raised terrace, was Bishop Patteson's iron cross, painted white and decorated with palm fronds. Behind the cross, presumably on the site where the bishop was killed, stood a rickety church. With its palm-thatch eaves, the church resembled the pool bar at a Club Med. I felt as though I was still floating, as though the magic was waiting for its moment.

We were led to the chief's house, an immaculate, split-level thatch hut. The ground level was lined with grass mats. On stilts, at waist height, was a sleeping room. The chief was away. A man who claimed to be the chief, but who was really only the assistant chief, came to introduce himself. Silas Loa was his name. He had thick jowls and tiny eyes. "You are on Nukapu now," he said, puffing his chest up under his floral shirt. "You will pray tonight. You will bow down before the bishop's cross before you enter church."

"Yes, of course we will," I said.

"Watch out for him," one of my friends whispered when Silas turned his back.

The village grew crowded. People arrived in dugout canoes and fiberglass long boats. There were church choirs in matching T-shirts and swaggering *bêche-de-mer* traders.

At dusk there was a memorial service. A choir from Pileni sang in exquisite harmony. People wore their best T-shirts. Some wore shoes. One boy had sneakers with LEDs imbedded in the soles. They flashed when he walked. The minister, who had come in a canoe from Nendo, retold the story of Patteson's death. "This is why you and I are Christians now," he said in Solomons pidgin. "Because someone laid down his life for us."

Later, as the half-moon crept up through the palms, we carried oil lamps to the clearing beneath the bishop's cross. The children performed a pageant. A dreadlocked altar boy starred as Patteson. The old folks gathered around me and whispered their versions of the bishop's death. The murderer was a Nukapu chief, insisted one codger. No, the murderer was from Matema, hissed his wife. And so on. Nobody could imagine why a palm frond with five knots had been placed on the bishop's corpse.

"What about Mr. Forrest?" I asked.

Nobody had ever heard of a Mr. Forrest.

What people agreed on was Patteson's supernatural legacy. The ocean floor where the bishop's body had lain for decades was moving, heaving, pushing the bishop's bones toward the surface. "The bishop wanted us to remember where he was buried, so he made a reef," said Silas solemnly. "We call it Patteson Shallows," said an old woman.

Then there was the site of the bishop's murder. It had been rising every year, too. It was the highest spot on the island. The iron cross that stood on that mound was the nexus of the bishop's power.

"Once a missionary told us that we did not need to go to the hospital if we were sick. We just need to go to Bishop Patteson's cross," said a man.

"The old, the sick, we just take them there—"

"For example," interrupted Silas, "one catechist had ten or twelve kids, and they were all dying, all in the space of a few weeks."

"Malaria?" I asked.

"No. A *kastom* sickness, which came because he had been fighting over land. When the man had only one son left, he took the boy and pushed him underneath the cross. He said, 'All my *pikinini* are dead, please, bishop, let me keep just this one. If my boy lives, he will work for God.' That boy was saved! Now he is a catechist in the church."

The bishop's ghost was being treated much like Melanesians had always treated their ancestor spirits. He was, indeed, becoming stronger in his death. His cross oozed *mana*. Why not? The bishop of Malaita, who had railed against the *mana*-ization of Christian symbols, would not have approved, but it didn't seem like such a bad thing for Patteson's ghost to exert a benevolent influence. Especially if it worked.

Silas moved closer. "You understand it was God's plan for the bishop to die here, not ours."

"Okay."

"And you see that we have helped you," he said. "So now you must help us. We want to find Bishop Patteson's family. His grandsons."

"Tell them we are Christian," pleaded the old lady. "Tell them we know the Master now."

"We want to build a special house for the cross," said Silas. "And we want to put a computer in it, so we can be on the Internet."

"For tourists," added someone else.

"But you would need electricity for a computer," I said, "and a telephone line . . ."

Silas was not listening. He leaned in toward me and lowered his voice. "And you should help me, too. The *bêche-de-mer* man has a crate of beer in his canoe. You should buy me some beer."

Beer was rare on the outer islands. When men got their hands on it, they drank as much as they could as fast as they could. To buy a crate of beer would be to catalyze an evening of chaos and tears. And besides, I didn't like Silas. I didn't like his bulging, suspicious eyes, or the way he took care to stand slightly higher than everyone else, or the way he pushed his face into mine.

I assured the people I would try to help them, and then I retreated to the real chief's house. Silas followed me. I felt his hand on my shoulder just as I was about to duck inside.

"Did you know that sometimes a column of light shoots up into the sky from the bishop's cross?"

"I'd like to see that," I said, pulling away.

"Of course it takes weeks of prayer to bring the light." Silas tightened his grip on my shoulder. His breath was heavy with betel.

I waited.

"A storm is coming. You are in danger," he said. "But I can help you in your journey. I can keep you safe. I am very powerful, because the bishop, the patron saint of Nukapu, gave me his power."

I did not want to hear this. It was not the end I wanted for my story.

"Bishop Patteson came to me in a dream once. He told me not to be afraid. He told me he would take special care of me. There was light shining from his face. Ever since, I have been able to use his power."

"Sure," I said. "You heal people."

"More than that." Silas stepped between me and the door of my hut. "Suppose I get in a fight with some man. Maybe he has hurt me or done something bad. I always warn him first: I tell him watch out, now something bad will happen to you. And then in a day or two, he will fall down, or cut himself, or get bitten by a shark. That's the power the bishop gave me."

"That doesn't sound very Christian to me."

"Ha! Don't you worry. You have promised to help us. So tomorrow I will pray under the cross for the bishop to protect you. Then, sometime—I can't promise you when—he will come to you in a dream. He will make you safe. He will bring you success."

"Thank you," I said, straining to free my shoulder from his grip.

"But remember your promise. You must find the bishop's grandchildren. You must tell them to send money. If you do not do that, something very bad will happen to you."

He squeezed harder. "Something very, very bad. Maybe you drown."

The three-quarter moon had climbed to its apex. It cast the village in silver light. Our shadows were sharp and black beneath us. Silas's eyes glistened. I despised him for what he was doing to Patteson's myth. A century after their conversion, the Nukapuans were now converting Christianity: Patteson had not banished the *tindalo*, the powerful ancestor spirits. He had become one. And here was Silas, threatening me with an invocation of the martyr's ghost. Patteson would surely be rolling in his saltwater grave. I crept inside and waited until the sound of Silas's footsteps faded away. One of my friends stirred on the floor.

"Don't worry, Charles," he whispered. "That man is a liar."

I knew it. All the night's talk rang false. Nukapu was not what it should have been.

The feast day was searingly hot. I tried to avoid Silas, but he was everywhere. There he was, announcing the Pileni Youth for Christ dance group (they wore grass skirts, waved their arms like the dancers at the Waikiki Hilton, and sang, "We are dancing in the light of God"); there he was, apportioning the feast (parcels of leaf-wrapped pork and sweet potato, baked in an earthen oven, they resembled the remains of Christmas presents after a house fire); there he was ordering people to sit down at their banana-leaf place mats and eat. Silas was always barking at people. And he always seemed to be watching me with one eye. He insisted I make a speech, so I stood up and told the people that Nukapu was "*wan gudfala Christian paradaes.*"

But when I saw the *bêche-de-mer* trader loading his boat, I collected my things and threw them in.

As I said my hurried good-byes, an old lady, who turned out to be Silas's grandmother, pulled me aside. The sun-baked skin on her face and arms was covered in tattoos. There were fish bones and stars, and on one arm, a name: Steven. Her earlobes had been stretched into long, flabby rings. She pulled the pipe from her mouth and hissed at me in her own language.

"She is telling you to remember that we are not heathens anymore," said the girl beside her. "There are no heathens left on the island. We are Christians. You must not be scared. We won't kill anymore white men."

The woman thrust a woven handbag into my arms and peered at me imploringly.

"I'm not scared," I said. "That's not why I'm leaving."

The trader pushed his boat free of the sand. I waded into the sea behind him. Silas charged into the water behind me.

"My friend. You won't break your promise, will you?" he said. "Because if you do . . . Ha! Ha!"

He slapped me on the back. I scowled at him and hopped into the boat.

"*Mi funi nomo!*"—I was only joking!—Silas shouted over the roar of the outboard as we pulled away. But he wasn't smiling.

I turned to the sea and did not look back. I wasn't scared. I was angry, breathless with disappointment, but also on the verge of understanding. I didn't need another word from Silas. I wanted to be alone.

I asked the *bêche-de-mer* trader to drop me on the deserted island I had seen near Pileni. All the boats returning from Nukapu would pass near it when the feasting was over in a day or so. I could just flag down one of those boats, I said, imagining it would be like hailing a cab. It was a foolish idea. The trader agreed to drop me only because he knew the island was not actually deserted.

To my dismay, a fisherman and his family were standing on the beach when we crossed the reef. They had paddled over from Pileni in dugout canoes. They had brought water jugs, cassava, babies, a portable stereo, and a shoe box full of gospel cassettes. They had built huts from sticks, palm leaves, and plastic bags. Now the music was blaring, the babies were bawling, and the white sand had been transformed into a minefield of buried shit. The men were tired. They had spent ten nights diving in the lagoon for *bêche-de-mer*. The slugs were now shriveling on racks above a fire tended by the fisherman's wife. Their insides oozed out like pus.

The fisherman offered me a shell full of turtle soup. I ate with him in the shade, but then I told him I wanted to be alone. This made him sad, but still he ordered his two sons to carry my back-pack away from their camp, through the young palms and oaks to the south end of the island, which he called Makalom.

The island was a temporary place, a perfect teardrop of sand that would surely disappear with the next big cyclone. A strong man could throw a coconut across its widest point. I had brought a tent. I pitched it where I could see the surf breaking on the reef, the smoke curling from Tinakula, and the palms of Pileni trembling like a clump of dandelions on the southern horizon. If I climbed a tree, I could probably see Nukapu, too. But I didn't do that, and I tried not to imagine Silas, who would surely still be licking the pig fat from his fingers and bragging about the special magic he had inherited from the martyred bishop.

I watched the family from my tent as daylight bled from the sky. After dark, the fisherman and his sons pushed their canoes out from the beach and drifted silently across the lagoon. They slid into the water, shattering the reflection of the moon. Their flashlights glinted, glimmered, and faded with each dive, illuminating the surface of the water from below. The surf burned white on the edge of the reef beyond them like a phosphorescent brush fire sweeping back and forth across a dark plain. Thunderheads boiled silver in the distance. Tentacles of vapor were reaching north across the sky. A storm was approaching.

I waited hours for the men to paddle back to their camp. When they did, I listened for their murmurs to cease, for the last gospel song to finish, for the babies to stop crying. Through the trees, I watched their fire spark and flicker and finally settle into an untended glow. I knew the fisherman and his family said their prayers. They thanked God, and probably their ancestors, too, implored them to bring more slugs and to keep the storms at bay for just another week.

Now, for the first time in four months, I was alone, facing the sea. A breeze sent shivers across the lagoon.

From the moment I had spotted Makalom, I had imagined ending my story there. I had imagined myself alone, knee-deep in the lagoon, understanding the weight and truth about stories and gods and ancestors. But it would not work. The story could not end with Silas's threats still rippling across the water. It was not the concept of the dead bishop's power that troubled me. It was the idea of Silas using Patteson's spirit like a curse-dispensing *kastom* stone, the idea that God could be reversed and reduced to a weapon. No. It wouldn't do.

The central struggle in Melanesia was no longer the fight between Christian and pagan mythology. The Christian God had pretty much won the battle. Paganism was on its last legs. The old spirits survived only in a few last pockets of resistance, like the wounded remnants of an army at the end of a long siege. Even in the Kwaio hills, Christian soldiers were hammering at the battlements of pagan ritual. But the old way of thinking, the way of *mana*, had survived and flourished within the Christian churches. The real fight now was the tug-of-war between *mana* and mysticism; between those who tried to claim and direct supernatural power, like children throwing rocks at their enemies, and those who were certain that the heart of their Christian myth was self-sacrifice and divine love. It was between Old Testament thinking—which was very much in keeping with *kastom* ideas about *mana* and which was increasingly popular among Christian evangelicals—and New Testament thinking, which rejected sorcery and magic in favor of a transcendent kind of vulnerability. The

Church of Melanesia claimed to have oriented itself unambiguously toward the mysticism of the New Testament. It was a profound distinction. The key to this philosophy was not commandment, reward, or punishment. It was not the directing of thunderbolts toward one's enemies. It was not the prophet Fred draining the lake on Tanna Island. It was certainly not Silas invoking the spirit of the bishop to draw favors from me or cast bad luck on his neighbors. It was not magic as technology, nor was it a sorcerer's stone. The key, which you do not have to be Christian to appreciate, was Jesus without his miracles, trudging out of Jerusalem with his cross on his back, toward death and rebirth. It was the shedding of power and worldly wherewithal. It was love. But most of all it was a story whose power came only through faith and its sister, imagination. Silas had gotten it wrong, and so, in my hunger for magic, had I.

I felt the magic draining away from my journey, felt the miracles of the Nonotongere and Langa Langa Lagoon becoming hollow. These were empty miracles, junk-food miracles. They had left me unsated, always hungry for more. What a fool I had been to hunt for magic glitter, more proof of *mana* among the Melanesian Brotherhood. The white *tasiu*'s words returned to me like shouts across the lagoon: The measure of a miracle's truth was the quality of the faith it inspired. Proof was the very opposite of faith.

Here, at the end of the world, on the empty edge of things, I felt a sudden and terrible clarity. The miracle for which my great-grandfather waited decades did not contain even a whiff of *mana*. His god did not bring rain or thunder or wealth when it appeared to him so many years after his return from Melanesia. There was only the briefest moment of light in his Irish garden, and a question—"Lovest thou me?"—which most certainly came from inside the bishop's own gut. The light and the voice were not proof of his faith but products of it, and yet they most certainly led him closer to the God of Love.

I know this now, because I have found a conclusion to my own story.

The last pieces of it arrived one afternoon, six months after I left Nukapu. I was sitting in my office on the far side of the Pacific Ocean, thinking about the day I had joined the *tasiu* on their mission to rescue Johnson Junior. I was considering Brother Francis, how he had murmured and chuckled and remained very small, so small that I had decided he was barely worth noticing until the moment he stepped forward and radiated something so good and true that the tension was washed from the afternoon and the men with anger and guns were made humble. And then I received the news I had been fearing for months.

After I left the Solomons in November 2002, the country began to fall deeper and deeper into darkness, despite all the Melanesian Brotherhood's efforts at disarmament and peacemaking. There was the corruption, of course, and the failed economy, and a general lawlessness. But these were nothing in comparison to the storm of violence that was building on the Weather Coast of Guadalcanal, where the warlord Harold Keke had gone berserk. Keke, the only militant leader not to have signed the peace accord in 2000, knew that his former allies in the Guadalcanal Liberation Front were joining forces with the police and that they intended to catch him, dead or alive. Anger, jealousy, and paranoia—and perhaps the bullet he had received in his skull back in '99—had pushed him beyond the bounds of sanity. Keke imagined treachery in every face. He had razed villages and murdered dozens of people, including some of his own followers. A wave of refugees poured north from the coast to report the atrocities. One man, who had escaped by trekking thirty miles through the mountains, told a reporter that every house in his village had been burned to the ground and that Keke's lieutenants had taken three men to the beach, where they were forced to parade naked and were beaten until all their bones were broken. Then the men were decapitated.

Others were kidnapped and carried to Keke's mountain camp, where they were tied up, beaten with sticks, and also dismembered. Heads, arms, and legs were dumped into mass graves like mannequin parts.

Keke escorted former allies to the altar of his village church, where he demanded that the congregation deliberate on each victim's loyalty before he cut off their heads. The blood trickled in the unceasing rain, through the soot-blackened mud of incinerated villages on darkness's darkest coast, barely a mountain away from Honiara.

In April, a pair of *tasiu* journeyed to the Weather Coast, bearing a message to Keke from the head of the order, the archbishop of Melanesia. Only one of them returned. The other died after three days of torture. The Melanesian Brotherhood was shaken but still not afraid. Brother Francis, along with five others, set out for the Weather Coast to retrieve the body of their dead comrade. The mission was a last chance to confront the warlord and convince him to return to the light before his fury spilled beyond the coast and infected the rest of the islands. The six brothers left their canoe on a beach near the village of Babanakira and hiked into the dripping jungle to search for Keke's base.

It was said that Keke had taken the six *tasiu* prisoner. It was said that Francis and his companions never stopped praying for their captor. It was true that, directed by the white *tasiu*, Richard Carter, thousands of Anglicans around the world began to pray, not just for the release of the captive brothers but for the return of Keke and his followers to the way of light.

People were confident the brotherhood would triumph, as they always had, through their God-given *mana*. But weeks and months went by. Keke captured five more brothers and two of their novices, and the kidnappings became a wound in the soul of an already weak nation.

By July, the government had given up. With even the Melanesian Brotherhood failing, it was time for foreigners to come and save Solomon Islanders from themselves. An Australian-led coalition of more than two thousand troops and police landed in Honiara. Keke welcomed the foreigners and invited the new acting police commissioner, an Australian, to meet with him. Keke informed the Australian that his men had already executed Brother Robin Lindsay, second-in-command of the *tasiu*; and young Brother Patteson Gatu-Young, who had once welcomed me to Tabalia with a song; and quiet Brother Alfred Hilly, who had unlocked the door for me late each night at Chester; and Brother Ini Ini Partabatu, who had confronted the Royal Solomon Islands Police about their beatings and extortion; and Brother Tony Sirihi, who had no parents.

And Keke had also executed one more: my friend Brother Francis Tofi of the half-smile, of the whispered prayer among the militants, of the calming breeze at the Tetere Police Post.

I turned from my computer screen to the light of afternoon and watched the buses and bank towers beyond my office window disappear behind the salty haze, and I did not know if I was crying for the dead, for myself, or for something shining and good that once called to me, dared me to believe, and then was gone again. I was swallowed by the useless, helpless urgency of *too late*, the thought that I had chased it all wrong, known it all wrong, and told it all wrong, too, and it was more than just a story, but now it had blown apart from the inside.

I laid out my photos and notebooks, pored over my interviews and my scribbled observations of the *tasiu*, sifted, peered between the lines, searching for an answer to the searing question of Francis's death. I read the histories again, and my great-grandfather's diaries, and Campbell and Jung and Frye and even the Bible, and I let the pieces of the story flap in the wind that blew through my open window and scatter themselves across the floor.

The answer came to me slowly, over days and weeks. The

pieces stirred, shifted, and the shattered tower of memory began to reassemble itself, like those films of building demolitions shown in reverse; bricks and slate and window shards coming together again from the rubble, only the story was different than before. It wanted to be seen with new eyes. It wanted a new ending. It wanted to be a story of transformation.

It began with temptation. Months before Brother Francis's death, the bishop of Malaita had told me he was worried about the brotherhood. The *tasiu* were the bridge between the old religion and the new. They represented Melanesians' ideas of holiness, but they also embodied their belief in *mana*. The bishop was concerned that all their alleged miracles—not to mention the sickness and death that sometimes befell those who challenged the *tasiu*—lured them toward the old thinking, the thinking of shamans and sorcerers, and away from a more mystical relationship with God.

Beyond my grief, which was shapeless and confusing, I resolved to believe that, on this level, the brothers' deaths were a kind of triumph. They knew Harold Keke was mad. They knew he had already killed dozens of civilians, one government minister, and at least one *tasiu*. And yet they journeyed alone to the darkest edge of their world. There, far from home and light and love, under the unceasing rain, amid the mud and the squalor, under the gaze of an illiterate psychopath, they had offered themselves up as martyrs.

Their deaths would mirror those of their heroes, of Bishop Patteson, Stephen Taroaniara, Edwin Nobbs, Fisher Young, and all the other fallen missionaries of Melanesia—and of Jesus. In one audacious leap, the brothers moved from *mana*, the hoarding of personal power advocated by the old cosmology, to self-sacrifice, the transcendental love and martyrdom of the new. They had abandoned the God of Power for the God of Love. And in their sacrifice, surely they would become more powerful, more illuminated, than they had been in their lives. That is the way martyrdom works. That is the geography of the hero's journey.

Richard Carter had tried to chart the brothers' mystery for me. He had tried to explain that the stories that surrounded them were people's attempts to get at the truth of things, truths that were so profound and elusive, so beyond language, that storytellers were forced to fall back on miracles to represent them.

There is truth in myth; not just allegory, but a hint of the divine we cannot name—I'm sure that's what the white *tasiu* meant. If this is so, then imagination is more than the ability to produce fiction. It is the expanse between the shores of historical fact and the truths of the soul. Mythmaking is an expedition to chart the hidden geography between matter and spirit. Miracles do contain truth, though, as Northrop Frye tried to explain, these were truths, above all, of the soul's relationship with the universe. The story becomes a communion, because the story is the journey.

It has always been the storyteller's role to claim the lives of heroes, squeeze them into form, polish them, and adorn them so that they achieve a kind of mythic luminescence—not to turn them into fairy tales, but to allow the ideals they represent to shine more brightly. It is what the missionaries, including my great-grandfather, did for Bishop Patteson: "He died with a smile on his face," said those who were not there to see Patteson's last gasp. It is what mythmakers did for Joan of Arc, what Steinbeck did for Zapata, what an entire nation did for John F. Kennedy, sweeping away his sexual adventures, amplifying his speeches. It is what the world is doing now for the Dalai Lama, what we will soon do for Nelson Mandela. Isn't it my job to do the same for Brother Francis? It is hard, when you are caught in the tide of the moment, to feel otherwise.

I am close to understanding these things. I am close to understanding what my great-grandfather meant when he implored me to trust the eyes of my soul and my spirit. These are the eyes that see the part of ourselves we call God.

I experienced three miracles in Melanesia.

The tempest that fell from the sky above the Nonotongere—that was a gift.

The vision of the shark boss and his circling shadow in Langa Langa—that was a decision.

The third miracle would have to be told in order to live.

I would like to trade my tempest and my circling shadow for another, clearer image of Brother Francis. Return with me now to the Tetere Police Post and the shade of that huge oak tree and the tension that showed in the twitching muscles of the young militants. Return with me to the very moment when Brother Francis stepped forward, removed his wraparound sunglasses, and began to pray. Would it be wrong for me to paint a faint, saintly glow around his head? It would be like the halo that surrounds the moon on a humid night, so faint it would be easy to believe I had imagined it. And the militants, didn't they remove their sunglasses, too, and didn't they wipe tears of shame from their eyes? Didn't the cicadas cease their incessant whirring for the first time in months? Didn't the wind rise, tear at the grass, and lift the dust so it swirled in a circle around Brother Francis, and weren't his whispers amplified by it? And weren't we all lifted? Didn't we all hover there, for a moment, just above the rustling grasses, at once humbled, helpless, and yet buoyed by holiness? Would it be wrong for me to tell the story that way? Because this would be closer to the truth of things.

And the miracles did not end on that afternoon.

Four days after admitting he had killed my friends, Harold Keke released the rest of his hostages and gave himself up. His followers turned in their machine guns. Keke's enemies among the police force and various militias also handed over hundreds of shotguns, pistols, and SR-88s to the Australian-led intervention force. Even Jimmy Rasta surrendered his arsenal. Within weeks, the country was proclaimed gun-free. It was the beginning of peace. There was dancing on Mendaña Avenue. At Saint Barnabas Cathedral, where the knotted palm leaves from Bishop Patteson's death shroud had been preserved in a glass case, thousands of islanders gathered to mourn and praise the fallen *tasiu*.

Richard Carter, now chaplain to the Melanesian Brotherhood, told the crowd that the *tasiu* had been instrumental in manifesting the new peace. It was the brothers' captivity that had precipitated the foreign intervention. It was the influence of the second group of captured brothers that had softened Keke's heart and encouraged him to surrender. God, said the white *tasiu*, was pouring out his grace through the martyrs' deaths. The curse of violence had been lifted from the nation. Meanwhile, the brotherhood itself had been transformed by the ordeal. The *tasiu* had been humbled and purged of pride. They had been allowed a glimpse through the mystery of things to the promise of the eternal.

Through their sacrifice, the martyrs had offered their country the greatest gift of all. They had laid the foundations of a new story, one far more potent, far deeper, than tales of bouncing bullets or magic walking sticks, one that reaffirmed the truths they had been telling each other for a century.

The specifics of the martyrs' final days were vague. People wanted details. They wanted pieces of their new myth. So the white *tasiu* shared with the crowd at the cathedral a tale that reflected the order's holiness. The story had come by e-mail, from a Canadian traveler. It described a tense negotiation between militants at a police post on the plantations east of Honiara; how one quiet *tasiu*, who seemed at first not at all powerful or charismatic, had stepped forward and brought the two enemy groups together in a whispered prayer. "He radiated something so good and true and bigger than the moment, and the tension was washed from the afternoon, and the men with anger and guns were made humble." And the people heard Carter's eulogy and knew the *ta-siu* had led them back into the arms of the God of Love.

When I read a transcript of the eulogy and recognized my own words in it, I realized that, regardless of what had really happened at the Tetere Police Post, Brother Francis's myth had begun its journey, and that if we told it well, it would grow through the decades until it was unquestionably true in its transforming power, as grand and shining as *The Light of Melanesia*. The story itself would be the miracle.

Epilogue

Do thou draw the canoe, that it may reach the land;
speed my canoe, grandfather, that I may quickly reach
the shore whither I am bound. Do thou, Daula, lighten
the canoe, that it may quickly gain the land, and rise
upon the shore.

—Florida Islanders' invocation
of a frigate-bird *tindalo*, in
R. H. CODRINGTON, *The Melanesians*

By dawn the storm had engulfed Makalom. The scrub oaks groaned in the wind. Palms hissed. The surface of the lagoon vibrated with exploding raindrops. The wall of surf that marked the fringe of the reef had grown, and so had the swell in the open ocean beyond. The sandbar that trailed from my side of the island had been consumed. I stood knee-deep in the water and scanned the blackened swell for boats, but the world had disappeared.

The fishermen's sons yelled at me from shore. "Nobody will leave Nukapu until the storm has passed. Nobody will rescue you!" The boys were drenched, grinning. "You will stay on Makalom many, many days, unless!" bellowed the elder of the two above the roar of the storm.

"Unless what?" I shouted back. I wanted to get as far as I could from Nukapu.

"Unless *yumi padel long* Pileni," shouted the younger. There was a village on Pileni, and a longboat with an outboard engine that could ferry me back to the trading post at Pigeon Island, then on to Santa Cruz.

"But how will we find Pileni?" I asked. "We can't even see past the edge of your reef."

The boys shifted in the sand, conferred with each other, considered the sky, then clapped their hands. "The waves will tell us which way to go!"

We pushed the fisherman's dugout canoe out into the shallows. I jammed my pack into the bow, and the boys passed me a crude, hand-carved paddle.

The surf had now wrapped itself around Makalom, rendering even the sheltered lee side treacherous. Each approaching wave sucked the reef plateau almost bare before rising to curl and collapse across the exposed coral. We measured the rhythm of the wave sets.

Three rollers, then two calves, then a set of seven.

A lull.

We charged, paddling for all we were worth across a sheet of foam, cutting diagonally over the collapsing shoulder of the next wave and high along the crevassed edge off the reef; on over the abyss, rising, falling, rising again through the foothills of the Pacific. We left the scant shelter of Makalom's wind shadow. The first gust hit us like an explosion, transforming the ocean into a confused stampede of chop, whitecaps, and spindrift.

"Pull, Charlie!" yelled the elder. "Pull!"

I pulled. So did the elder, and his exhalations were like the snorting of a bull. The younger, wide-eyed and delirious with the excitement of the moment, held his paddle like a rudder at the stern. The wind came from the southeast. The waves came from the east. They peeled over the bow, filling the canoe with warm water. It rolled, but it did not tip.

We pulled until my shoulders ached, until blisters rose on my hands and knees. We pulled until Makalom became a silhouette behind us, then a phantom, then nothing but a memory pressed into vapor. The sky collapsed. The line of the horizon disappeared. The universe beyond the veil of mist and spray became formless, malleable, a thing of conjecture. The world was reduced to the roll of the canoe, the plunging of our paddles and also the swell, which existed to guide us. We pulled through the folds, keeping them at an angle, trusting the message they brought from the edge of the world. We pulled, knowing our faith would conjure an island from the mystery of the sea.

A Note on Language and Spelling

Most conversations relayed in this book were conducted in Bislama or Solomon Islands pidgin. Many of those exchanges have been translated into English to avoid confusion. I was assisted in the translation, and also in correcting the spelling and syntax of Bislama and Solomons pidgin, by Helen Tamtam of the University of the South Pacific and Richard Carter of the Melanesian Brotherhood. However, I have deviated from their advice in several respects and have certainly introduced errors along the way.

I have generally used the most common (and mostly phonetic) modern spelling for Bislama and Solomons pidgin words, but in some cases I have fallen back on the spellings used by earlier traders and travelers. For example, I use *rubbish* instead of *rabis* or *ravis*, to mean "of bad character," to reflect that word's metaphorical origin. I use *savve* to mean "to know/to be able to" rather than the now more popular—yet confusing for English speakers—*save*.

When the same words appear in both Bislama and Solomons pidgin, I have stuck with the first Bislama spelling, rather than switching to the Solomons standard, for consistency. For example, the word *you* is spelt *yu* throughout the book, rather than switching to *iu* once we reach the Solomons.

My apologies to those who are working to standardize both languages.

Acknowledgments

I owe first thanks to my mother and my favorite storyteller, Frances Montgomery, for keeping the old myths alive, and to my family and friends for encouraging, forgiving, and supporting me through my geographical and emotional absences.

Many people shared their homes and their lives with me in the United Kingdom, Fiji, Vanuatu, and the Solomon Islands. I hope this story respects their truths. In the Solomons, thanks go especially to the members of the Melanesian Brotherhood, and in particular: Brothers Harry Gereniu, Albert Wasimae, Clement Leonard, John Blythe, and, for help with pidgin and other mysteries, Brother Richard Carter. Thanks also to Bishop Terry Brown and his household, David MacLaren, Geri and Alvin Gaines, Roni Butala and his *wantoks*, John Palmer, Grant and Jill Kelly, John Roughan, Ben Hepworth, Robert Iroga, Henry Isa of the National Museum, Johnson Honimae, Morris Otto Namoga, and Andrew Nihopara at the Solomon Islands Visitors Bureau. In Vanuatu, I was assisted by the Anglican Diocese of Banks and Torres, Jirus Karabani, Alfred of Mota, Sabina Hess, Don Fockler, Rona Dini, Eli Field, Ralph Regenvanu at the Vanuatu Kaljoral Senta, and Linda Kalpoi and Natasha Motoutorua at the Vanuatu Tourism Office. The wise and patient Helen Tamtam of the University of the South Pacific taught me Bislama and performed triage on my translations. Laura Palmer and Alex Wolf offered refuge in Fiji.

Alastair Macaulay saved me from the wilds of North London. Catherine Fitzpatrick and Paul Hatton provided shelter and surf lessons in Sydney.

I was assisted in research by the shining Catherine Wakeling, archivist for the United Society for the Propagation of the Gospel, John Pinfold at Rhodes House Library, Richard Palmer at Lambeth Palace Library, Allan Anderson at the University of Birmingham, Fergus King, Ben Burt, David Hilliard, Robert Withycombe, Thorgeir Storesund Kolshus, Viscount David Montgomery, Tarcisius Tara Kabutaulaka, Manfred Ernst, Adele Plummer, and Pierre Maranda.

Support from the following magazine editors opened doors for me across the Pacific: Jim Sutherland at *Western Living*, Matthew Mallon at *Vancouver Magazine*, Chantal Tranchemontagne at *enRoute*, James Little at *Explore*, Anne Rose at *WestWorld*, Ian Hanington at the *Georgia Straight,* and Aryn Baker at *Time Asia*. Crucial support also came from Air Pacific, Solomon Airlines, Air Vanuatu, and VanAir.

Friends, family, and colleagues read and critiqued my early proposal and various chapters of the book. Thanks to Michael Scott, Carol Toller, Daffyd Roderick, Erik and Kathi Lees, Andrew Mayer, Colin Thomas, Michael Prokopow, Edward Bergman, Kevin Griffin, Jeff Hoover, Deborah Campbell, James MacKinnon, Brian Payton, Alisa Smith, and in particular Chris Tenove, who offered regular doses of savage and necessary criticism. The Vancouver FCC kept the creative fires stoked. Jorge Rivero-Vallado showed me new ways to imagine language and stories.

I am grateful to Scott McIntyre for giving me the means. My editors, first Saeko Usukawa at Douglas & McIntyre, then Christopher Potter, Courtney Hodell, and Catherine Heaney at HarperCollins, led me to an infinitely stronger manuscript. My agent, Anne McDermid, worked miracles for me on two continents with the help of her team, Rebecca Weinfeld, Jane Warren, and Martha Magor. The journey was kick-started with financial support from the Canada Council for the Arts and the B.C. Arts Council, but I would never have considered it without constant encouragement and badgering from Michael Scott, who was the first to believe.

Selected Bibliography

Manuscript Sources

Harold Turner Collection on New Religious Movements, University of Birmingham, Selly Oak, England. Essays and papers on Pacific cults and millenarian movements, missiology, and religious syncretism.

Lambeth Palace Library, London, England. Archbishops' Papers (Benson, Davidson, Tait, Frederick Temple); *Church Times*, 1895–1901; and other miscellaneous papers.

Mitchell Library, Sydney, Australia. Western Pacific High Commission Archives, Patteson Memorial Endowment Fund of the Melanesian Mission, Papers, 1871–1906.

Rhodes House Library, Oxford, England. United Society for the Propagation of the Gospel Archives, Codrington Papers, Patteson Papers, reports from missionaries, Wilson letters to Montgomery, 1894–1906.

Viscount David Montgomery Private Collection. Notes and diaries of Bishop H. H. Montgomery.

South Pacific Journeys

Amherst of Hackney, Lord, and Basil Thompson, eds. *The Discovery of the Solomon Islands by Alvaro de Mendaña in 1568*. Vol. 2. London: Hakluyt Society, 1901.

Coates, Austin. *Western Pacific Islands*. London: Her Majesty's Stationery Office, 1970.

Davidson, J. W. *Peter Dillon of Vanikoro*. Melbourne: Oxford University Press, 1975.

Edwards, Philip, ed. *Journals of Captain Cook*. Abridged. London: Penguin, 1999.

Jack-Hinton, Colin. *The Search for the Islands of Solomon, 1567–1838*. Oxford, England: Clarendon Press, 1969.

London, Jack. *Cruise of the Snark*. New York: Macmillan, 1919.

McAuley, James. "Captain Quirós." In *Collected Poems*. Sydney: Angus & Robertson, 1971.

Markam, Sir Clements, trans. and ed. *Voyages of Pedro Fernandez de Quirós, 1595 to 1606*. Vol. 2. London: Hakluyt Society, 1904.

Montgomery, H. H. *The Light of Melanesia*. London: Society for Promoting Christian Knowledge, 1896.

Shineberg, Dorothy, ed. *The Trading Voyages of Andrew Cheyne, 1841–1844*. Canberra: Australian National University, 1971.

Theroux, Paul. *The Happy Isles of Oceania*. New York: Ballantine, 1992.

History of the Melanesian Mission

Hilliard, David. *God's Gentlemen: A History of the Melanesian Mission, 1849–1942*. St. Lucia, Australia: University of Queensland Press, 1978.

Macdonald-Milne, Brian. *The True Way of Service: The Pacific Story of the Melanesian Brotherhood, 1925–2000*. Leicester, England: Christians Aware and the Melanesian Brotherhood, 2003.

Sarawia, George. *They Came to My Island*. Sioata, Solomon Islands: St. Peter's College, 1996.

Whiteman, Darrell. *Melanesians and Missionaries*. Pasadena, Calif.: William Carey Library, 1983.

Williams, C. P. S. *From Eton to the South Seas*. London: Melanesian Mission, n.d.

Solomon Islands

Bennett, Judith. *The Wealth of the Solomons*. Honolulu: University of Hawaii Press, 1987.

Honan, Mark, and David Harcombe. *Lonely Planet: Solomon Islands*. 3d ed. Hawthorne, Calif.: Lonely Planet, 1997.

Hviding, Edvard. *Guardians of Marovo Lagoon: Practice, Place, and Politics in Maritime Melanesia*. Honolulu: University of Hawaii Press, 1996.

Kabutaulaka, Tarcisius Tara. *Beyond Ethnicity: The Political Economy of the Guadalcanal Crisis in Solomon Islands*. Suva: Australian National University, 2001.

Keesing, R. M., and Peter Corris. *Lightning Meets the West Wind*. Melbourne: Oxford University Press, 1980.

Tippett, A. R. *Solomon Islands Christianity: A Study in Growth and Obstruction*. London: Lutterworth Press, 1896.

Vanuatu

Adams, Ron. *In the Land of Strangers: A Century of European Contact with Tanna, 1774–1874*. Canberra: Australian National University, 1984.

McClancy, Jeremy. *To Kill a Bird with Two Stones: A Short History of Vanuatu*. Port Vila: Vanuatu Cultural Centre, 1985.

Paton, J. G. *John G. Paton, Missionary to the New Hebrides: An Autobiography*. London: Hodder & Stoughton, 1893.

Rice, Edward. *John Frum He Come: A Polemic Work about a Black Tragedy*. New York: Doubleday & Company, 1974.

Rush, John, with Abbe Anderson. *The Man with the Bird on His Head: The Amazing Fulfillment of a Mysterious Island Prophesy*. Seattle: YWAM Publishing, 1997.

Tryon, Darrell. *Bislama: An Introduction to the National Language of Vanuatu*. Canberra: Pacific Linguistics, 1987.

ANTHROPOLOGY, MYTHOLOGY, THEOLOGY

Arens, William. "Rethinking Anthropophagy." In *Cannibalism and the Colonial World*, edited by F. Barker, P. Hulme, and M. Iversen. Cambridge, England: Cambridge University Press, 1998.

Bidney, David. "Myth, Symbolism and Truth." In *Myth: A Symposium*, edited by T. Sebeok. Bloomington: Indiana University Press, 1974.

Brunton, Ron. *The Abandoned Narcotic: Kava and Cultural Instability in Melanesia*. Cambridge, England: Cambridge University Press, 1996.

Campbell, Joseph. *Myths to Live By*. New York: Bantam, 1972.

Carter, Richard. *Liturgy beyond Words: Symbolic Exchange with the Transcendent God*. Leeds, England: University of Leeds, 2001.

Codrington, R. H. *The Melanesians: Studies in Their Anthropology and Folklore*. Oxford, England: Clarendon Press, 1891.

Evans-Pritchard, E. E. *Theories of Primitive Religion*. Oxford, England: Clarendon Press, 1965.

Frazer, James. *The Golden Bough: Abridged Edition*. New York: Macmillan, 1940.

Frye, Northrop. *The Double Vision: Language and Meaning in Religion*. Toronto: University of Toronto Press, 1991.

Kulick, Don, and Margaret Willson, eds. *Taboo: Sex, Identity and Erotic Subjectivity in Anthropological Fieldwork*. London: Routledge, 1995.

Leenhardt, Maurice. *Do Kamo: Person and Myth in the Melanesian World*. Chicago: University of Chicago Press, 1978.

Lévi-Strauss, Claude. "The Structural Study of Myth." In *Myth: A Symposium*, edited by T. Sebeok. Bloomington: Indiana University Press, 1974.

Loeliger, Carl, and Garry Trompf, eds. *New Religious Movements in Melanesia*. Suva, Fiji: University of the South Pacific and the University of Papua New Guinea, 1985.

Michaud, Jean. "Ethnological Tourism in the Solomon Islands: An Experience in Applied Anthropology." *Anthropologica* 36, no. 1 (1994).

Obeyesekere, Gananath. *The Apotheosis of Captain Cook: European Mythmaking in the Pacific*. Princeton, N.J.: Princeton University Press, 1992.

———. "Cannibal Feasts in Nineteenth-Century Fiji: Seamen's Yarns and the Ethnographic Imagination." In *Cannibalism and the Colonial World*, edited by F. Barker, P. Hulme, and M. Iversen. Cambridge, England: Cambridge University Press, 1998.

Rivers, W. H. R., ed. *Essays on the Depopulation of Melanesia*. Cambridge, England: Cambridge University Press, 1922.

Sahlins, Marshall. *Islands of History*. Chicago: University of Chicago Press, 1985.

Spong, John Shelby. *Rescuing the Bible from Fundamentalism: A Bishop Rethinks the Meaning of Scripture*. San Francisco: HarperSanFrancisco, 1991.

Worsley, Peter. *The Trumpet Shall Sound: A Study of "Cargo" Cults in Melanesia*. London: Schocken, 1968.

Henry Montgomery and Family

de Montgomery, B. G. *Origin and History of the Montgomerys*. Edinburgh: William Blackwood and Sons, 1948.

Hamilton, Nigel. *The Full Monty*. Vol. 1, *Montgomery of Alamein, 1887–1942*. London: Penguin, 2001.

M. M. *Bishop Montgomery: A Memoir*. Westminster, England: Society for the Propagation of the Gospel in Foreign Parts, 1933.

Montgomery, Brian. *A Field-Marshal in the Family*. London: Constable, 1973.

Montgomery, H. H. *Foreign Missions: Handbooks for the Clergy*. London: Longmans, Green, 1904.

———. *Life's Journey*. London: Longmans, Green, 1916.

————. *Mankind and the Church: Being an Attempt to Estimate the Contribution of the Great Races to the Fulness of the Church of God*. London: Longmans, Green, 1907.

————. *Visions*. Westminster, England: Society for the Propagation of the Gospel in Foreign Parts, 1910.

————. *Visions*. 3d ser. Westminster, England: Society for the Propagation of the Gospel in Foreign Parts, 1915.

OTHER SOURCES

Conrad, Joseph. *Heart of Darkness, with The Congo Diary*. London: Penguin, 1995.

The Holy Bible, Authorized King James Version. London: Collins' Clear-Type Press, 1928.

Honigsbaum, Mark. *The Fever Trail: In Search of the Cure for Malaria*. New York: Farrar, Straus & Giroux, 2002.

Hyam, Ronald. *Empire and Sexuality*. New York: Manchester University Press, 1990.

A Melanesian English Prayer Book with Hymns. Honiara, Solomon Islands: Church of Melanesia, 1965.

Niutestamen: The New Testament in Solomon Islands Pijin. Suva, Fiji: Bible Society of the South Pacific, 1993.

Said, Edward. *Culture and Imperialism*. New York: Knopf, 1993.